FREE
KNOWLEDGE

FREE
KNOWLEDGE
CONFRONTING THE COMMODIFICATION OF HUMAN DISCOVERY

EDITED BY
PATRICIA W. ELLIOTT
& DARYL H. HEPTING

 University of Regina Press

Printed and bound in Canada at Marquis.

The text of this book is printed on 100% post-consumer recycled paper with earth-friendly vegetable-based inks.

Cover design: Duncan Campbell
Text Design: John van der Woude Designs
Copy editor: Kirsten Craven

Library and Archives Canada Cataloguing in Publication
Cataloguing in Publication (CIP) data available at the Library and Archives Canada web site: www.collectionscanada.gc.ca and at www.uofrpress.ca/publications/Free-Knowledge

10   9   8   7   6   5   4   3   2   1

University of Regina Press, University of Regina
Regina, Saskatchewan, Canada, S4S 0A2
tel: (306) 585-4758   fax: (306) 585-4699
web: www.uofrpress.ca

The University of Regina Press acknowledges the support of the Creative Industry Growth and Sustainability program, made possible through funding provided to the Saskatchewan Arts Board by the Government of Saskatchewan through the Ministry of Parks, Culture, and Sport. We also acknowledge the financial support of the Government of Canada through the Canada Book Fund and the support of the Canada Council for the Arts for our publishing program. This publication was made possible through Culture on the Go funding provided to Creative Saskatchewan by the Ministry of Parks, Culture, and Sport.

To all those who work tirelessly to share knowledge so that all may benefit.

CONTENTS

PROLOGUE: FREE KNOWLEDGE, SEEDS, AND OTHER BEINGS

Brewster Kneen

The mere conjoining of these two words—"free" and "knowledge"—raises a plethora of conflicting thoughts and visions.

Does the word "free" mean without cost or price? Or is the knowledge to which free refers simply floating about in the air, going where it will on a breeze, waiting to be captured by some entrepreneurial capitalist who will claim ownership and seek a patent on that fragment of ... of what?

Knowledge, actually, is all about relationships, both historical and contemporary, just as life itself is. Consider its base, the verb "know." We use this word colloquially with great frequency and in many quite different ways. For example: I am certain, I understand, I am familiar with. A dictionary gives us an interesting variety of meanings of the word "know":

1. To perceive directly, grasp in the mind with clarity or certainty. 2. To regard as true beyond doubt. 3. To have a practical understanding of, as through experience. 4. To have fixed in the mind. 5. To have experience of. 6a. To perceive as familiar; recognize. 6b. To be acquainted with....9. Archaic, To have sexual intercourse with.[1]

The last definition—the archaic one—may be closer to the profound meaning of "know" than any of the others because it makes it very clear that knowing is about relationship.

The same source also gives us the confusing definition: "To possess knowledge, understanding, or information,"[2] as if the three words were interchangeable. Information is not, however, the same thing as knowledge and understanding, though in practice we seem not to recognize this. The verb "possess" also raises a flag with its implication that knowledge is a commodity that can be possessed. Information, detached as it is, may be eligible for possession, and dispossession, as is a fourth category, data, being of an even lower order than information. Knowledge, however, being contextual and relational, cannot be so regarded.

There is also the question of "knowledge" in the singular. It seems to be an assumption of the Western monoculture mind that there is a single objective category of knowledge, like a big bank out of which we withdraw pieces of information/knowledge that become the currency of a capitalist economy. This currency then constitutes the means of acquiring property, both material and abstract. For example, a genetically engineered seed may be patented, but the patent itself is also a tradeable commodity. Actually, it is not the seed itself that is patented but certain "objective" characteristics of it introduced or identified through genetic engineering. The seed is thus treated as a (possibly self-reproducing) mechanical object. What is patented is the description of certain parts of this machine. We should not regard any of this as knowledge.

The acquisition of a patent is a kind of deal with the bank. The patent claimant agrees to make a deposit of information in return for monopoly control over, and profit from, this information. The bank agrees to make this information available to the public, but if use is made of it,[3] the owner of the patented information must be paid for it. In other words, it is no longer free, whether this refers to an "improved" crank handle or an "improved" seed, and it is still information, not knowledge, in spite of all the talk about a "knowledge economy."

A very serious implication of holding that there is only one bank of knowledge is that this one is deemed to be universal and therefore there is only one universal way of knowing, one epistemology. One might even claim that this is the "civilized" way; all else is barbaric. If there is only a single large bank of knowledge, then there must be only one set of rules, officially at least—one language—in which to conduct the business of depositing or withdrawing knowledge. Globally, for now at least, English, and the culture it expresses, is that language, which further limits the presumed "universality" of knowledge.

But how do we know there is only one way to know, only one legitimate epistemology? We cannot know that, so we simply state this as a fact and use whatever means necessary to impose it, using the practices of colonialism and imperialism to impose this cultural artifact on any contesting or resisting peoples. It is very much like laws and rights. The usual response to the question "But where did the law come from?" is "It's just there."[4] In the case of rights, the customary response is "They are inherent in the human being." Both answers obviously beg the question, leaving us to wonder why the question is not actually answered—or if it cannot be answered because it is the wrong question.

Accompanying this monoculture epistemology is a belief in development and progress. By definition, an arrow points in one direction only: there can be only one progress, that is, progress toward a singular goal of civilization (the "civilizing" mission to the "barbarians"). It is a great way to tidy up the world and overcome the confusion of diversity.

Seeds—those embryos of food and life—provide a good subject with which to distinguish between data, information, and knowledge. Is the seed just an envelope of genetic information? Or is it a collection of stories? Or must we regard the seed as a being with which we must converse with respect? French sociologist Bruno Latour cautions,

> *Let us remember that non-humans are not in themselves objects, and still less are they matters of fact. They first appear as matters of concern, as new entities that provoke perplexity and thus speech in those who gather around them, discuss them, and argue over them.*[5]

Think of the stories the seed could tell if only we were prepared to listen. The stories would be all about the many changing relationships of the seed in the variety of contexts it and its ancestors have experienced and lived through. They could also tell of their relatives that fell by the wayside, unable to adapt to a changing environment, or picked off by an alien pathogen. In listening to the stories, we might gain some knowledge of the seed, that is, some understanding of its life and the relationship we have with the seed, particularly if we have the sensibility to question it and listen to it. Then we would know it as a subject in its own right, a companion, not an object to be captured, enslaved, and, quite possibly, tortured. Latour writes,

> *As soon as we stop taking non-humans as objects, as soon as we allow them to enter the collective in the form of new entities with uncertain boundaries,*

entities that hesitate, quake, and induce perplexity, it is not hard to see that
we can grant them the designation of actors.[6]

I was taught in school that history was about "facts" that we were supposed to memorize: significant battles and their winners and losers; kings and queens; empires and colonies; great inventors and their inventions; nothing that I can remember about knowledge, and very little about all the other creatures inhabiting the world with us. We were also supposed to learn about Western civilization, industrialization, and the accumulation of wealth. In biology it was about Linnaean classification into genus and species, with lineages all neatly laid out. I always found this intimidating and forgettable as I was always more interested in sequences of events, cause and effect, and relationships than I was in names and dates—I figured I could always look these up if need be. Then when I was researching for my book, *The Rape of Canola*, I found that the identity of varieties of rapeseed had changed. Upon inquiry as to how this could be, I was told that this was common as researchers discovered that where they had put a variety was not where it belonged. Facts were not quite facts. In other words, there was considerable arbitrariness in the "science" of classification. Or was it that in nature nothing stands still? What one knew for sure yesterday might not be true today. One might be tempted to conclude that facts and objects are not reality but are social constructs.

Perhaps that information, wrongly described as knowledge, is about the seed of an ancient plant that has been described and characterized as if it was some kind of object by some corporate or university employee labelled "scientist." The description would be of its appearance; its morphology or external form, for purposes of identification; and of its physiology, what it does, how it functions. But that information would not be sufficient to characterize the seed. This would require a delving into, and exposing of, the seed's genetic and agronomic characteristics. It is this kind of information that might be eligible for a patent if it has been genetically engineered ("invented") and can be claimed to be unique and novel, thanks to the genetic engineering.

But who can know if it is unique and novel, two requirements of a patent claim? How can anyone claim to know that? One cannot know this, despite the claims of specious "inventors." All that one can truthfully claim is that the seed differs from those it has been compared with, likely just other varieties of the same species. So what does the holder of the "breeder's right"—or patent—on the seed really know about the seed? Not very much, actually.

This is partly because the seed is a life form—or, as other cultures would say, alive and unstable—a subject, an actor, not a dead object.

While the practitioner of Western reductionist science, including, in particular, a "genetic engineer," might amass genetic information about the seed, he cannot be said to know the seed, or even to have knowledge about the seed.

> *The only thing that can be said about them [nonhumans] is that they emerge in surprising fashion, lengthening the list of beings that must be taken into account.[7]*

To claim knowledge of the seed would include "knowing" how to grow it under what conditions and how to cook, eat, and preserve it—all relational activities.

The village seed keeper in Andhra Pradesh, India, or the Andean subsistence farmer, on the other hand, may know a great deal about the seed. She may be knowledgeable about the best conditions for growing the seed, from weather to soil quality, the best conditions for harvesting, as well as its taste and how to cook or prepare it for a variety of foods. She will know how to store it to keep it viable for the next season's planting and she will identify it by feel, smell, and appearance. For her, the seed is not an object but a friend, a companion with whom she converses. And she knows the company the plant likes to keep, the companion plants in whose presence it thrives and is happiest. A master gardener in North America would hold similar knowledge.

What I am suggesting here is that the question of knowledge—and, with it, information—is first of all a cultural question. Information may be objective, that is, verifiable by others, but it does not constitute an object, a thing. Information by itself is nothing, does nothing.

Knowledge, on the other hand, assumes and acknowledges an "other" as a being. There is no abstract knowledge; it is relational.

> *If the world, like the Andean one, is constituted by persons and not by subjects and objects, its members are not interested in "knowing" the other, because they do not see the other as a thing or object and also because they are not interested in acting upon it and transforming it. The focus is on mutual attunement...for inasmuch as mutual conversation flowers, nurturing flows. Dialogue here does not end in an action that falls upon someone, but in a reciprocal nurturing...*
>
> *One converses with the mouth, the hands, the sense of smell, vision, hearing, gestures, flowerings, the colours of the skin, the taste of the rain,*

the colour of the wind, etc. Since all are persons, all speak. The potatoes, the llamas, the human community, the mountains, the rain, the hail, the huacas (deities) speak. Language is not a verbal representation which encapsulates the named person ... The word makes present the named one, it is not, as it is said, a representation.[8]

This profound cultural understanding of what it means to know something can also be found in relation to a nonbeing, in this case, how to irrigate:

One can know how to irrigate, but the way in which to do it at any particular moment depends on a combination of circumstances; it will not be a repetition of what has been done before, but will arise from an attunement with the circumstances of the moment ... That is why a peasant is not interested in teaching others how something is done. What he or she does is to show the way he or she does it.[9]

Science, as understood and practised in the West, is one specific epistemology based on the singular philosophy of reductionism: the whole is the sum of its parts, and the more finely the whole can be reduced to its constituent parts, the more one can "know" about it. Thus, as an organism is deconstructed and reduced to a collection of genes or a strand of DNA, it is assumed that one knows more and more about the organism. This assumes that the organism is really an isolated object and that everything there is to know about it is contained within it. (Henry Ford got his idea of organizing the building of cars on an assembly line from the slaughterhouse industry in Chicago where he saw animals being deconstructed on a disassembly line—stationary workers and a moving chain.)

In reductionist philosophy, the organism is functionally autonomous and has nothing to do with other beings, other plants, or seeds or animals. However, this approach has never explained how organisms, plants, people, and seeds relate to, and interact with, others. It offers no knowledge about life. What Western reductionist science is all about is control and management. What it seeks to know about the organism is how to make it do what its "owner" (or manager) wants. Genetic engineering, the prime example of this attitude, is prepared to be as intrusive and violent as necessary to shape the organism into a useful slave.

Several politically loaded terms are used to refer to seeds in the self-replicating form, the form in which they are planted, harvested, and consumed as food. These terms all reduce the seed to a utilitarian object, a packet of genetic information to be used in commercial plant development, including, now, genetic engineering: plant germplasm; plant genetic resources; common heritage of mankind.

Until about seventy-five years ago, plant germplasm was not viewed as capable of being anybody's property, and, legally speaking, germplasm was not considered a commercial commodity. However, it did provide the basis for tradeable commodities such as corn, wheat, soybeans, and other food crops. To transform "plant genetic resources" (germplasm) into commodities and commercial goods simply required moving the line between public and private through legal manoeuvring. It was the Chakrabarty case, in the United States in 1980, that "opened the door to patents in living organisms by its focus on human intervention as a crucial factor in determining patentability ... The judgment emphasized a very *particular* form of human agency and simultaneously eclipsed and obscured other types of human agency [traditional plant breeding] that the genetic structure of the major food crops grown by traditional agriculture represents."[10]

> *The irony is that germplasm's value stemmed precisely from its non-commodification. Plant genetic diversity has been an invaluable resource to humans in preserving and developing a reliable food supply, and farmers could openly access germplasm for thousands of years in local and decentralized fashion.*[11]

Outside of Western materialist societies, the idea of being able to "own" seeds is absurd and unacceptable to virtually everyone. Seeds, as the basis of life, are simply unknowable. Yet seeds have the unique characteristic of being both the product and the means of production, and in the past half-century there has been a big push to privatize the seed—to move the seed from being effectively "free" to being owned.

The New Serfdom

While the traditional gardener/farmer who plants ("unowned") seeds does "own" the product—that is, it is hers to eat or sell—with hybrid seeds, and now genetically engineered, patented seeds, farmers no longer own the means of production. They become, in effect, renters of the means of production for a season, and whether they even own the product of the rented seeds they planted is now a contested issue. The intimate relationship of the traditional farmer and seed keeper with her seeds is broken: knowledge of the seed is kept in the mind of the seed keeper and farmer, but the information in the seed becomes the private property of a corporation.[12]

Having bought up most of the smaller seed companies, including vegetable seed companies, the very small number of corporations that control a growing percentage of the seeds of major grain and oilseed crops, as well as vegetables, really know very little about what they are selling, though they know very well what they are doing. What they have is information about the package of seeds, agrotoxins, and fertilizers they are selling, like patent medicines, and the directions on the label apply universally. The crop producers ("farmers") need only follow the directions on the label. The loss of farmers' knowledge is palpable.

What Reductionist Science Cannot Know

Now, however, reductionist science is being compelled to recognize the new field of epigenetics, which studies how organisms are influenced by their environment, or context. To put it colloquially, epigenetics is about how plants and animals talk to and influence each other at the level of the gene. This realization makes a hash of the long-held belief that the genetic structure of an organism could only be intentionally altered, with the alterations becoming heritable traits, by internal manipulation of the genetic material through chemical or radiological mutation or, more recently, genetic engineering.

> What this field [epigenetics] has been revealing in the most striking ways is that the cell and organism are a whole and determine, not only how genes will be expressed, but even what is to count as a gene at any given time...We can use the word "gene" only as a convenient way of referring to an almost unfathomable complex constellation of cellular events...[I]n order to understand the important developments now under way in biology, it's more useful to take "epigenetics" in its broadest sense as "putting the gene in its living context."[13]

Of course, as indicated above, millions of people have known this forever. They never knew about, or accepted, the reductionist mythology in the first place. But it is not just at the level of the gene that there is communication between organisms. Nor is it just humans who talk to each other, or just animals in the same family. As sheep farmers for many years, I know that we talked to our sheep, particularly when we had to intervene during the lambing process, and we eventually learned to listen for what they were trying to tell us. And, of course, my border collie working companion and I conversed in a variety of ways, and she with the sheep. The sheep knew well when Jule was "working" them, but they would simply ignore her if she was walking by my side through the flock. When she was old, arthritic, and tired, she lay on the back step one evening, not her usual place to lie. I sat on the step observing her. She lifted her head, looked me in the eye, and said, "I am tired, I am through." I said, "I understand," and moved her to her customary spot in the porch. In the morning, she was in her usual relaxed sleeping position, no longer alive.

On another occasion, I looked up the road along a pasture to see a rather ornery cow, which we could never get near, standing in the middle of the road. I slowly walked up the hill to her and she did not move. When I got close, I could see that she had a nasty infected wound on her leg. She allowed me to lead her slowly down to the barn and let me dress her wound, which took several days to heal, during which time she remained calm. Once healed, she took up her wild ways again. I was sure she had realized she needed help, so she "called" to us by standing patiently in the middle of the road until I saw her. She had obviously known that she had to get my attention before she could "tell" me her problem. In turn, I knew that I had a responsibility to her. The context was an unspoken relationship between two beings.

The sheep, the cattle, even a dog, can be and are owned, narrowly speaking. Owning is not knowing, however, although herders and good livestock farmers know well the animals they are responsible to and for. They may also have a little or a lot of information about them, particularly if they are dairy animals or breeding livestock where their lineage is important. On the other hand, I had virtually no information about my dog, Jule, except from whom I had gotten her, and that she was a good working dog. But after years together, Jule and I knew each other very well. I had, I would say, a good knowledge of her—and it was literally priceless. Though not, I think, free.

This brings to mind the words of Lynda Kitchikeesic Juden:

It is difficult to imagine a profit-based venture forming a good relationship with a medicinal plant. Practitioners of traditional knowledge know that respecting the plant is often essential to the efficacy of the medicine, which is not a miracle chemical compound but a measure of curative energy that draws its medicinal qualities from the relationship between the plant and the people or the person. And you can't buy a person's power.[14]

Notes

1   Nelson Canadian Dictionary of the English Language (Scarborough, ON: Nelson Thomson Learning, 1997).
2   Ibid.
3   "Use" may be qualified in a number of ways, from personal to commercial, private or public.
4   See Judith N. Shklar, Legalism: Law, Morals, and Political Trials (Cambridge, MA: Harvard University Press, 1986).
5   Bruno Latour, Politics of Nature (Cambridge, MA: Harvard University Press, 2004), 66.
6   Ibid., 76.
7   Ibid., 79.
8   Grimaldo Rengifo Vasquez, as quoted by Frédérique Apffel-Marglin, The Spirit of Regeneration: Andean Culture Confronting Western Notions of Development (London, UK: Zed Books, 1998), 26.
9   Ibid., 180.
10 Keith Aoki, Seed Wars (Durham, NC: Carolina Academic Press, 2008), 42.
11 Ibid., 7.
12 See Brewster Kneen, The Rape of Canola (Toronto: NC Press, 1992).
13 Steve Talbott, "Can Biologists Speak of the 'Whole Organism'?" In Context, no. 22 (Fall 2009): 17–22, http://www.natureinstitute.org/pub/ic/ic22/index.htm.
14 Lynda Kitchikeesic Juden, "Correspondence," Nature 421, no. 313 (January 23, 2003), doi:10.1038/421313c.

INTRODUCTION

Patricia W. Elliott and Daryl H. Hepting

Broadly speaking, this collection looks at the question of knowledge: how it is generated and shared, and to what purpose. This includes both applied knowledge and what contributor Arthur Schafer refers to as "knowledge for its own sake" (page 46)—for one can hardly exist without the other. The devaluing and withdrawal of public support for the latter, and simultaneous profit-seeking commandeering of the former, leads us toward a future when human knowledge, in all its myriad forms, is diminished in the public sphere.

In particular, alarms are being sounded around the globe, and across multiple sectors and disciplines, over the rapidly unfolding appropriation of public knowledge for private benefit. A recent example is a report released by the Canadian Association of University Teachers (CAUT) in November 2013, which outlined deeply troubling relationships between Canadian universities and their external research partners. CAUT researchers analyzed twelve collaboration agreements between Canadian universities and corporations, donors, and governments. The roster of partners included some of the country's major corporate interests in the energy, pharmaceutical, and manufacturing sectors, such as Imperial Oil, Pfizer, and Bombardier Aerospace. CAUT's research aimed

to determine how closely collaboration agreements adhered to the group's recommended broad principles for effective collaboration agreements.

One such principle is central to the subject of this book: "Protect the
university's commitment to the free and open exchange of ideas and discoveries."[1] How well—or, more precisely, how poorly—this open exchange
was faring on Canadian campuses could be gleaned from the outset; when
CAUT's researchers sought copies of the collaboration agreements, just two
of the twelve documents were publicly available, leaving the researchers to
seek the remainder through access to information requests. In several cases,
documents arrived with significant sections redacted.

Once the pieces were gathered, a disturbing picture emerged: notions
of academic freedom, collegial governance, and peer review were largely
absent from or, in some cases, directly supplanted by the terms of collaboration agreements. In some cases, government and corporate sponsors held
vetoes and majority decision-making power over the allocation of university
resources and staffing, as well as the right to delay publication of results.
The agreements also typically assigned intellectual property rights to corporations and universities rather than to creators, and placed external con-
trols on the public announcement of discoveries. CAUT's analysis presented
a sobering challenge to the public perception that "a university produces
knowledge for the general public not for any particular individual, corporate
or organizational interest, including its own material interest."[2]

These revelations rang true at our own institution, the University of
Regina, which had just undergone the painful experience of publicly acknowl-
edging that a highly touted carbon capture research project was fraught
with conflicts of interest and lax accountability, as revealed in a series of
CBC investigative journalism reports.[3] The International Performance
Assessment Centre for the Geologic Storage of Carbon Dioxide (IPAC-CO2)
was established at the University of Regina with the support of Royal Dutch
Shell and the provincial and federal governments. In 2005, the centre negotiated a carbon capture technology licensing agreement with HTC Purenergy,
Inc., which in turn signed a global licensing agreement with Doosan Babcock
Energy of the UK, and Doosan Heavy Industries and Construction of South
Korea in 2008. The Purenergy announcement stated, "Saskatchewan developed technology will now be offered and presented to customers through
twenty Doosan commercial offices world wide with significant emphasis on
the opportunities within the People's Republic of China."[4]

How and if the University of Regina was to be included in the profits of
this university-generated technology became the subject of legal proceedings

in March 2013.[5] Once revealed, these and other developments contributed to what can only be described as a crisis of confidence in the university's academic mission, leading to the calling of the first, full, University Council gathering in more than thirty years. At the council meeting, some three hundred faculty, students, and professional staff discussed not only financial accountability issues but also the nagging sense that the university was adrift from its core public service mission, as described in the university motto, "As One Who Serves," and in its values statement: "We employ our expertise to serve each other and society. We illuminate socially relevant problems. The knowledge we generate enriches the community."[6] In this case, the incident contributed to a positive and ongoing institution-wide discussion of the role of the university, and of the value of knowledge in service of the public good.

While these events unfolded, the seed for this book had already been planted some years earlier (and appropriately) in the field of agriculture. On a miserable winter night in 2004, Terry Pugh and Terry Boehm of the National Farmers Union (NFU) travelled to Regina to speak to a small but enthusiastic crowd about the NFU's Seed Saver campaign. One of the editors of this book, Daryl Hepting, had been asked to organize the talk for the Council of Canadians. The event poster read:

Do farmers have the right to save and plant the seeds that they have helped to develop over thousands of years? Are seeds intellectual property to be patented? Percy Schmeiser vs Monsanto[7] was just the beginning. Find out what the recent Seed Sector Review means for YOU!

As a computer scientist, Hepting was intrigued by what he heard that evening. There were obvious parallels to be drawn between the struggles of farmers and software developers seeking to freely share their knowledge. He had just been reading about Microsoft's expression of "fear, uncertainty and doubt" regarding open GNU/Linux.[8] There appeared to be a double standard at play: spreading openness through GNU Public License software was bad but spreading "closedness" through Monsanto's seed patents was good. But good for whom?

Taking this question forward, Hepting and University of Regina colleagues Roger Petry, Claire Polster, David Gerhard, Patricia Elliott, and Philip Fong organized the conference, "Free Knowledge: Creating a Knowledge Commons in Saskatchewan," in November 2005. This title involved a certain conceit: the participants were not creating a knowledge commons but were rather helping to understand, publicize, and defend the concept. The posters went up, and people began wondering what it was all about. While the term "knowledge commons" had been kicking around the Internet and academic conferences for nearly a decade, the group learned it had yet to break through to public consciousness. "What is a knowledge commons?" was a question asked of the organizers many times as the event approached.

In our view, a *knowledge commons* is a public place where knowledge is made freely accessible for the public good. The terminology is based on the concept of a European village commons, where grazing land was shared for public use—but where it was also open to overuse and exploitation. To this end, movements to "reclaim" the commons are, as Bollier explains, essentially movements to restore balance in relationships among those who inhabit an arena of shared knowledge, to avoid practices of exploitation and overextraction that make a commons unsustainable.[9] Bollier further suggests that the term is, in fact, more appropriately referred to in the full plural sense, in that knowledge commons are diverse and variable, defying a single description.[10] Hess and Ostrom add:

> *Trying to get one's hands around knowledge as a shared resource is even more challenging when we factor in the economic, legal, technological, political, social and psychological components—each complex in their own right—that make up this global commons.*[11]

With these concepts in mind, panellists were invited to the conference from many walks of life, such as farming, rural development, the fine arts, software development, medicine, academia, Indigenous Traditional Knowledge (TK), the media, and environmental organizations. It was an excellent beginning to ongoing linkages that have since spread from local, to national, to global.

The idea for a book that would reflect the topic's inherent diversity and global scope germinated during Hepting's sabbatical in 2007–2008, motivated by a visit to Regina by Ralph Nader. The original call described the intended scope of this volume: "The increasing privatization of knowledge is changing our society in important ways, but for the benefit of very few. Of interest are essays that deal with current challenges, and promising alternatives, in specific sectors such as (but not limited to) farming and food, computer software, medicine, media, arts, and libraries. Essays dealing with, for example, TK, economics, or the historical context of this issue are also welcome."

The road to the final volume has been a long one, with plenty of interesting correspondence. Our goal was to link locally generated discussions to the global arena by inviting national and international contributors to mingle their experiences with ours. We sought out voices working to emancipate the flow of knowledge in diverse fields, including pirate radio, co-operative education, TK, and open source technology. The response was enthusiastic and encouraging. However, we also received an important reality check; Eben Molgren, legal counsel for the Free Software Foundation, asked why people should spend their days working on books when they could be undertaking action. It was a valid question that presented a strong challenge to all of the participants in this project. Every contributor to this volume is undertaking actions in their daily lives, in fields ranging from media to medicine. Our answer to Molgren's tough question is that stories about the actions being taken need to be shared, so they can be sustained and enhanced. We hope this book serves that purpose and inspires further action.

The book begins with a prologue by Brewster Kneen, a farmer and public intellectual who was also the first to speak at our long-ago Free Knowledge conference. At the time, we felt his words adequately captured the simplicity, complexity, and beauty of the commons, and we wanted to hear more. His contribution to this volume begins by placing diverse perspectives at the foundation of knowledge commons theorizing, with his observation that placing two simple words side by side—"free" and "knowledge"—unleashes a wide spectrum of "conflicting thoughts and visions." Kneen cautions against conceptualizing knowledge as a single, universal bank, leading to "monoculture epistemology" (page ix). Such an epistemology comes with the trappings of cultural and species imperialism, he argues. He advises us to instead look to the humble seed as a guidepost for differentiating between information and knowledge, and overcoming human-centric conceit in the bargain. A scientist who describes, classifies, and perhaps even patents a seed does not unlock its true stories. In contrast, a subsistence farmer is acutely aware of a seed's history and relationship to its surroundings; the seed is not a mere object but is a companion to be tended. From this, Kneen argues that all knowledge is relational—an essential concept missing from reductionist science that seeks to manage and control organisms as objects. The idea of the organism as a packet of genetic information that can be owned and patented fails to express the deep knowledge farmers have of seeds and animals, and, indeed, is an abhorrent concept to much of the world's population.

From Kneen's thought-provoking prologue, the collection moves into four parts. Part I sets out some of the essential dilemmas of an increasingly corporatized academy. Despite the widespread use of buzz phrases such as "knowledge mobilization" and "knowledge use" in today's academic institutions, it stands to reason that much actual knowledge is left behind when the academy marches lockstep into the narrow, self-interested realm of patentable research. However, there is more at stake than knowledge loss, according to Joel Westheimer. Universities were founded on the ideal of scholars working together toward a common end, he writes. When this mission is lost, so, too, is a powerful democratic mandate that understands— not perfectly, but at least in principle—that knowledge and learning should serve the public interest.

The implications of losing this path are clearly evident in the two articles that follow Westheimer's contribution, both of which focus on corruption in medical research. Physician Sally Mahood echoes Westheimer's concern for the future integrity and reliability of the academy in a corporatized world: "Open communication and knowledge sharing, long considered the lifeblood of scientific endeavour, are lost in the competitive atmosphere of rival firms," she observes (page 27). Further, corporate encroachment on scientific knowledge distorts the direction of research, resulting in a wide variety of treatments for erectile dysfunction and baldness, while research on tuberculosis and malaria is neglected. She notes, in particular, that patent protection and privately held drug information have disastrously restricted access to HIV drugs in Africa.

In the following chapter, noted medical ethicist Arthur Schafer illustrates the life-and-death consequences of Faustian private-sector bargains in his review of the Vioxx scandal, where evidence of damaging side effects of a popular arthritis medication was suppressed. In an environment of "marketing dressed up as science," he writes on page 43, the pursuit of university-industry partnerships leads to the erosion of independent, critical perspectives that the public expects of university researchers. Consequently, by the time Vioxx was withdrawn from the market in 2004, millions of patients had been exposed to a drug that increased the risk of heart attack by 400 per cent, and over one hundred thousand Vioxx users suffered heart attacks and strokes. These examples from the medical field form a powerful argument for a return to public science in the public interest.

How might this be accomplished? Claire Polster looks to the university itself as an important arena of reform in the reordering of how knowledge is created and to what end. There is much at stake: "The public university cannot be sustained when its lifeblood—public knowledge—is diminished" (page 59). As one potential solution, Polster suggests the introduction of mandatory, nonexclusive licences that would prohibit university-based research from being appropriated by private interests. Under this proposal, all university-generated knowledge—whether publicly or privately financed—would have to be placed in the public domain. Polster argues that not only would this prevent conflicts of interest and abuses of the public trust (as illustrated in the Vioxx scandal), it would contribute to protecting and revitalizing the knowledge commons beyond the university. Polster realistically concedes that such an across-the-board solution is likely to raise a number of objections and alternative proposals, ranging from tinkering with legislation to the establishment of nonprofit oversight boards. While such debates and questions are welcome, she concludes that we must first "successfully build a consensus that the privatization of knowledge in Canada's universities should come to an end" (page 63).

Helpfully, while the enslavement of knowledge for profit appears to be a dominant paradigm in the twenty-first century, it is certainly not the only paradigm. Part II is meant to provide some examples of how people have worked together to share and disseminate knowledge on a more equitable, empowering basis—as well as their struggles to maintain and build on such movements. While we may congratulate ourselves for being very cutting-edge with our current-day discourse, today's knowledge commons advocates are hardly the first pioneers of the concept. Indeed, the idea of knowledge for the common good has been the guiding principle of co-operative education over many decades, writes Mitch Diamantopolous. "The modern co-operative movement is fundamentally rooted in the political struggle over who defines, owns, produces, and distributes economic knowledge, and for whose purposes," he writes (page 74). Through adult education programs, local meetings, and progressive publications, early co-operators aimed to break the knowledge monopoly held by capitalist entrepreneurs. Diamantopoulos argues that the success of this approach led to a thriving co-operative sector in Quebec—just as its gradual neglect led to an erosion of co-operative development in Saskatchewan. It is a fascinating history that illustrates how the degree of attention paid to active knowledge mobilization and dissemination plays a central role in advancing—or impeding—the success of alternative institutions.

In the sphere of media, Marian van der Zon takes a close look at the creation of alternative media institutions, focusing on unlicensed, low-power radio, popularly called pirate radio. She opens with an observation that "our 'public airwaves' are not truly public at all" (page 102). State control of the broadcast frequency spectrum is the norm, leading to media that is tailored to reproduce dominant ideologies and social constructs, she argues. In this environment, commercially oriented knowledge monopolies grow strong, while diverse, community-based knowledge is devalued and suppressed.

Van der Zon's own hands-on experience in pirate radio has convinced her of the importance of keeping knowledge, via access to the media, free. "It is perhaps in emancipating knowledge that we emancipate ourselves," she writes (page 107).

Returning to the sphere of the university, Patricia W. Elliott examines participatory action research as a form of knowledge sharing that is ultimately connected to academic reform, shaking up the paradigm under which knowledge has traditionally been held and transmitted within the academy. Action research "challenges the templates we use, forcing us to acquire new knowledge about the world from new sources," the author observes (page 128). It also challenges current accepted trends in knowledge dissemination, including the priority given to academic journals as the primary "knowledge product" of university-based research. To community research partners, such journals represent a closed, inaccessible world that is not held accountable to community-based peer review. Elliott argues that, ultimately, genuine community engagement amounts to a reordering of power relations on many levels. "It should come as no surprise, then, that [action research] may upset the status quo not only within marginalized communities but also within power centres, including our universities," she cautions (page 131). The chapter includes suggestions for reform, as well as examples of existing campus-based initiatives aimed at accomplishing the wider social imperatives embedded in all action research projects. Whether you are a marginalized citizen or a stressed-out scholar, the reward, Elliott posits, is a more humane and just world for all.

Elliott's chapter introduces the concept of community self-determination over knowledge collection and dissemination. To wit, if a researcher regards community participants as equal partners in knowledge generation, it stands to reason that community members would then also play a major role in determining the management and end use of their knowledge, in the service of mutual social benefit. This view offers some distinction from the free/open source movement, which holds the premise that knowledge should be universally and freely accessible to all, including the freedom to modify, reconfigure, and redisseminate knowledge products on a global scale. The problematic edge to carte blanche appropriation was made abundantly clear on April 23, 2013, when a group of scientists connected to a private synthetic biology venture, Genome Compiler, turned to the popular crowd-funding website Kickstarter as a means to finance the creation of a glow-in-the-dark houseplant. The group proposed to insert computer-written genetic code into Arabidopsis plants, which would then be distributed to citizens who made donations to the research. Buoyed by the popular film

Avatar and its bioluminescent forest, the campaign far exceeded its original goal of $65,000, raising $484,013 in two months.[12]

Not surprisingly, the campaign also raised questions about the wisdom of creating and releasing synthetic organisms outside the guidance of scientific peers and public regulators. The technology-monitoring ETC Group launched an international "kick-stopper" campaign to shut down the plant give-aways, drawing on the UN Convention on Biological Diversity's call for a "precautionary approach…to the field release of synthetic life, cell, or genome into the environment."[13] Although an online petition against the project was signed by fourteen thousand people, the campaign reached its planned end date on June 7, 2013, without interference.[14] The following month, Kickstarter quietly introduced a ban on handing out genetically modified reward gifts via its website.[15] However, the science itself continued outside the Kickstarter campaign, with an online website for pre-ordering the plants, as well as souvenir t-shirts and a "How-To" instruction book for creating synthetic life forms.[16]

This incident alone should give us pause on the path to knowledge freedom. Accordingly, Part III of our collection places an important codicil on the knowledge commons. Many Indigenous groups would outright reject unfettered deployment and modification of their traditional knowledge (TK). Part III raises a model of the commons that accepts sovereign collective control over culturally based knowledge. This is driven by historical experience that has shown knowledge can be swiftly colonized, devalued, and diminished in an "open" marketplace of ideas, leaving whole populations bereft of key teachings that previously enabled their survival.

Speaking from the perspective of a Kiche-Mayan timekeeper, Leonzo Barreno looks at the Mayan calendar as an example of a knowledge system that was essential to the understanding of time-space-energy among the Kiche-Maya and other Mayan groups. Under colonialism, this knowledge system was devalued, suppressed, and replaced by a European cultural monopoly, an experience shared by Indigenous peoples throughout the Americas. Now, after more than five hundred years of oppression and genocide, many Mayan people link their continuing survival on this planet to the recovery of the knowledge embodied in texts such as the Cholq'ij calendar, along with recovery of Mayan languages and ceremonies. "The reasons why Mayan intellectuals, professionals, students, and activists are choosing to learn their ancient knowledge are debatable," Barreno states. "The fact, nonetheless, is that the uses of Mayan languages and the expansion of Mayan ceremonies are becoming part of the modern Mayan struggle" (page 146–7).

Beyond the specific historical experience of Mayan groups, Barreno's chapter implies a message to all the world's people about the importance of maintaining diverse knowledge systems as a key component of human survival. This speaks to Kneen's opening statement that we must be prepared to view the commons from multiple perspectives and experiences, as well as Bollier's advice that not every commons looks and functions the same way.

Indeed, alternative models of knowledge sharing have existed for millennia. Within Indigenous societies, customary laws and cultural protocols have long regulated the use of TK effectively and consistently, notes Gregory Younging, a creator's rights scholar and member of the Opaskwayak Cree Nation. In recent centuries, the parallel development of European-based intellectual property rights systems has provided ample opportunity for interaction and conflict between two very different knowledge systems. Younging's chapter includes a fascinating roster of legal case studies in which Indigenous communities fought to retain their collective ownership of cultural products, such as petroglyphs and traditional stories. In most situations, the court cases centred on the commercialization and/or patenting of TK by non-Indigenous profit-seekers. As Younging observes, Indigenous knowledge has contributed greatly to humanity. It is therefore distressing to see such knowledge become a prize to be won or lost in court battles.

In answer to this distressing scenario, Younging teamed up with Jane Anderson, a research fellow at the Australian Institute of Aboriginal and Torres Strait Islander Studies, to explore the potential to incorporate Indigenous knowledge traditions in the creation of new protocols for research and intellectual property. "In the absence of formal legal intellectual property mechanisms for recognizing and protecting rights in Indigenous cultural knowledge, and in ever increasing contexts where relationships with Indigenous peoples are sought, or where Indigenous knowledge is used, protocols are providing a productive tool for negotiating new kinds of equitable relationships," they write (page 181). Drawing on examples from Australia to the Arctic, their chapter examines the pragmatic utility of protocols that have been developed over the past decade, as well as their shortcomings. "Whilst protocols offer a practical possibility for protecting Indigenous knowledge, they can also be unintelligible, general, and useless," they note, concluding that reflexive practice must become part of the march toward protocol development (page 191).

Part IV of the book presents some by-no-means-exhaustive forays into advancing theoretical understandings and practical reforms. The need for reform is clear: Joshua Farley and Ida Kubiszewski warn that today's markets are not equipped to deliver the research we need to survive in a post-carbon economy. As fossil fuels decline, major advances are needed in low-carbon energy technology. Meanwhile, there has been a concerted global effort to confine the free flow of knowledge via increased patent and intellectual property protection. Today's firms lock down potentially useful discoveries with patents they do not plan to use, simply to keep others from using them, Farley and Kubiszewski note. In the rush for consumer dollars, innovation slows and little heed is paid to the needs of future generations. Farley and Kubiszewski critically examine the alternatives, including public sector provision, science prizes, and commons-based peer production, and find all are hampered by the current economic paradigm. Open source/open access paradigms hold the advantage of allowing scientists to work full-time for the public good, if adequately funded. The authors predict that scientists will migrate to nonmarket alternatives as they become viable and respected, for one reason alone: "We suspect that in general scientists prefer to find cures for life-threatening diseases or improve technologies that mitigate environmental catastrophes rather than develop cosmetics for the rich" (page 217).

Indeed, as Roberto Verzola of the Philippines observes, the idea that another person might profit from your knowledge at your expense tends to hinder the natural flow of knowledge sharing. He notes that today's imposed, artificial model of knowledge scarcity hampers the natural flow of knowledge from farmer to farmer, generation to generation, even species to species. Yet the natural state of knowledge is one of abundance and sharing, not scarcity and propriety, he argues, pointing to examples from agriculture to the development of the Internet. He adds, "Today, the single biggest obstacle to the full realization of abundance in the information sector is the legal system of intellectual property rights" (page 224). His highly original conceptualization of abundance challenges us to reorder the traditional dictums of economics, including "the fundamental assumption of scarcity as gospel truth" (page 232). Unleashing the natural cascade of knowledge will lead to advances in fields ranging from human services to renewable energy, he theorizes. It is a hopeful message that sets this remainder of the book's chapters on the path toward solutions geared at liberating human knowledge for the common good.

Speaking from the standpoint of an organic farmer trying to grapple with the corporatization of agricultural knowledge, Doug Bone offers a series of needed policy changes for government to consider. Bone states that, like most small-scale Canadian farmers, he simply wants to make a decent living and to be able to pass the land undamaged to the next generation. However, powerful market forces conspire against these modest goals. "From a corporate standpoint, sustainable and subsistence farming are forms of resistance and threats to their bid to dominate the food system," he writes (page 250). In response, powerful transnationals work to co-opt political and regulatory regimes, and to enslave agriculture with chemical dependency. However, it is possible to resist this agenda by demanding a series of policy initiatives from provincial and federal governments, which are outlined in the chapter.

The last word in this collection belongs to a thinker grounded in library science, befitting the library's role as steward and shepherd of the knowledge commons. Author Heather Morrison sees an unprecedented opportunity to disseminate library holdings through the Internet, provided the principles of open access are protected and promoted. "The expansion of access to knowledge made possible by the web is almost incomprehensible," she writes, citing the example of the thesis paper, once relegated to a single library copy in the scholar's home institution but now instantly available around the globe (page 257). Yet barriers remain, including online subscription fees that economically exclude libraries and scholars in developing countries. As well, there is a distinction to be made between full open access (free of charge) and *libre* open access (free of copyright restrictions). Morrison advocates author retention of copyright, which ultimately allows self-archiving for the purpose of full open access—meaning the author has the legal right to make an article available for free, even if the publishing journal requests a fee for the same article. Morrison observes that a number of research funders now encourage researchers to provide open access to their work, tipping off a backlash from some of the larger, more lucrative publishing concerns. Yet despite a well-heeled lobby to restrict open access, the number of open access journals continues to grow, evidence that the movement has strength. Morrison notes that publications by scholars in developing countries populate the list of open access journals, suggesting a rebalancing of the knowledge monopoly is in the works. As well, the open access movement is expanding from open access journals to open access databases and open education, including the production of free textbooks.

The book would be too heavy to lift if it contained all the stories that need to be told. If anyone would care to take on a second volume, we would suggest, for starters the story of Drugs for Neglected Diseases Initiative (http://www.dndi.org), an organization working to develop an alternative model for the research and development of new drugs for neglected diseases; Avaaz.org, a "global web movement to bring people-powered politics to decision-making everywhere"; the case of Steve Kurtz, founding member of the award-winning art and theatre collective Critical Art Ensemble, who was accused of bioterrorism; Richard Littlemore's take on who pays the price when details of science and public policy are dictated by the highest bidder; Elizabeth Royte's analysis of the crisis of bottled and tap water; and Ian Mauro's work with Inuit people to document their knowledge of climate change.

As it stands, our final chapter provides an optimistic starting point for further exploration, suggesting that—despite the myriad pressing concerns this collection has raised regarding the present corporate stranglehold on knowledge production—in the long view, the knowledge commons is on the rise and knowledge privateers are in retreat.

Notes

1   CAUT, *Open for Business: On What Terms? An Analysis of 12 Collaborations between Canadian Universities, Corporations, Donors and Governments* (Ottawa: CAUT, 2013), 3.
2   Ibid., 189.
3   CBC News, "Officials Shocked by Flow of Money in U of R Carbon Dioxide Project," February 20, 2013, http://www.cbc.ca/news/canada/saskatchewan/officials-shocked-by-flow-of-money-in-u-of-r-carbon-dioxide-project-1.1322740.
4   HTC Purenergy, "HTC Purenergy Signs Global Licensing Agreement with World Leading Power Plant Equipment Supplier and Constructor," September 2008, http://www.htcenergy.com/mediaCenter/News/2008/news090308.html.
5   Geoff Leo, "U of R sues over 'misappropriated' CO2 technology," March 28, 2013, http://www.cbc.ca/news/canada/saskatchewan/u-of-r-sues-over-misappropriated-co2-technology-1.1305896.
6   University of Regina, *mâmawohkamâtowin: Our Work, Our People, Our Communities. Strategic Plan 2009–2014* (Regina, University of Regina, 2009), 2.
7   For background on this case, see Democracy Now, "Percy Schmeiser vs Monsanto: The Story of a Canadian Farmer's Fight to Defend the Rights of Farmers and the Future of Seeds," 2010, video posted at http://www.democracynow.org/2010/9/17/percy_schmeiser_vs_monsanto_the_story.
8   Glyn Moody, "A Brief History of Microsoft FUD," 2009, LXer–Linux News, http://lxer.com/module/newswire/view/57261/index.html.
9   David Bollier, "The Growth of the Commons Paradigm," in *Understanding Knowledge as a Commons: From Theory to Practice*, ed. Elinor Ostrom and Charlotte Hess (Cambridge, MA: MIT Press, 2006), 27–41.
10 Ibid.
11 Elinor Ostrom and Charlotte Hess, "A Framework for Understanding the Knowledge Commons," in *Understanding Knowledge as a Commons: From Theory*

to Practice, ed. Charlotte Hess and Elinor Ostrom (Cambridge, MA: MIT Press, 2006), 41.

12   Antony Evans, "Glowing Plants: Natural Lighting with No Electricity," https://www.kickstarter.com/projects/antonyevans/glowing-plants-natural-lighting-with-no-electricity.

13   United Nations Environment Programme, Convention on Biological Diversity, *Decision Adopted by the Conference of the Parties to the Convention on Biological Diversity at Its Tenth Meeting, X/37 Biofuels and Biodiversity*, October 2010, para. 16, http://www.cbd.int/doc/decisions/cop-10/cop-10-dec-37-en.pdf.

14   Dan Nosowitz, "Is Kickstarter Hostile to Science?" *Popular Science*, August 9, 2013, http://www.popsci.com/science/article/2013-08/kickstarter-anti-science.

15   Duncan Geere, "Kickstarter Bans Project Creators from Giving Away Genetically-Modified Organisms," *The Verge*, August 2, 2013, http://www.theverge.com/2013/8/2/4583562/kickstarter-bans-project-creators-from-giving-GMO-rewards.

16   Glowing Plant: Natural Lighting without Electricity, http://www.glowingplant.com/.

PART 1

KNOWLEDGE FOR PROFIT: THE COMMODIFICATION OF EDUCATION AND RESEARCH

HIGHER EDUCATION OR EDUCATION FOR HIRE? CORPORATIZATION AND THE THREAT TO DEMOCRATIC THINKING

Joel Westheimer

Teaching critical thinking and the importance of public engagement is the university's democratic mission, and today's universities are failing to deliver.

Just over ten years ago, I was fired, which is not in and of itself interesting. After all, many people lose their jobs every day, especially in times of economic turbulence. For better or worse, however, most endure such indignity in privacy. My case, for better or worse, made its way to the *New York Times*. Under the headline "New York University Denied Tenure to Union Backer," the *Times* reported that the U.S. government's National Labor Relations Board "charge[d] New York University with illegally denying tenure to a professor who had testified in favor of allowing graduate students to unionize."[1] The *Chronicle of Higher Education* headline read, "A Promising Professor Backs a Union Drive and Is Rejected for Tenure."[2] Smaller papers and magazines made similar observations. I was more concerned at the time with wanting my job back than with thinking about the broader implications (the cacophony of negative publicity heaped on NYU offered a sense of just desserts, to be sure). But thrust into the public position as I was did raise one particular concern for my scholarly interests in democratic education.

Nearly every news story cast my lot as an isolated incident of vengeful retri-
bution by a few university administrators rather than as a case of something
much larger than one professor (me) or one university (NYU).

Since then, I have been happily employed by the University of Ottawa and
am pleased to report that my children have not gone hungry. But whether
others view my earlier dismissal as scandalous or justified, I find the following irrefutable: the forces that set the process in motion and enabled it to
continue are an inevitable by-product of dramatic changes the academy has
been facing in the past several decades. These changes have little to do with
individual university employees and much to do with changes in the structures and workings of the academy itself—not only NYU but also private and
public universities across the United States and Canada. Universities now
model themselves after corporations, seeking to maximize profit, growth,
and marketability. As a result, the democratic mission of the university as
a public good has all but vanished. And many of the (never fully realized)
ideals of academic life—academic freedom (in my case, freedom of political
expression), intellectual independence, collective projects, and pursuit of the
common good—have been circumscribed or taken off the table altogether at
a growing number of college and university campuses across North America.

The effects of corporatization on the integrity of university research—
especially in the sciences—has been well documented elsewhere. Readers
of this volume are already likely familiar with the many cases of scientific
compromise resulting from private commercial sponsorship of research by
pharmaceutical and tobacco companies. Indeed, faculty throughout North
America are already deluged with requests or demands to produce research
that is "patentable" or "commercially viable." Sometimes these entreaties
are couched in gentler (some might argue more insidious) terms such as
"knowledge mobilization" or "knowledge use." What I want to focus on here,
however, are implications that are less well explored but equally dangerous:
the ways the academy's shift toward a business model of education delivery
impedes our collective ability to preserve and promote a democratic way of
life. As in so many other arenas in our society today, where democratic interests are pitted against economic ones, democracy seems to be losing.

Three developments stemming from the pursuit of a corporate model of
education pose threats not only to the historic ideal of a liberal democratic
education but also to the future of democratic thinking itself. They are the
elimination of critical thinking and a culture of criticism; the weakening of
intellectual independence and democratic faculty governance; and the promotion of a meritocracy myth that drives the work of graduate students and

junior and senior faculty alike. The first two erode democratic thinking by curbing the habits of mind and heart that enable democracy to flourish—what John Dewey called the "associated experience[s]" essential to democratic life.[3] The last—the meritocracy myth—attacks the heart of these associated experiences by diminishing the power of the community to nurture collective meaning and worth.

The Impact of the Corporate Campus on Critical Thinking

*Within the unique university context, the most crucial of all human rights...
are meaningless unless they entail the right to raise deeply disturbing questions and provocative challenges to the cherished beliefs of society at large
and of the university itself...It is this human right to radical, critical teaching and research with which the University has a duty above all to be concerned; for there is no one else, no other institution and no other office, in
our modern liberal democracy, which is the custodian of this most precious
and vulnerable right of the liberated human spirit.[4]*

This excerpt from the mission statement of the University of Toronto might be hailed as a shining example of the centrality of university campuses in promoting and preserving critical thinking as the engine of progress in any democratic society. Except for one thing: institutional leaders at the university that drafted these words do not believe them and do not abide by them. The University of Toronto is the site of two of the most notoriously blatant violations of these principles in the past decade: the well-publicized cases of the University of Toronto's Nancy Olivieri, who in the late 1990s was sued by the drug company Apotex for going public with data that cast doubt on an experimental drug, and David Healy, who in 2000 had an offer of a clinical directorship and professorship at University of Toronto withdrawn after he publicly questioned the safety of the popular antidepressant Prozac. Both incidents revealed the university's unwillingness to stand up to corporate funders and protect academic freedom and the integrity of critical inquiry.

Unfortunately, the Olivieri and Healy cases do not stand alone. Over the years, there have been scores of examples of scientific and social scientific research essential to public welfare being undermined by private influence.[5] The balance of private funding of clinical medical research in Canada reached majority territory by 2004, when a Canadian Association of University Teachers (CAUT) report found more than 52 per cent of funding was from corporate sources.[6] The trend is easiest to spot and most publicly alarming in the medical sciences, since lives are at stake. But there is cause for concern as well in the humanities and social sciences, where publication of inconve- . nient truths can be discouraged by university higher-ups.

The harm to the reputation of the university as a reliable source of (especially "scientific") information, untainted by private conflicts of interest, has been documented extensively. But the ways these changes affect the campus life of faculty and students has been considered far less. As universities turn to business models—becoming certification factories rather then institutions of higher learning—democratic educational ideals are fast becoming obsolete. Consequently, professors find it more difficult in their teaching to foster critical thinking as a necessary underpinning of democratic participation. The "shopping mall" university, where students seek the cheapest and fastest means for obtaining the basic skills and certification they need, is becoming a familiar metaphor and model for university administrators, students, and parents.[7] Courses not directly related to job training look more and more like useless dust to be eliminated. Meetings among faculty about which program of courses might yield the most robust understanding of a field of study, and of the debates and struggles that field entails, are rapidly being replaced by brainstorming sessions about how to narrow the curriculum to fit into, for example, two weekends in order to *incentivize* matriculation and increase student enrollment.

The Weakening of Intellectual Independence and Democratic Faculty Governance

The state of affairs I describe above pertains mostly to the emaciated pedagogical potential of the newly corporatized university. But ultimately, what faculty—and especially junior faculty—are being asked to give up is their own intellectual independence. The creeping corporate climate of some university departments and schools can easily lead to the substitution of bureaucratic allegiance, in the form of "budget alignment" or "optimization" in the new parlance, for scholarly inquiry as the cornerstone of academic life. In some cases, the effect on the intellectual life of a department might be plain to see. In some schools and faculties, elected department chairs— who traditionally served terms of a few years and then eagerly returned to their intellectual pursuits within the department—have been replaced by chairs *appointed* by university higher-ups with no, or at best perfunctory, input from department faculty. Some stay in these positions for a decade or more with ever-diminishing interest in, or focus on, scholarly inquiry. In an article titled "Tenure Denied" (where I described more fully my experiences at NYU), I told of a colleague at a Midwestern university whose department chair suggested to the faculty that research questions that the department wanted investigated should be agreed on by a committee (made up of senior faculty and administrators) and posted on a website—and that faculty should align their research with one of those questions.[8] Requiring research to be streamlined according to central criteria (doubtless related to funding opportunities) makes perfect sense if one treats an academic department as a profit centre. But it turns scholarly life into something less than we all hope it to be.

At times, the mere fact that departmental faculty are pursuing an active, diverse, and uncontrolled set of research agendas may be perceived negatively by school administrators. While such departments continue to recruit promising scholars on the basis of their research production, the departmental leadership is caught in a bind. They need such scholars for the department's reputation and grant-getting ability, but once there, these scholars may pose some threat to the order of business within the department (and to the security of the chair who has likely already traded the kind of professional security earned from scholarly inquiry and production for the kind won by allegiance and loyalty to university higher-ups).

Appointed chairs can slowly and steadily shift faculty focus from scholarly pursuits that advance a field to those that advance the chair, a possibility especially troubling to junior faculty seeking tenure. Much as external pressures on the corporate university constrain and refocus academic research, so, too, do internal incentives on the departmental level. As in much of university politics, junior faculty are the most vulnerable. Faculty governance in departments that have remade themselves along corporate culture lines can become little more than a parody of pseudo-democratic (or simply nondemocratic) governance, in which faculty simply (and always) endorse administrative positions. Faculty managers' and department chairs' only convictions are those that do not ruffle administrative feathers of those higher up. And the chill that blankets departments in which power has been centralized results in the further entrenchment of antidemocratic tendencies.

Under these conditions, the university starts to look less like a place of free exchange of ideas and more like a Hobbesian Leviathan, a place that boasts, as former State University of New York (SUNY) New Paltz President Roger Bowen warns, "a settled, conforming, obedient citizenry—not dissenters who challenge convention."[9] In these departments, junior faculty either conform or withdraw from departmental life after being tenured. The bottom line is raised to the top. Research that promotes the financial and hierarchical health of the administration is rewarded while independent scholarly thought is punished. Institutions of higher education become ones of education for hire. Undue administrative influence over research agendas, appointed department chairs and the further erosion of democratic governance, and the hiring of part-time and clinical faculty with no time for scholarly inquiry and little job security are all threats to both critical inquiry and university democracy.

Before moving on to my final point, I want to point out that these conditions are created not only by university administration but also by a complicit faculty who would rather not sacrifice research time to engage in something as time-consuming as democratic governance. In other words, a repressive hierarchy is not required for nondemocratic decision making to flourish. Were university administrators to honour democratic faculty governance fully, would faculty step up to the plate? Under a corporate model of governance, appointed department chairs may stay in their positions for a decade or more. A democratic model, however, would require those deeply engaged in scholarship and research to be willing (or required) to take on leadership positions in administration, in addition to their roles as teacher and scholar. Countering an increasingly hierarchical and corporatized model of university governance requires commitments of time and energy that many faculty members now shun but that a just workplace requires.

The Corporate Benefits of the Meritocracy Myth

One final characteristic of the newly corporatized campus I want to address is the complicity of the professorial (and graduate student) culture. The pervasive culture of increasing individualism results in a story we tell ourselves that goes something like this: "We work in a merit-based system. If I do my job correctly—if I'm a good graduate student or a good professor, and I'm smart and I do my work well—I will be rewarded with a plum teaching assignment, and I will be part of the academic elite and get a job." This is an unfortunate state of affairs for two reasons. The first is economic and concerns the entrenched system of academic labour. The simple reality is that for the majority of disciplines, the claim that the system is merit-based is just not true. There are vastly more qualified, hardworking individuals than there are tenure-track and tenured academic positions for them to fill. At a certain level of proficiency, it becomes the luck of the draw.

But the second cost of an emphasis on individualism in the form of the meritocracy myth might be more insidious. Faculty focused only on individualized measures of professional success miss out on the collective action that has an extensive history in democratic societies and that has sustained and driven countless scholars, artists, scientists, and activists: working together toward a common end. Merit-based rewards encourage faculty to work behind office doors, estranged from colleagues. As my colleague Marc Bousquet points out in his book *How the University Works*, believing in the fantasy of merit results in a great loss to everyone, including those dubbed meritorious.[10]

The corporate university, on the other hand, advances and benefits from the illusion that each of us will attain rock star status in the academy. Some readers might recall the episode of the television show *The West Wing* when fictional President Jeb Bartlett explains why Americans seem to vote against their own interests by protecting a tax system that benefits only the super rich: "It doesn't matter if most voters don't benefit," he explains. "They all believe that someday they will. That's the problem with the American dream. It makes everyone concerned for the day they're going to be rich."[11] And so it goes for the star system in the academy. The more graduate students and professors believe that their hopes for professional satisfaction lie in superstar recognition for their individual work rather than in collective meaning-making and action, the easier it is for democratic life in the university to be compromised.

Conclusion

The language of individual entrepreneurship has become all-pervasive across many sectors of society. It has, therefore, become increasingly difficult for faculty, administrators, students, and public officials even to talk about the public role of universities in a democratic society. This was not always the case. Universities in Canada, as elsewhere, were founded on ideals of knowledge and service *in the public interest*. Universities had a noble mission—if not always fulfilled—to create knowledge and foster learning that would serve the public good and contribute to social welfare. Academic workers at all levels and of all kinds need to fight to regain this central mission. What is the role of the university in fostering civic leadership, civic engagement, and social cohesion? How can education reinvigorate democratic participation? How can colleges and universities strengthen our communities and our connections to one another?

I sometimes ask my education students to consider how schools in a democratic society should differ from those in a totalitarian nation. It seems plausible that a good lesson in chemistry or a foreign language might seem equally at home in many parts of the world. Every nation wants its educational institutions to prepare students for active participation in the workforce. So what would be different about teaching and learning in a Canadian classroom than in a classroom in a country governed by a one-ruling-party dictatorship? Most of us would like to believe that schools in a democratic nation would foster the skills and dispositions needed to participate fully in democratic life; namely, the ability to think critically and carefully about social policies, cultural assumptions, and, especially, relations of power. Many schoolteachers and university professors, however, are concerned that students are learning more about how to please authority and secure a job than how to develop democratic convictions and stand up for them.

There are many powerful ways to teach young adults to think critically about social policy issues, participate in authentic debate over matters of importance, and understand that people of good will can have different opinions. Indeed, democratic progress depends on these differences. If universities hope to strengthen democratic society, they must resist focusing curriculum and research on skills training, workforce preparation, and the commercialization of knowledge to the benefit of private industry. They must instead participate in the rebuilding of a public purpose for education. How to do so is a matter of professorial imagination.

This chapter is adapted from the previously published essay, "Higher Education or Education for Hire? Corporatization and the Threat to Democratic Thinking," Academic Matters: Journal of the Ontario Confederation of University Faculty Associations *(April–May 2010), and printed here with permission.*

Notes

1   Karen W. Arenson, "Labor Board Rules That NYU Denied Tenure to Union Backer," *New York Times*, February 28, 2002, B2.
2   Piper Fogg, "NLRB Readies Complaint against New York U. for Firing Professor Who Backed Union," *Chronicle of Higher Education* 47, no. 48 (August 10, 2001): A8–A9.

3   John Dewey, *Democracy and Education* (New York: Macmillan, 1916), 360.
4   University of Toronto, *Mission and Purpose*, Approved by Governing Council, October 15, 1992, http://www.utoronto.ca/about-uoft/mission-and-purpose.
5   Lawrence C. Soley, *Leasing the Ivory Tower: The Corporate Takeover of Academia* (Cambridge, MA: South End Press, 1995); Janice Newson and Howard Buchbinder, *The University Means Business* (Aurora, ON: Garamond Press, 1988); David L. Kirp, *Shakespeare, Einstein, and the Bottom Line: The Marketing of Higher Education* (Cambridge, MA: Harvard University Press, 2004); James Turk, ed., *Universities at Risk: How Politics, Special Interests and Corporatization Threaten Academic Integrity* (Toronto: James Lorimer and Company, 2008); and Jennifer Washburn, *University, Inc.: The Corporate Corruption of Higher Education* (New York: Basic Books, 2005).
6   Philip Welch et al., *Defending Medicine: Clinical Faculty and Academic Freedom*, November 2004, http://www.caut.ca/docs/reports/defendingmedicine.pdf?sfvrsn=0.
7   See, for example, Kevin Mattson, "The Right's War on Academe and the Politics of Truth," in *Universities at Risk: How Politics, Special Interests and Corporatization Threaten Academic Integrity*, ed. James Turk (Toronto: James Lorimer and Company, 2008).
8   Joel Westheimer, "Tenure Denied: Anti-Intellectualism and Anti-Unionism in the Academy," *Social Text* 20, no. 4 (Winter 2002): 47–64.
9   Roger W. Bowen, "The New Battle between Political and Academic Cultures," *The Chronicle of Higher Education*, June 22, 2001, http://chronicle.com/article/The-New-Battle-Between/32233.
10 Marc Bousquet, *How the University Works: Higher Education and the Low-Wage Nation* (New York: New York University Press, 2008).
11 *The West Wing*, Season 3, Episode 3, "Ways and Means," originally aired October 24, 2001.

PRIVATIZED KNOWLEDGE AND THE PHARMACEUTICAL INDUSTRY

Sally Mahood

Medical knowledge intended to treat and prevent human illness and suffering is being hijacked by the corporate sector.

The pharmaceutical industry—with its ubiquitous and pervasive influence in the fields of medical research, pharmaceutical development, physician practice, and the education of health professionals—stands as a particularly informative example of the distorting impact of privatized knowledge. Knowledge of medical interventions to prevent and treat human illness and suffering, which should be a shared and accessible human resource, lies in the private corporate domain. The resulting impacts on health expenditures, medical research, and social policy are enormous, and provide a disturbing example of the hijacking of public resources and the public interest by the corporate sector.

The pharmaceutical industry is highly profitable.[1] It is dominated by a few large transnational corporations (such as Pfizer, Merck, Novartis, Sanofi-Aventis, GlaxoSmithKline) that have monopoly patent protection. Within the industry, there is constant pressure to develop new patent-protected drugs, and increasingly intense competition between one another, and from generic drug producers. Brand name producers frequently litigate to keep low-cost generic competitors off the market, and the increasingly powerful generic drug industry follows suit with legal challenges to patents before they expire. One might think, and certainly the industry itself claims, that such competition results in greater creativity and progress, and in better, cheaper access to pharmaceuticals. The evidence, however, contradicts such a claim.

Open communication and knowledge sharing, long considered the lifeblood of scientific endeavour, are lost in the competitive atmosphere between rival firms. Instead, competition restricts the sharing of results, causes needless repetition and duplication, and leads to concealing and/or delaying publication of findings to protect commercial interests. The driving force is market profitability, not finding solutions to human problems. The impacts are profoundly negative.

Despite the vast sums spent on medical and drug research within the industry, only a small proportion of so-called new drugs is new. Approximately 11 per cent are actually new compounds or improvements on older drugs.[2] This was evident in a review of Canadian drug patenting during a period of highly accelerated growth in industry sales. Between 1990 and 2003, of the 1,147 newly patented drugs appraised by the Canadian Patented Medicine Prices Review Board, only 6 per cent met the criterion for a breakthrough drug (the first drug to effectively treat an illness or provide substantial improvement over existing drug products).[3] A concurrent 2005 U.S. study found there had actually been a decline in the number of new drugs being developed and that only 18 per cent of the drug industry's budget went to basic research for breakthrough drugs.[4] The majority of so-called new drugs were in fact "me-too" drugs, minor variations on existing drugs that offer little advantage but add cost, and allow a new patent and thus increased market share and profitability. In British Columbia, for example, 80 per cent of rising drug costs were attributed to "me-too" drugs, not new and innovative drugs previously unavailable.[5]

The first major impact is on drug costs. The cost of a drug has little to do with its development costs but is instead based on what the market will bear. Canadians spent an estimated $34 billion on drugs in 2013, helping make drugs "one of the fastest growing major categories of health system spending" between 2001 and 2013.[6] In particular, in the decade before 2005, drug costs rose 72 per cent while costs for hospitals and doctors rose just 22 per cent.[7] Although the relative pace of drug spending has since slowed, the impacts remain profound. Drugs consumed 16.4 per cent of all health care dollars by 2013, a larger piece of the health care pie than the 14.8 per cent consumed by physician services.[8]

As previously stated, cost effectiveness studies indicate that, overall, patients actually gain very little from an additional sixth or seventh coronary heart disease-treating drug, or a fourth or fifth lipid-lowering statin drug.[9] However, achieving market dominance with a "new" version of such a drug can make or break a company. Meanwhile, drug companies aggressively market their products to both consumers and physicians, encouraging them never to treat cheaply what can be treated expensively.

By the mid-1990s, the annual industry budget for drug advertising exceeded that spent on all undergraduate and postgraduate medical education combined, and was equivalent to the entire budget of the U.S. National Institutes of Health (NIH).[10] The industry spends more on sales and marketing than on research and development,[11] and the cost of this marketing is passed on to patients. Companies (such as IMS Canada) buy personal prescribing records, pharmacy databases, and physician prescribing profiles to target marketing to high-volume physician prescribers. The industry itself has reported spending $6,000 to $11,000 per physician per year on marketing.[12]

The impact on physician behaviour is pervasive. Companies do not promote the best drug in a category but instead the newest and most expensive. Directly or indirectly, the pharmaceutical industry now funds most continuing medical education for medical professionals.[13] The industry hires influential doctors, termed "key opinion leaders," to educate and influence other physicians in their prescribing choices. Many leading specialists are paid generously to do such work, and the industry even evaluates its subsequent return on investment in such key opinion leaders in terms of subsequent sales. The industry sponsors educational events and underwrites medical conferences or publications, including clinical guidelines for treatment that set practice standards for doctors. It pays for travel and lodging, doles out honoraria and gifts, provides free samples of new drugs, and employs an army of "detail" men and women to hawk its products.

All of this is highly effective. There are extensive data to prove that doctors are influenced, even if they believe they are not. Their prescribing habits and behaviour are predictable. Those who rely heavily on the pharmaceutical industry for their drug information have the poorest prescribing habits,[14] and, not incidentally, higher morbidity and mortality in their patients.[15] The organized medical profession is deeply divided on these issues. Many doctors persist in portraying industry marketing as "educational and informative," express a sense of entitlement to industry largesse, and deny its obvious impact. Even educational institutions and professional bodies have been slow to address the issues of conflict of interest between physicians and the drug industry.

The impact on the discipline of medicine itself has been even more far-reaching. Industry's efforts to broaden the application of drugs and to expand the definition of what is a treatable medical condition have had a dramatic impact. Common conditions are "medicalized" (e.g., premenstrual dysphoria, sexual dysfunction, restless legs, social phobia versus shyness). Companies create concern in the population about diseases such as high cholesterol or osteoporosis in order to increase drug sales. In a health-obsessed society, they push diseases in order to push drugs.[16]

Many approaches are used to facilitate sales. Industry funds "illness clubs" and patient advocacy groups around particular medical conditions. Organizations such as the Heart and Stroke Foundation, the Canadian Diabetes Association, the Osteoporosis Society, and the Arthritis Society all enjoy significant industry funding. Consequently, there is significant industry involvement in defining disease criteria and setting treatment standards. Some of these organizations are legitimate grassroots organizations, although significantly, if innocently, heavily influenced by the industry.

Professional bodies are also heavily funded by the drug industry. Thirty per cent of the American Psychiatric Association's $62.5 million financing in 2006 came from the pharmaceutical industry.[17] Journalists and marketers frequently find converging interests and, in general, media coverage of drug issues emphasizes benefits and minimizes drug risks. News outlets may also use freely provided "video news releases," which are, in fact, prepackaged promotional videos produced by corporate publicists for the pharmaceutical industry, designed to appear as independently produced news.[18] Such videos also allow the industry to bypass regulations prohibiting drug advertising or mandatory disclosure of adverse drug side effects.

The history of the marketing of drugs such as Fen Phen or Vioxx illustrates the problem. Fen Phen was a drug for obesity marketed by Wyeth. The company's own data showed the drug gave only a 3 per cent advantage over the placebo, and that the average weight loss on the drug was 5 per cent. The company invested in a campaign to promote obesity as a major health issue and paid $54 million to launch the drug, including grants to the American Academy of Family Physicians, the American Diabetes Association, and the North American Society for the Study of Obesity. This funded lavish conferences with high-profile academic consultants (key opinion leaders), editorials in major medical journals, and the hiring of communication firms to write articles for medical journals promoting obesity treatment (to the tune of $20,000 per article). The firm subsequently paid university researchers to edit drafts and put their names to already largely completed articles, sometimes such that the authors did not even know Wyeth was involved. After Fen Phen was withdrawn from the market because of dangerous side effects, the company spent another $100 million on a public relations campaign to convince the public that the response had been overblown, convening an expert panel of cardiologists and paying Arthur Weyman of Harvard $5,000 per day as an honorarium to chair the panel.[19]

Merck & Co. spent $161 million to advertise their drug rofecoxib (Vioxx),[20] more than the amount spent on advertising Nike, Budweiser, and Pepsi combined.[21] The marketing avalanche resulted in the drug being prescribed broadly and inappropriately, often at patient insistence. Researchers at the University of Chicago subsequently showed that two-thirds of the patients prescribed drugs in this class did not need them or benefit from their therapeutic advantage.[22] As Arthur Schafer discusses in Chapter 3 of this collection, Merck was forced to pull this top-selling pain medication from the market in September 2004, after research showed the drug increased the risk of heart attacks and strokes. The Vioxx story again shows how promotional review articles were designed, executed, and ghostwritten by company employees, with "guest authors" signing their names and lending their reputations, all for a fee.[23] Prestigious medical journals publishing these articles were unaware of the true authorship. Further, Merck did not disclose in a clear and timely fashion the full extent of the potential health risks posed by Vioxx.[24] The company even took legal action to stop an independent drug bulletin in Spain from publishing safety concerns several years prior to the company's withdrawal of the drug.[25]

Even without such clearly unethical approaches and lack of research integrity, industry marketing contributes to a drug-intensive approach to the treatment of disease. The result is tremendous allocation of health resources to drugs and away from other approaches to treatment or prevention. For example, there is often more emphasis on cholesterol-lowering drugs than smoking prevention or cessation, even though smoking cessation gives much more "bang for the buck" in preventing disease. This medication-intensive approach is constantly reinforced by direct to consumer (DTC) advertising, the aggressive marketing of drugs to patients in the name of consumer education. DTC advertising campaigns manipulate the public's lack of sophistication in assessing medical evidence, and bypass the medically trained professional acting as a "learned intermediary."

The privatized nature of drug information and pharmaceuticals is also a powerful driver of global health inequality. There is more profit to be made developing and selling "lifestyle" drugs to wealthy North Americans than essential drugs to the world's sick or poor. The medical research agenda is diverted from the serious health needs of the world in favour of the relatively minor lifestyle concerns of the privileged.

According to the World Health Organization's most recently available data, in 2012 there were some 207 million cases of malaria and 627,000 deaths, mostly among young children in Africa,[26] but none of the major companies maintain in-house research on malaria. There were an estimated nine million reported cases of tuberculosis in 2013, and 1.5 million deaths, but medical science has not developed any new antituberculosis drugs in the last forty years.[27] Research on tuberculosis and malaria is neglected in favour of yet another drug for erectile dysfunction or baldness. The profit margin on Viagra is 98 per cent,[28] and so it seems market forces rule in setting the scientific agenda. Vaccine development and production for pandemic illnesses that threaten vast numbers of the world's population have been sacrificed to the rule of profit. The obstruction of access to HIV drugs in Africa is a tragic example of the dangers of patent protection and privately held drug information, an obscene example of the victory of private profit over public good.[29]

The impact of the privatized nature of pharmaceutical knowledge, however, has an even more insidious impact on medical scientific evidence itself, an erosion of objectivity and credibility that is perhaps less well appreciated by the public. As public funding of medical research has declined over the last two decades, the drug industry has become the single largest funder of health research in Canada, the United Kingdom, and the United States, such that 60 per cent of all researchers work under contract with industry.[30] Cash-strapped universities and teaching hospitals market themselves to wealthy drug companies, and governments actively encourage researchers and institutions to commercialize.

The fact that this process comes with strings attached has become increasingly clear. He who pays the piper calls the tune, and the evidence of the deleterious impact on science is mounting. Marcia Angell, former editor of the *New England Journal of Medicine*, notes that industry influence has so distorted the medical literature that this is the "misinformation age of medical research."[31]

We now know that there is a clear relationship between the source of funding for a study and its outcome.[32] Meta-analyses funded by the industry are five times more likely than those funded by other sources to report findings favouring a study drug when these conclusions are not supported by the results.[33] The Women's Health Initiative,[34] a publicly funded study of the impact of hormone replacement therapy on menopausal women, found precisely the opposite conclusions than those found by the privately funded industry research on the subject.

Physicians increasingly follow clinical practice or treatment guidelines, recommendations from expert bodies that specify standards of care in drug prescribing and purport to represent an objective consensus on evidence and treatment. It is of significant concern that 60 per cent of those who develop medical guidelines for treatment receive research funding from the drug industry.[35] Many argue that such conflicts of interest are unavoidable when the community of "experts" is small and exclusive. Agencies such as the U.S. Food and Drug Administration (FDA) even allow "waivers" of conflict of interest in recognition of expertise in an area. However, such conflicts of interest do have an impact on decision making and compromise the objectivity of scientific advice. In this light, consumer advocacy organizations have asked the NIH to review independently their cholesterol-lowering guidelines following the revelation that eight out of nine of the guideline authors had undisclosed financial associations with the manufacturers of statin drugs used to treat high cholesterol.[36]

The deformation of objective scientific inquiry is accomplished by many other means. Research study design can itself be loaded in favour of, and therefore guarantee, a preferred outcome in drug trials.[37] Drugs can be compared to subtherapeutic doses of a competitor's drug to suggest superiority, or the duration of a drug trial can be shortened if concerns exist about long-term safety. Supervised clinical trials in which participants are paid to comply, or noncompliant patients are excluded, do not reflect real-life outcomes and can exaggerate the benefits of a drug. Data can be manipulated in many ways. There is now clear evidence that the industry participates in selective or delayed dissemination of study results whereby only study results that are favourable are released or published, and others are quietly relegated to the closely guarded company filing cabinet.[38] The result is publication bias in favour of certain drug treatments. It is clear from the Vioxx scandal in the United States that even the safety of patients is not a deterrent to these practices, and that the public watch dogs, such as the FDA, are appallingly ineffective.

Academic fraud is also commonplace. The *Journal of the American Medical Association* recently published two damning studies based on court documents that confirm that a significant number of key academic articles in medicine are ghostwritten by industry, who then pay honoraria to prestigious academics to sign their names as authors for publication.[39] Quite apart from the academic dishonesty of such a bogus authorship practice, it speaks volumes about the corrosive influence the industry has on research evidence, evidence on which medical practitioners base their clinical decision making.

University and hospital research careers increasingly depend on attracting and maintaining drug industry funding, and the pharmaceutical industry also engages in scientific harassment of scientists who "won't play ball." In Canada, we have several examples in recent years of attempts by pharmaceutical companies to suppress research findings or stifle scientific discussion. As already mentioned in Chapters 1 and 2 of this book, Dr. Nancy Olivieri at Toronto's Hospital for Sick Children faced professional censure for refusing to co-operate with her funding company's demands to suppress unexpected risks in her study findings.[40] Dr. David Healy, a leading British psychiatrist, had his offer of employment from the University of Toronto's Centre for Addictions and Mental Health withdrawn because he publicly expressed concerns about the safety of SSRI antidepressants, which offended the university's leading corporate donor, Eli Lilly.[41] Ann Holbrook, a physician/scientist who evaluated drugs for the Ontario Ministry of Health, was harassed and intimidated in the courts by AstraZenica PLC (the makers of the drug Losec) when she authorized guidelines favouring two cheaper, but equally effective, drugs for use by Ontario physicians.[42] Bristol Myers Squibb Canada, using the courts, tried to prevent the Canadian Coordinating Office for Health Technology Assessment from releasing its summary report on statin drugs for the treatment of high cholesterol.[43] A British Columbia task force, with strong representation from the pharmaceutical industry, has recently recommended the dismantling of the *Therapeutics Initiative*, the province's independent prescription drug evaluator that provides evidence-based drug information to the province's practitioners.[44] Examples such as these create a "chill effect" on other scientists, publishers, and agencies, and such celebrated cases may represent only the visible tip of an iceberg.

More ominous perhaps is the fact that drug regulation agencies and procedures have been increasingly made more responsive to commercial interests and, as a result, industry even increasingly funds the activities of its own watchdogs. Canada's Health Protection Branch, now called Health Canada, largely dismantled its own in-house drug safety research capacity and instituted a cost-recovery policy whereby industry pays for its own drug reviews through user fees. The industry suggests this approach gives patients faster access to new treatments, but one fears that examples such as the Vioxx disaster and the role of the FDA will be quickly forgotten, as increasingly business is disguised as science.

Conclusion

Universities have a social obligation to promote knowledge and protect the acquisition of knowledge from the vagaries of commercial interest. However, the privatized nature of drug information and the influence of the industry permeate every aspect of medicine and its institutions. In turn, this erodes public trust and the legitimacy of medical practice. What are the alternatives?

The industry argues that drug research and development are risky endeavours that necessitate the behaviours it engages in. In fact, the industry spends much more on marketing than it does on research and development,[45] and while the final product, the profits, and much of the generated "intellectual property" are privately owned by industry, much of the upstream research and academic facilities are, in fact, government-funded or subsidized. We should remember that some of the most significant drug-related discoveries of the twentieth century (insulin, penicillin, the polio vaccine) were developed in public, not-for-profit institutional laboratories.

Some efforts are clearly underway to improve the integrity of medical research and limit the more unpalatable consequences of the pharmaceutical industry's practices. Proposals to raise the bar on drug approvals, and requirements that industry prove new products are not just better than placebos but better than currently existing drugs, would discourage the "me-too" drug phenomenon. Mandatory registration of clinical trials is proposed to create a public record of all research being undertaken, and in order to make selective publication of study results more difficult. There is, however, clear acknowledgement that selective study designs, data misrepresentation and analysis, and selective reporting will be difficult to control.

Both the NIH in the United States and the Canadian Institutes of Health Research have new conflict of interest guidelines in place. However, these are still largely voluntary and aimed at ensuring disclosure of, rather than eliminating, conflict of interest. Disclosure has been of limited success as a strategy, an increasingly empty ritual to ease the conscience. Conflicts of interest in this setting are not so much about secrecy as they are about power.

Medical journals are attempting to address the problems of academic fraud, ghostwriting, and "guest authorship," and proclaim editorial independence. The success of these endeavours remains to be seen. Academic bodies in medicine are slowly calling for restrictions on industry handouts to physicians and physicians-in-training, and calling for some distancing between educational and promotional activities. However, there are not as yet national guidelines or enforceable policies in this regard, and those that exist are largely voluntary.[46]

Clearly, the privatized drug industry has brought scientific advances to humankind. These advances, however, have been highly promoted, often exaggerated, and clearly pursued in a manner that is wasteful of human intellectual energies and unresponsive to public health and public policy needs. Furthermore, access to the benefits of these advances is often denied to those most in need of them by virtue of the private ownership of knowledge and the profit motive embedded in the drug industry.

One cannot help but question the current belief that medicine and the public good are best served by a system of for-profit, privatized knowledge and drug development. I would argue that public ownership and investment in pharmaceutical and medical scientific knowledge would be a model more in keeping with intellectual and research creativity, drug affordability, and our national and international public health and social policy goals in disease treatment and prevention. Some experts have even argued persuasively that it would be less expensive to fund drug research and development from public sources and that the overall savings in drug costs would more than compensate for these additional costs. Public science in the public interest would also certainly allow us to re-establish control over the health research agenda and address issues of research integrity, patient safety, and academic freedom.

Such a solution would be far-reaching in its potential impacts and vigorously opposed by powerful interests within and outside of the industry and the professions. In the end, however, such an approach will accomplish much more than our current meagre efforts to rein in the monster in our midst.

Notes

1   Return on equity averages 30 per cent per year as reported in F. Carey et al., "Drug Prices: What's Fair?" *Business Week*, December 10, 2001, 60–68. Pfizer is a $48-billion-a-year business and made $9.1 billion in profits in 2002 (see J. Simmons, "King of the Pill: Pfizer Is Biggest Drug Company Ever. Can It Become the Best?" *Fortune*, April 14, 2003). See also, N. Pattison and L. Warren, *Drug Industry Profits: Hefty Pharmaceutical Company Margins Dwarf Other Industries* (Washington, DC: Public Citizen Congress Watch, June 2003), accessed August 12, 2008, http://www.citizen.org/documents/Pharma_Report.pdf.

2   Eleven per cent of new drugs approved fall into this category according to the independent French drug bulletin *Prescrire International*. See "Industrial

Interests versus Public Health: The Gap Is Growing," *Prescrire International* 13, no. 70 (2004): 71–76.

3   S. G. Morgan et al., "Breakthrough Drugs and Growth Expenditure on Prescription Drugs in Canada," *The BMJ* 331 (October 8, 2005): 815–816; Patented Medicine Prices Review Board, *Annual Reports* (1988–2003) (Ottawa: Patented Medicine Prices Review Board), archived at http://www. collectionscanada.gc.ca/webarchives/20061122085818/http://www.pmprb-cepmb.gc.ca/english/view.asp?x=91.

4   D. W. Light and J. Lexchin, "Will Lower Drug Prices Jeopardize Drug Research? A Policy Factsheet," *The American Journal of Bioethics* 4, no. I (2004): W3–W6; T. H. Lee, "Me-Too Products: Friend or Foe?" *New England Journal of Medicine* 350, no. 3 (2004): 211–212.

5   Morgan et al., "Breakthrough Drugs."

6   Canadian Institute of Health Information (CIHI), *Drug Expenditure in Canada, Prescribed Drug Spending in Canada, 2012: A Focus on Public Drug Programs.* (Ottawa: CIHI, 2014).

7   CIHI, *Drug Expenditure in Canada 1985–2005*, National Health Expenditure Database (Ottawa: CIHI, 2005).

8   CIHI, *Drug Expenditure in Canada, Prescribed Drug Spending in Canada.*

9   R. Mickleburgh, "Costly Drugs Overprescribed," *Globe and Mail*, May 26, 1994, A2

10 S. Wolfe, "Why Do American Drug Companies Spend More than $12 Billion a Year Pushing Drugs? Is It Education or Promotion?" *Journal of General Internal Medicine* 11 (1996): 637–639.

11 Pfizer spends roughly 39 per cent of its revenues on sales and marketing as noted in L. Clifford, "Tyrannosaurus Rx," *Fortune* (Europe) 142, no. 10 (2000): 84–91. See also M. A. Gagnon and J. Lexchin, "The Cost of Pushing Pills: A New Estimate of Pharmaceutical Promotional Expenditures in the United States," *PLOS Medicine* 5 (2008), accessed August 12, 2008, http://medicine. plosjournals.org/perlserv/?request=get-document&doi=10.1371journal.pmed. 0050001#journal-pmed-0050001-b004; W. Kondro, "Brandname Companies Fail to Meet Research and Development Commitments," *Canadian Medical Association Journal* 175, no. 4 (2006): 344.

12 D. Shapiro, "Drug Companies Get Too Close for Med School's Comfort," *New York Times*, January 20, 2004, F5.

13 A. Reiman, "Separating Continuing Medical Education from Pharmaceutical Marketing," *Journal of the American Medical Association* 285 (2001): 2009–2012; P. Hebert, "The Need for an Institute of Continuing Health Education," *Canadian Medical Association Journal* 178, no. 7 (2008): 805–806.

14 J. Lexchin, "Interactions between Physicians and the Pharmaceutical Industry: What Does the Literature Say?" *Canadian Medical Association Journal* 149, no. 10 (1993): 1401–1406; T. S. Caudill et al., "Physicians, Pharmaceutical Sales Representatives and the Cost of Prescribing," *Archives of Family Medicine* 5, no. 4 (1996): 201–206.

15 W. Davidson et al., "Physician Characteristics and Prescribing for Elderly People in New Brunswick: Relation to Patient Outcomes," *Canadian Medical Association Journal* 152, no. 8 (1995): 1227–1234.

16 R. Moynihan and A. Cassels, *Selling Sickness: How the World's Biggest Pharmaceutical Companies Are Turning Us All into Patients* (Vancouver, BC: Greystone Books, 2006).

17 B. Carey and G. Harris, "Psychiatric Association Faces Senate Scrutiny over Drug Industry Ties," *New York Times*, July 12, 2008, A13.

18 J. Lenzer, "When Drug News Is No News," *The BMJ* 332 (2006): 919; *Center for Media and Democracy Report*, accessed August 13, 2008, http://www.prwatch. org/fakenews/execsummary.

19 A. Mundy, *Dispensing with the Truth* (New York: St. Martin's Press, 2001), 159, 181–182.

20 C. Elliott, "Pharma Goes to the Laundry: Public Relations and the Business of Medical Education," *Hastings Center Report* (Hoboken, NJ: Wiley-Blackwell, September/October 2004), 18–23.

21 A. Ellner, "Rethinking Prescribing in the United States," *The BMJ* 327 (2003): 1397–1400.

22 "Marketing Drugs to Unsuitable Patients," editorial, *New York Times*, January 28, 2005, A22.

23 J. S. Ross et al., "Guest Authorship and Ghostwriting in Publications Related to Rofecoxib: A Case Study of Industry Documents from Rofecoxib Litigation," *The Journal of the American Medical Association* 299, no. 15 (2008): 1800–1812.

24 B. M. Psaty and R. A. Kronmal, "Reporting Mortality Findings in Trials of Rofecoxib for Alzheimer Disease or Cognitive Impairment: A Case Study Based on Documents from Rofecoxib Litigation," *The Journal of the American Medical Association* 299, no. 15 (2008): 1813–1817.

25 L. Gibson, "Drug Company Sues Spanish Bulletin over Fraud Claim," *The BMJ* 328 (2004): 188.

26 World Health Organization (WHO), "Malaria Fact Sheet No. 94," updated March 2014, http://www.who.int/mediacentre/factsheets/fs094/en/.

27 WHO, *Global Tuberculosis Report* (Geneva: WHO, 2014).

28 Ibid.

29 S. Lewis, *Race against Time* (CBC Massey Lectures Series) (Toronto: House of Anansi Press Inc., 2005).

30 P. Baird, "Getting It Right: Industry Sponsorship and Medical Research," *Canadian Medical Association Journal* 168, no. 10 (2003): 1267–1269.

31 M. Angell, *The Truth about the Drug Companies: How They Deceive Us and What to Do about It* (Mississauga, ON: Random House, 2005).

32 M. Bhandari et al., "Association between Industry Funding and Statistically Significant Pro-Industry Findings in Medical and Surgical Randomized Trials," *Canadian Medical Association Journal* 170, no. 4 (2004): 477–480.

33 P. A. Rochon, "A Study of Manufacturer-Supported Trials of Nonsteroidal Anti-Inflammatory Drugs in the Treatment of Arthritis," *Archives of Internal Medicine* 154, no. 2 (1994): 157–163; K. Fister, "At the Frontier of Biomedical Publication: Chicago 2005," *The BMJ* 331 (2005): 838–840; A. W. Chan and D. G. Altman, "Identifying Outcome Reporting Bias in Randomized Trials on PubMed," *The BMJ* 330 (2005): 753–756.

34   J. E. Rossouw et al., "Risks and Benefits of Estrogen Plus Progestin in Healthy Postmenopausal Women: Principal Results from the Women's Health Initiative Randomized Controlled Trial," *The Journal of the American Medical Association* 288, no. 3 (2002): 321–333, accessed August 12, 2008, http://www.whi.org/findings/ht/eplusp.php; G. Heiss et al., "Health Risks and Benefits 3 Years after Stopping Randomized Treatment with Estrogen and Progestin," *The Journal of the American Medical Association* 299, no. 9 (2008): 1036–1045.

35   N. K. Choudry, H. T. Stelfox, and A. S. Detsky, "Relationships between Authors of Clinicial Practice Guidelines and the Pharmaceutical Industry," *The Journal of the American Medical Association* 287, no. 5 (2002): 612–617.

36   J. Lenzer, "Scandals Have Eroded U.S. Public's Confidence in Drug Industry," *The BMJ* 329 (2004): 247.

37   Bhandari et al., "Association between Industry Funding"; Rochon, "A Study of Manufacturer-Supported Trials"; Fister, "At the Frontier of Biomedical Publication"; and Chan and Altman, "Identifying Outcome Reporting Bias."

38   J. E. Bekelman, Y. Li, and C. P. Gross, "Scope and Impact of Financial Conflicts of Interest in Biomedical Research: A Systematic Review," *The Journal of the American Medical Association* 289, no. 4 (2003): 454–465; E. H. Turner et al., "Selective Publication of Antidepressant Trials and Its Influence on Apparent Efficacy," *New England Journal of Medicine* 358, no. 3 (2008): 252–260.

39   "Marketing Drugs to Unsuitable Patients."

40   J. Downie, J. Thompson, and P. Baird, *The Olivieri Report: The Complete Text of the Report of the Independent Inquiry Commissioned by the Canadian Association of University Teachers*, 2nd ed. (Toronto: James Lorimer and Company, 2001).

41   A. McIlroy, "Prozac Critic Sees U of T Job Revoked," *Canadian Medical Association Journal* 164, no. 13 (2001): 1879; A. Silversides, "Hospital Denies That Withdrawal of MD's Job Offer Was Related to Drug Company Funding," *Globe and Mail*, November 17, 1999, A:5.

42   M. Shuchman, "Drug Firm Threatens Suit over MD's Product Review," *Globe and Mail*, November 17, 1999, A:5; D. Hailey, "Scientific Harassment by Pharmaceutical Companies: Time to Stop," *Canadian Medical Association Journal* 162, no. 2 (2000): 212–213.

43   Andrew A. Skolnick, "Drug Firm Fails to Halt Publication of Canadian Health Technology Report," *The Journal of the American Medical Association* 280, no. 8 (1998): 683–684.

44   A. Silversides, "Highly Lauded Drug Assessment Program Under Attack," *Canadian Medical Association Journal* 179, no. 1 (2008): 26–27.

45   W. Kondro, "Industry Handouts: Enough Is Enough," *Canadian Medical Association Journal* 178, no. 13 (2008): 1651–1652.

46   Heiss et al., "Health Risks and Benefits."

THREE

PSEUDO-EVIDENCE-BASED MEDICINE: WHEN BIOMEDICAL RESEARCH BECOMES AN ADJUNCT OF PHARMACEUTICAL MARKETING

Arthur Schafer

We have made a Faustian bargain. With the best of intentions, we have sold our souls for company gold and, in the process, have put the integrity of our research and the credibility of our universities into serious question.

Prologue: Anatomy of a Scandal

I begin this chapter by anatomizing a research scandal whose aetiology can, in significant ways, be traced to the new entrepreneurial spirit prevailing in our universities. Later, I will argue that, with the ever-growing importance of university-corporate "partnerships," scandals involving the integrity of university research may be expected to multiply in Canada, as they have elsewhere. The resulting loss of public trust is likely to be devastating to our universities and to the wider community that they serve.

I have chosen the Vioxx scandal to illustrate the ways in which the integrity of university research is threatened by the entrepreneurial university and the new class of entrepreneurial academics who labour in its laboratories and teaching hospitals. The Vioxx story beautifully illustrates the perils that may befall university research when it is funded by for-profit corporations. Sadly, there is no shortage of other examples one could have chosen instead.

The VIGOR Trial: Cox-2 Inhibitors in the Dock

The Vioxx scandal encompassed the world's third-largest drug company, Merck, and the world's most impactful medical journal,[1] the *New England Journal of Medicine* (NEJM), as well as its editor Dr. Jeffrey Drazen. It also involved, in the role of first author, a Canadian scientist, Dr. Claire Bombardier, from the University of Toronto's faculty of medicine. Since this is the same faculty and the same university that were earlier implicated in the Nancy Olivieri and David Healy scandals,[2] some readers may infer that the research environment at the University of Toronto is ethically tainted to a degree greater than that which might be found elsewhere in Canada. Whether or not this conclusion is sustainable, it is certainly true that when it comes to attracting massive corporate funding, the University of Toronto is far and away the most successful university in Canada. I shall argue that corporate funding of university research is very close to the heart of virtually all these scandals.

In November of 2000, the NEJM published the VIGOR (Vioxx gastrointestinal outcomes research) trial. The trial appeared to demonstrate that those patients who were randomized to Vioxx experienced fewer stomach bleeds than those who received an older and much cheaper drug called naproxen.[3] Publication of the VIGOR trial in the prestigious NEJM launched Vioxx on its career as a blockbuster arthritis drug, with annual sales exceeding a billion dollars. The University of Toronto was very proud of the fact that Dr. Bombardier was the lead author of this article.

Vioxx (rofecoxib) belongs to a class of drugs known as COX-2 inhibitors. They are used primarily for the treatment of arthritic pain. When these drugs were first introduced to the marketplace, they were heavily promoted by their respective companies and were widely hailed by the mass media as "miracle aspirin." The miracle was alleged to be the comparative absence of serious adverse effects. Promotional advertising for Vioxx and its main competitor in this class, Celebrex, ran to well over $300 million annually.

Vioxx was not finally withdrawn from the market until September of 2004, when additional clinical trials, such as the ADVANTAGE (Assessment of Differences between Vioxx and Naproxen to Ascertain Gastrointestinal Tolerability and Effectiveness) trial, provided damaging evidence of the cardiac risks posed to patients taking the drug.[4] The trial that ultimately guaranteed the withdrawal of Vioxx from the marketplace was the APPROVe trial, discussed below. Meanwhile, tens of millions of Americans and millions of Canadians unsuspectingly used Vioxx for arthritic pain before the drug was exposed as being scientifically and ethically suspect.[5] Vioxx was withdrawn from the market in 2004. The demise of Vioxx came about only after it was indisputably shown to carry unacceptable risks of heart attacks and strokes.

The miasma of scandal that surrounds Vioxx did not arise simply because it was found to be much more dangerous than first advertised. Rather, the scandal arose because university (and company) researchers responsible for the conduct and publication of the clinical trial were discovered to have interpreted their data in an intellectually questionable manner and, worse, to have suppressed vital data that would, if disclosed, have enabled doctors and patients to make a better informed choice about whether to recommend or use the drugs.

It is important to note that, as reported by Dr. Bombardier and her colleagues, the research subjects enrolled in the VIGOR trial who took 50 mg of Vioxx per day developed much more serious cardiovascular complications than those taking the comparator drug, naproxen. The VIGOR trial, for example, showed a 400 per cent greater risk of experiencing heart attacks, strokes, and blood clots for subjects who were randomized to Vioxx, compared to those in the naproxen arm of the trial. The study's authors explained, or perhaps one should say "explained away," this elevated risk by claiming that Vioxx was not responsible for the surplus of heart attacks and strokes. Instead, they claimed naproxen was protective. They also claimed, falsely, that the serious heart and stroke complications occurred exclusively in patients with a history of cardiovascular disease. If true, this would suggest that Vioxx might have had a favourable risk-benefit ratio for patients having no previous history of cardiovascular disease.[6]

Given the importance of the issue, one would have expected the VIGOR authors to provide some evidence to support their hypothesis that naproxen was protective against heart attacks and strokes. They provided none. In February of 2001, the United States Federal Drug Administration (FDA) cast serious doubt on the claim that naproxen had been protective, which led, inexorably, to the conclusion that Vioxx was harming many patients. Curiously (and embarrassingly), the editors of the NEJM, when they were refereeing the article prior to publication, somehow failed to challenge the VIGOR authors to justify their sanguine hypothesis. Nor did the editors invite a more skeptical interpretation of the data from independent scientists.

Fortunately, rescue from company "spin" was at hand. Some alert scientists discovered that the VIGOR authors had failed to report several heart attack deaths in their NEJM publication even though they had supplied the correct data to the FDA.[7] (As we will see later, it was a similar case of data suppression, in the APPROVe and ADVANTAGE trials, discussed below, that proved to be the final straw for Vioxx.) These additional data showed that patients taking Vioxx were several times more likely to suffer from heart attacks and strokes than patients taking naproxen. Even worse, from the company's point of view, the Vioxx deaths, which had been suppressed from the NEJM article, were deaths that occurred in patients with no history of heart disease. This fact kicked the legs out from under the company's specious claim that only those with a history of heart disease were at elevated risk from taking Vioxx.

The investigators did not correct the scientific record. Their failure to do so was compounded when Dr. Jeffrey Drazen, esteemed editor of the NEJM, declined an opportunity to publish a letter submitted to the journal by independent scientists. The suppressed letter would have alerted readers to the misleading nature of the data originally published. Years later, when the full extent of the harm done to tens of thousands of patients became undeniably clear, Drazen and his fellow editors at the NEJM justified their refusal to publish a timely correction with the intellectually (and morally) feeble excuse that it is the responsibility of authors, not journal editors, to correct data.[8]

Overall, if one considers serious complications—defining "serious complications" as those which lead to hospitalization, permanent disability, or death—the subjects who were given Vioxx had 21 per cent more serious complications (of all kinds: gastrointestinal, cardiovascular, and other) than did those who were given naproxen. Tens of thousands of patients died unnecessarily because this salient fact was not adequately publicized; well over 100,000 suffered heart attacks and strokes.[9]

In sum, if all the data from the VIGOR study had been properly disclosed and properly analyzed, the publication of the trial in NEJM would in all likelihood have dealt a death blow to the marketing and sale of Vioxx. Instead, the death blow came several years later—after tens of thousands of unnecessary deaths—with the publication of a second Merck-sponsored Vioxx clinical trial, known as APPROVe.

Merck decided to sponsor the APPROVe clinical trial in the hopes that it would demonstrate that Vioxx was effective as a treatment for patients with colon polyps. The trial involved 2,600 patients. Significantly, all were pre-screened to ensure that no one who had any sign of cardiovascular disease was enrolled in the trial. Whether by design or not, this meant that it was less likely that dangerous cardiovascular side effects would be discovered and revealed. Disastrously for Merck, but luckily for arthritis patients who had been unwittingly taking Vioxx, despite the calculated exclusion of high-risk patients, the APPROVe trial demonstrated that 3.5 per cent of the patients assigned to rofecoxib (Vioxx) had myocardial infarction or stroke, as compared with only 1 per cent of the patients assigned to the placebo. This 350 per cent increase in cardiovascular disease experienced by patients randomized to Vioxx led to the discontinuation of the trial and, shortly thereafter, to the permanent withdrawal of Vioxx from the marketplace.[10]

A third clinical trial, the ADVANTAGE trial, also sponsored and funded by Merck, displayed some of the same ethically dubious features as the VIGOR study, but it is worth considering separately, partly because it helps to establish and reinforce the pattern of unethical behaviour in university-industry research partnerships and partly because it introduces some new and disturbing wrinkles to the already toxic mix.

The first point to note is that the ADVANTAGE trial was not a genuine scientific study.[11] Under the guise of science, the marketing department at Merck set up this "study" with the primary purpose of inducing an additional six hundred doctors to prescribe the drug to their patients. In other words, the study was really marketing dressed up as science. (Marketing departments call these pseudo-trials "seeding trials," but to lay people and to many physicians they appear to be scientific research.) Ironically, however, ADVANTAGE demonstrated—what the company had been denying strenuously since its earlier VIGOR trial—that Vioxx carried significant heart attack risks: five ADVANTAGE research subjects taking Vioxx experienced heart attacks, compared with only one in the naproxen arm of the study. Second, although Merck insisted that this number of heart attack deaths did not reach a level of statistical significance, the number of reported deaths was later discovered to have been understated. In an instance of unethical data suppression comparable to that which occurred when the VIGOR study was first published, the ADVANTAGE study authors did not reveal that two additional Vioxx patients died from heart attack. Worse, the number of unreported heart attack deaths was likely three rather than two. Internal company records reveal that Merck's top scientist, Dr. Edward Scolnick, pressured a colleague to change his views about the cause of one patient's death, which was subsequently recorded as "unknown" rather than cardiac.[12] When all these additional Vioxx cardiac deaths are included in the study's total, they undermine the company's claim that there was no statistical significance to the number of deaths. As if these ethical breaches were not enough, it should also be noted that the lead author of the ADVANTAGE trial, Dr. Jeffrey R. Lisse, an academic rheumatologist from the University of Arizona, later admitted that he was little more than a ghost author: "Merck designed the trial, paid for the trial, ran the trial," Lisse admitted to a *New York Times* reporter. "Merck came to me after the study was completed and said, 'We want your help to work on the paper.'"[13]

When university students put their names to work that they have not done themselves, they are failed for plagiarism. Surprisingly, a significant number of university scientists seem comfortable accepting drug company money in exchange for putting their names to studies that have been designed and carried out by company employees.[14] Prominent academics thus pad their resumes at the same time as they pad their wallets and, in the process, lend their scholarly prestige to the company's products. Frequently, these academic "lead authors" have not even had access to the raw data on which the study's conclusions are based. As a result of the Vioxx scandal and a host of others, many medical journals now require that the lead author take explicit responsibility for the data presented.

Sadly, almost no one emerges with much credit from the Vioxx saga. The drug company, which massively marketed this "miracle" treatment for arthritic pain both to doctors and directly to consumers, made billions of dollars. But, when the facts eventually emerged, the company experienced a serious loss of public trust. Merck now faces a staggering number of expensive lawsuits. The company continues to insist that it took all reasonable measures to determine whether Vioxx carried undue cardiovascular risks and is defending its conduct in all of these lawsuits. Medical journals and their editors, in particular the *NEJM* and its editor Dr. Jeffrey Drazen, were seen by some critics as being incompetent at best, and collusive at worst, in what turned out to be a terrible human tragedy.[15] The medical community allowed itself to be "sold" on these miraculous new drugs, often persuaded of their merits over fine dinners at luxury resorts. The after-dinner talk would generally be delivered by a respected colleague—in drug industry lingo, a key opinion leader (KOL)—who is also a highly paid consultant to the companies. In consequence of such "education," doctors write millions of prescriptions and their unwitting patients pay a fortune of money for drugs that claim to have a superior safety profile but which are, in fact, inferior to older and much cheaper pain control drugs.

None of this is likely to have enhanced public trust in "evidence-based medicine" or the medical profession that claims to practise it. When the evidence on which evidence-based medicine relies has been massaged or otherwise tainted, then it scarcely provides a reliable tool for medical decision making. In the interests of truth-in-advertising, perhaps the medicine practised in this era of corporate-university partnerships should be referred to as "pseudo-evidence-based medicine."

Finally, and from our point of view most significantly, university scientists, who are professionally obligated to pursue and to publish the truth were instead responsible for withholding data unfavourable to the products of their commercial sponsors. They withheld data and they also misinterpreted the data that they chose to disclose, spinning that data in such a way as to give the impression that their sponsors' drugs had a safety profile superior to older and cheaper drugs.[16] The opposite was true.

Although I have been focusing attention on a single drug manufactured by a single drug company, there is ample evidence that similar problems are to be found with respect to many different drugs and classes of drugs produced and sold by the world's leading drug companies. York University drug researcher Joel Lexchin and colleagues have done a comprehensive meta-analysis of the tendency of drug company sponsorship to produce biased research results. Lexchin concludes, "There is some kind of systematic bias to the outcome of published research funded by the pharmaceutical industry."[17]

Canadian universities, like their American counterparts, tend to measure success by the extent of corporate financial support that their researchers attract. Our universities and teaching hospitals aspire to be world-class research institutions and, in pursuit of this objective, they vigorously solicit money (in support of research but also for new buildings and laboratories) from the world's wealthiest and most powerful drug companies. The pharmaceutical industry has come to be accepted by our research universities as a vital "partner." Handsome new buildings mushroom on campuses across the country, built with funds donated by these companies. However, when one discovers the cost to research integrity that seems to be an inescapable risk of such partnerships, the bargain may come to seem Faustian, with an unacceptable quid pro quo: the loss of research integrity and, eventually, the loss of public trust.

What Are Universities for?

I have been discussing some of the ethically dubious practices in which university scientists have engaged under the aegis of drug industry sponsorship. Now let us go back to basics for a moment to ask: What are universities for?

Universities are places where scholars pursue *knowledge for its own sake*. Hence, the venerable metaphor of the "ivory tower." University research is (primarily) curiosity-driven. Indeed, the intellectual vitality of universities derives from the fact that scholars are largely autonomous—beholden to no one, least of all the wealthy and powerful elites of society. The knowledge gained by university research is then freely disseminated to colleagues, students, and the wider community. For this reason, universities are a vital source of critical perspective on many of the issues that matter most to society. This critical perspective is possible only because universities and the scholars who work in them are fearlessly independent of governmental, church, or corporate control.

Well, this is the story we tell ourselves; or it is the story we used to tell ourselves. The paradigm of the university as a place of independent scholarship derives in some measure from the Enlightenment. We know, of course, that the Enlightenment ideal of the university as a centre for pure scholarship, untainted by the pursuit of wealth, power, and status, was never entirely true. When the Church or other ruling elites/classes controlled universities, there was never a shortage of academics who sought promotion via "scholarship," which told power whatever power wanted to hear. *La trahison des clercs* was a phrase made popular by Julien Benda in 1928 to describe the kind of betrayal intellectuals commit when they advance their self-interest (by providing legitimation to ruling elites) at the expense of the more dangerous enterprise of devoting one's scholarly energies to the disinterested search for truth.[18]

Granting this point, and thereby conceding that there may never have existed a "golden age" of scholarly purity, one might nevertheless insist that there was a time when the percentage of dross mixed in with the gold was less prominent than it is today. It is impossible to deny the claim—and many, within and without the university, want to trumpet rather than to deny it—that we are now living in an era when universities are regarded, perhaps first and foremost, as engines of economic prosperity. We constitute an important part of national "manpower policy." Our graduates, many of them, end up working in the corporate trenches. Our intellectual patents generate wealth for the biotech companies we have formed or with which we have struck up commercial alliances. Universities themselves often demand and receive an ownership share of these companies, from which arrangement they hope to receive substantial profits. It is now expected, indeed it is demanded, that university research findings should move rapidly from the academic laboratory or teaching hospital to the real world of bottom-line corporate profitability. Arguably, the modern university, in its role as corporate handmaiden, has acted in a way that restricts rather than expands the scope for critical scholarship.

Scientific research in Canadian universities is extensively funded by industry. This is especially true for pharmacological research, which attracts strikingly large sums of money from the drug industry. It is important to remind ourselves, however, that these university-corporate partnerships are a comparatively recent phenomenon. Thirty or forty years ago, most research funds came from governments and from quasi-governmental funding bodies (known as "granting agencies"). Today, although governments continue to invest large sums of money in scientific research (albeit a much smaller percentage of the total than in the past), the marked trend is toward private funding.

Not to put too fine a point on it, this means that academics who seek to pursue a career doing scientific research at a Canadian university had better ensure that their projects will be attractive to potential corporate sponsors. University careers depend heavily upon the ability to attract a continuous stream of research dollars. Pity the naive researcher whose cancer research project involves treating patients with a diet of broccoli sprinkled with lemon juice. Which pharmaceutical corporation would fund such a profit-threatening idea? Which university would give tenure or promotion to a researcher who could not attract corporate funding, however brilliant and socially beneficial her research project might be? Which government agency would support such research in the absence of a legitimating corporate partner? It may be an exaggeration to say that universities have transmogrified into the R&D departments of economically powerful corporations, but the exaggeration, if any, is mild.

The gravamen of my argument is this: we have made a Faustian bargain. With the best of intentions, we have sold our souls for company gold and, in the process, have put the integrity of our research and the credibility of our universities into serious question. Data are fast accumulating that demonstrate that when corporations fund research the results of that research are powerfully biased by the corporate agenda. A worrying series of academic scandals, one of which (the Vioxx saga) has been discussed in some detail above, shows that when universities become closely allied with the marketplace, their vigilance in the promotion and protection of research integrity may be less than stellar. In other words, when the search for truth turns into the pursuit of profits, the end result is often very far from beneficial to society.

At the outset of this chapter, the Vioxx study was analyzed to illustrate the manner in which powerful drug companies are able, via their funding of university research, to successfully develop and market drugs for which the risk-benefit ratio is known from the outset to be dubious at best. University investigators, whose careers depend on drug company sponsorship, seem to be doing research that often has greater affinities with marketing than with the pursuit of scientific truth. To understand better how this problem arose, it will now be necessary to explore the key concept of "conflict of interest."

Conflicts of Interest

The best short definition of "conflict of interest" is as follows:

> *A person is in a conflict of interest situation if she is in a relationship with another in which she has a moral obligation to exercise her judgment in that other's service and, at the same time, she has an interest tending to interfere with the proper exercise of judgment in that relationship.*[19]

When university researchers accept corporate funding for their research projects, they clearly put themselves in a conflict of interest situation. Drug researchers, for example, have an ethical obligation to put the interests of truth (and patient safety) ahead of the interests of the corporations that are funding their projects. When, however, the researcher's career depends upon the direction of her findings, then there is a worrying danger that the objectivity of the researcher may be biased or skewed. Thus, if a researcher stands to gain monetary and/or career success by demonstrating the safety and efficacy of a sponsor's new drug, but stands to lose research funding and perhaps her job if she finds that the new drug is unsafe or ineffective, then she is in a conflict of interest situation.

The suggestion here is not that researchers who have a conflict of interest will necessarily behave in a (consciously) corrupt fashion. Only a small minority of investigators is likely to be guilty of deliberately skewing their investigations so as to produce dishonest results in an effort to please their corporate sponsors. The real danger is that financial benefit or career self-interest have a marked (albeit unconscious) tendency to generate biased research findings. There is a deal of social science evidence that demonstrates that "even when individuals try to be objective, their judgments are subject to an *unconscious and unintentional* self-serving bias"[20] (emphasis mine). Moreover, we now have a substantial body of empirical evidence that confirms that when it comes to biomedical research, financial conflicts of interest are associated with significant effects.

The study that first drew wide attention to the issue was published in 1998 by H. T. Stelfox and colleagues.[21] Their goal was to investigate the question of whether industry sponsorship of biomedical research might influence the outcome of that research. To answer this question, they studied published articles on the safety of calcium-channel blockers—a class of drugs used to treat high blood pressure. Stelfox and colleagues first divided authors according to their financial relationship with pharmaceutical companies and then, separately, classified (as "supportive," "critical," or "neutral") their findings on the issue of whether these drugs were safe. What they found was that "96 per cent of supportive authors had financial relationships with the manufacturers of calcium channel antagonists, as compared with 60 per cent of neutral authors and 37 per cent of critical authors."[22] In other words, there was a striking association between the conclusions reached by investigators (with respect to the safety of calcium-channel blockers) and the financial relationship of those investigators with pharmaceutical manufacturers.

More recent studies have repeatedly demonstrated that industry-sponsored studies are significantly more likely to reach conclusions that favour their sponsors' products than studies that are independently funded.[23] To cite Lexchin again,

Research sponsored by the drug industry was more likely to produce results favouring the product made by the company sponsoring the research than studies funded by other sources. The results apply across a wide range of disease states, drugs and drug classes, over at least two decades and regardless of the type of research being assessed—pharmacoeconomic studies, clinical trials, or meta-analyses of clinical trials.[24]

The proliferation of studies pointing to the important impact of funding source on the results of biomedical research should be of serious concern to those who support industry-university partnerships.

It might be helpful to reflect that in fields far removed from biomedical research there is a sharp awareness of the dangers posed by conflicts of interest. Referees are not permitted to accept benefits or gifts from team owners; police are not allowed to accept benefits or gifts from crime suspects; judges are not permitted to accept benefits or gifts from litigants; professors are not allowed to accept benefits or gifts from students. That is because referees, police officers, judges, and professors are obligated to exercise their judgment impartially according to professional standards. When we hope for future benefits, our self-interest may skew our professional judgment. Moreover, gifts and benefits make the recipient beholden to the gift-giver. The well-established anthropological phenomenon of reciprocity operates powerfully, though (again) often not in a conscious, deliberate manner, to motivate us to return kindness for kindness, gift for gift.

Although most people recognize that the powerful combination of self-interest and reciprocity can bias the judgment of others, often in ways of which the recipient is scarcely aware, few of us are willing to acknowledge that we could ourselves be "bought" in this way. The vehemence with which most researchers deny that their judgment could have been skewed by the acceptance of drug company funding or other financial benefits from these companies reflects a common misunderstanding. Researchers become indignant because they believe that someone is accusing them of deliberate corruption. What many seem not to recognize, however, is that when one allows oneself to be placed in a conflict of interest situation, one tends almost automatically, at a subconscious level, to weigh arguments and evidence in a biased fashion.[25]

At present, the public appears not fully to appreciate that financial and career conflicts of interest have become the norm for university researchers in many different fields, including but not limited to the fields of academic medicine, agriculture, and climate change. Not only is it the case that most of our leading university scientific researchers benefit from sponsorship by industry, it is also the case that the very universities and teaching hospitals in which these scientists work accept substantial amounts of money from the same corporate sources, usually in the form of corporate "donations." Indeed, it is these corporate donations that make possible the proliferation of many fine new research buildings on Canadian university campuses. They also fund the expensive equipment and technical staff without which the buildings would be empty shells.

The connubial relationship between universities and the world of business is seen by many, including a significant portion of university administrators and governing boards, as something to be welcomed and fostered. Revenue generated by such partnerships (in the form of royalties on joint ventures, funds for salaries, equipment and support staff and the aforementioned donations to erect new buildings) is seen as providing the leverage that universities and teaching hospitals need in order to achieve "excellence" or, even better, to become "world class." The alternative to university-industry partnerships is seen as mediocrity and stagnation. University administrators are persuaded that if they do not aggressively pursue corporate research funds and corporate donations, then their competitor universities/hospitals, both nationally and internationally, will win the race for gold and glory.

University administrators believe sincerely that their strenuous efforts to harness corporate wealth on behalf of university expansion make an important contribution to the promotion of the university's fundamental objective: benefit to humankind through the advancement and dissemination of useful knowledge. It is also true, however, that in their ceaseless quest to raise money, university administrators can easily lose sight of the proper goals of a university. Means and ends are easily confused, with the means (rapid growth) coming to displace the end they were meant to promote (advancement of the public good via the advancement of knowledge).

Conclusions

Many members of the biomedical research community are persuaded that in this era of rapidly escalating costs, industrial sponsorship of university research is the best (and perhaps the only viable) path toward the advancement of science. They see, or claim to see, a synergy between the expansion of corporate profits and the flourishing of scientific creativity. For example, the creation of beneficial new drugs is often cited as evidence to demonstrate that the commercialization of university research is a highly positive development for society as well as for science.

Critics tend to be less sanguine than university administrators about the outcome of increasingly close ties between universities and for-profit corporations. They argue that it was government funding rather than corporate funding that promoted innovative and socially beneficial research. Corporate funding of university research has instead led us to a point where many of the new drugs coming to market are nothing more than "me-too" drugs—invariably more expensive than their predecessors (which have come off patent) but no more efficacious and often more dangerous.[26] Big Pharma's big investment in university research is producing fewer and fewer "new molecular entities."[27] In short, the number of golden eggs produced by the corporate goose is disappointingly exiguous. Even more worrying, adverse effects from prescription drugs now occupy the number four place on the list of leading causes of death in the United States.[28]

Critics worry about the marked divergence between the fundamental raison d'être of industry, on the one hand, and universities, on the other. If we ask, "What are corporations for?" the simple answer is that corporations are for the maximization of shareholder profits. By contrast, although today's multiversity may aspire to be all things to all people, it nevertheless continues to be the case that the "bottom line" for any university worthy of being so called must continue to be the pursuit of truth.

Corporations owe a fiduciary duty to their shareholders. That duty is to maximize profitability. Realistically, given the competitive global economy in which most corporations now operate, it is short-term rather than long-term profitability that dominates the thinking of corporate officials. If quarterly profits do not satisfy market expectations, then stock values will decrease, sometimes precipitously, and heads may roll. The fundamental commitment of the university, by contrast, is to seek truth even when that truth may have an adverse effect upon the corporate bottom line.

Once it is recognized that our current way of funding biomedical research is both vastly expensive and sadly unproductive of beneficial new molecules, it becomes a matter of some urgency to contemplate alternative funding arrangements. When it is also recognized that corporate funding has drastically undermined the integrity of both our researchers and our research institutions, the urgency is further increased.

Since the fundamental problem arising from university-corporate partnerships is the problem of conflict of interest, and since many of the reforms suggested as tools for "managing" this conflict—reforms such as disclosure of the conflicts—have proven ineffectual, the most promising solution to the problem turns out also to be the most simple: an outright prohibition of corporate funding for university research. The "sequestration thesis," which I propound, insists that university researchers must be entirely sequestered from the process of commercialization.

If we as a society want public science in the public interest, it will have to be funded through public tax dollars.[29] The "partnership" between universities and their researchers, on the one hand, and for-profit corporations, on the other, is almost pre-ordained to produce research findings that promote the interests of the corporations, even when, as not infrequently happens, those interests clash with the best interests of both patients and the wider community.

Hitherto, the community of university researchers has been viewed by society at large as an invaluable source of independent information and critical analysis. University-industry partnerships, as we have seen, threaten seriously to corrode the independence of university research and thereby its integrity. Once the true nature and extent of corporate financial sponsorship becomes widely recognized and understood by the rest of society, the credibility of university research is likely to suffer irreparable harm. Loss of public trust is a heavy price to pay for the short-term benefits that come when universities float on a sea of corporate largesse.

This chapter is an abbreviated and slightly modified version of "The University as Corporate Handmaiden: Who're Ya Gonna Trust?" in Universities at Risk: How Politics, Special Interests and Corporatization Threaten Academic Integrity, *ed. James Turk (Toronto: James Lorimer and Company, 2008). It is printed here with permission from the Harry Crowe Foundation (https://www.crowefoundation.ca/) and James Lorimer and Company.*

Notes

1   Its impact factor, at 44, is almost double that of its nearest rival. See Richard Smith, "Lapses at the New England Journal of Medicine," *Journal of the Royal Society of Medicine* 99, no. 8 (August 2006): 380–382.

2   Arthur Schafer, "Biomedical Conflicts of Interest: A Defence of the Sequestration Thesis—Learning from the Cases of Nancy Olivieri and David Healy," *Journal of Medical Ethics* 30 (2004): 8–24.

3   C. Bombardier et al., "Comparison of Upper Gastrointestinal Toxicity of Rofecoxib and Naproxen in Patients with Rheumatoid Arthritis," *New England Journal of Medicine* 343 (November 23, 2000): 1520–1528.

4   J. R. Lisse et al., "Gastrointestinal Tolerability and Effectiveness of Rofecoxib versus Naproxen in the Treatment of Osteoarthritis, the ADVANTAGE Study: A Randomized, Controlled Trial," *Annals of Internal Medicine* 139 (2003): 539–564.

5   More than twenty-five million Americans took Vioxx between 1998 and 2004. See Alex Berenson, "Evidence in Vioxx Suits Shows Intervention by Merck Officials," *New York Times*, April 24, 2005; Lisse et al., "Gastrointestinal Tolerability."

6   See an excellent discussion of the cardiovascular risks posed by Vioxx in Chapter 3 of John Abramson, *Overdosed America: The Broken Promise of American Medicine* (New York: Harper Collins, 2004). Abramson also points out that the subjects of the VIGOR trial were quite unrepresentative of the majority of people for whom doctors prescribed Vioxx. More than half of the subjects in the trial were on steroids. This little-noticed fact is of great importance because the study shows significant reductions in risk of serious GI complications only in those patients who were on steroids. For the others (i.e., most of the people who ended up taking Vioxx) there was no statistically significant reduction of GI complications.

7   D. Armstrong, "Bitter Pill: How the *New England Journal* Missed Warning Signs on Vioxx," *Wall Street Journal*, May 15, 2006, A1. See also Smith, "Lapses at the New England Journal of Medicine"; G. D. Curfman, S. Morrissey, and J. M.

Drazen, "Expression of Concern Reaffirmed," *New England Journal of Medicine* 353 (2005): 2813–2814.

8   Armstrong, "Bitter Pill"; Smith, "Lapses at the New England Journal of Medicine"; Curfman, Morrissey, and Drazen, "Expression of Concern Reaffirmed."

9   Abramson, *Overdosed America*.

10   Eric J. Topol, "Failing the Public Health—Rofecoxib, Merck and the FDA," *New England Journal of Medicine* 351 (October 21, 2004): 1707–1709.

11   Theoretically, the ADVANTAGE trial was meant to show that Vioxx caused fewer stomach problems than naproxen, but this had already been demonstrated by the VIGOR study, which had a much larger number of subjects. Dr. Edward M. Scolnick, a top Merck scientist between 1985 and 2002, admitted as much in an internal company memo: "Small marketing studies which are intellectually redundant are extremely dangerous," he wrote. See Berenson, "Evidence in Vioxx Suits."

12   Ibid.

13   Ibid.

14   S. Sismondo, "Ghost Management: How Much of Medical Literature Is Shaped behind the Scenes by the Pharmaceutical Industry?" *PLOS Medicine* 4, no. 9 (September 25, 2007): e286, doi:1374/journal.pmed.0040286.

15   Merck bought nine hundred thousand reprints of the article to use in marketing Vioxx, more than one for every doctor in America. The revenue to the NEJM is estimated to be in the range of three-quarters of a million dollars. See Smith, "Lapses at the New England Journal of Medicine."

16   If either the data suppression or the scientifically skewed interpretations were done deliberately, intentionally, or knowingly, then the scientists involved could be seen as corrupt. If these problems arose because of an unconscious desire to please commercial sponsors, then a charge of corruption might not stick. Instead, the researchers would be guilty of unprofessional conduct for allowing themselves to be in the kind of conflict of interest situation that tends to undermine research integrity. The conflicts of interest inherent in corporate sponsorship of academic research are now so pervasive that many now regard them as professionally acceptable because they are unavoidable and because "everyone is doing it."

17   J. Lexchin, K. A. Bero, and B. Djulbegovic, "Pharmaceutical Industry Sponsorship and Research Outcome and Quality: Systematic Review," *The BMJ* 326 (2003): 1167–1174.

18   J. Benda, *La Trahison des Clercs* (Paris: Editions de la Nouvelle Revue Francaise, 1928).

19   M. Davis, "Conflict of Interest," *Business and Professional Ethics Journal* 1 (1982): 17–27.

20   J. Dana and G. Lowenstein, "A Social Science Perspective on Gifts to Physicians from Industry," *The Journal of the American Medical Association* 290 (2003): 252.

21   H. T. Stelfox et al., "Conflict of Interest in the Debate over Calcium-Channel Antagonists," *New England Journal of Medicine* 338 (1998): 101–106.

22   Ibid.

23   See, for example, J. E. Beckelman, Y. Li, and C. P. Gross, "Scope and Impact of Financial Conflicts of Interest in Biomedical Research," *The Journal of the American Medical* Association 289 (2003): 454–465.

24   Lexchin, Bero, and Djulbegovic, "Pharmaceutical Industry Sponsorship."

25   Dana and Lowenstein, "A Social Science Perspective on Gifts."

26   See, for example, M. Angell, *The Truth about the Drug Companies* (New York: Random House, 2004); S. Krimsky, *Science in the Private Interest* (Lanham, MD: Rowman and Littlefield, 2003); J. P. Kassirer, *On the Take* (Oxford, UK: Oxford University Press, 2003); and J. Abramson, *Overdosed America*.

27   Angell, The Truth about the Drug Companies.

28   Arthur Daemmrich, *Pharmacopolitics: Drug Regulation in the U.S. and Germany* (Chapel Hill, NC: University of North Carolina Press, 2004), cited by Philip Mirowski, "Johnny's in the Basement, Mixin' Up the Medicine: Review of Angell, Avorn, and Daemmrich on the Modern Pharmaceutical Predicament," *Social Studies of Science* 37 (2007): 311.

29   For a range of possible answers to the question, "From where will the vast sums of money needed to fund research come?" see Schafer, "Biomedical Conflicts of Interest," 22–24.

FOUR

THE PRIVATIZATION OF KNOWLEDGE IN CANADA'S UNIVERSITIES AND WHAT WE SHOULD DO ABOUT IT

Claire Polster

The erosion of the knowledge commons contributes to the privatization of the university itself. How can we reverse the trend?

In this chapter, I briefly address the problem—for the public domain and the public interest—that stems from the university's growing involvement in the privatization of knowledge. I then offer and defend a solution to this problem and invite further discussion and elaboration of it. To clarify, I use the term "the privatization of knowledge" to refer to two things. First, I am referring to the privatization of the results of university research—that is, the conversion of the publicly subsidized knowledge produced in our universities into intellectual property that is privately owned and exploited by individuals, universities, and/or corporations. Second, I am referring to the privatization of the process of university research, as research sponsors (predominantly from the business sector) pay a small portion of the costs of academic research in return for the right to shape the topic and design of research projects and/or to acquire ownership of their results.[1] Rather than just one problem, it seems to me that there are actually two main problems for the public domain that stem from the university's growing involvement in the privatization of knowledge. On the one hand, it contributes, in a number of direct and indirect ways, to the erosion of the commons of knowledge—that pool of freely available knowledge to which we all may contribute and from which we all may draw. On the other hand, it contributes to the privatization of the university itself, or to its transformation from a public-serving institution into a private-serving institution or knowledge business. These two problems are closely related and mutually reinforcing. Below, I briefly address each in turn and then outline a strategy that responds to both.

The university's involvement in the privatization of knowledge contributes to the erosion of the commons of knowledge in a variety of mutually reinforcing ways. For example, as universities become more involved and invested in the production and exploitation of intellectual property, either on their own or in collaboration with others, it becomes more difficult and less rewarding for academics to participate in public—i.e., free knowledge—production. This is because university involvement in intellectual property contributes to rising research costs (given that knowledge that was once free to use must now be paid for—often at monopoly prices). At the same time, it also reduces some of the institutional resources available to academics engaged in public knowledge production. These include research funds (as more direct and indirect funds within universities and government are being allocated to commercially oriented research and related activities), colleagues (more of whom are becoming involved in private knowledge production and thus cannot or will not collaborate), and time (more of which is spent dealing with various obstacles to research posed by intellectual property rights, such as the obligation to ensure against patent infringement). Public knowledge production also becomes more problematic as those academics involved in the privatization of knowledge reap greater institutional rewards and perks including power, prestige, release time, and discretionary funds, at the expense—both literal and figurative—of their publicly oriented colleagues. Thus, we are seeing increasing numbers of faculty being either enticed or compelled into the privatization of knowledge, which makes it progressively more difficult for those who would rather not do this to resist (Polster, 2000).

There are numerous other ways in which the university's involvement in intellectual property erodes the knowledge commons. For example, not only do those academics involved in private knowledge production make withdrawals from our common bank of knowledge without depositing anything in return, but they also slow the rate at which other academics and members of society may replenish our knowledge commons. They do this by refraining from attending or speaking at scientific meetings and conferences, delaying reporting research findings in scientific media, and withholding their knowledge from the students in their classrooms and the citizens in their communities in order to protect their own and/or others' intellectual property claims. They also do this by wasting precious scientific resources as they duplicate work being done by others also in secret (Polster, 2000). As well, entrepreneurial academics and their corporate partners may actively impede others from contributing to the commons of knowledge when, with the encouragement and assistance of their lawyers, they apply for patents that are as broad and open as possible, and when they hoard and restrict the use of intellectual property for private profit, as has been done, among many other things, with a key breast cancer gene (Washburn, 2005, p. xi).[2]

In addition to eroding the knowledge commons, our universities' involvement in the privatization of knowledge is helping to privatize our universities themselves, to render them less and less like public institutions and more and more like private corporations. In terms of research, university involvement with the private sector is skewing the scientific agenda in the direction of business needs and interests and away from the needs and interests of other social groups—particularly disadvantaged social groups. This is occurring in many fields of investigation, including medical research that is focusing more on the relatively minor but highly profitable "lifestyle" concerns of the rich, such as erectile dysfunction, as opposed to the more widespread and serious diseases of the poor, such as malaria and tuberculosis (Mahood, 2005). Research partnerships with industry are also transforming the knowledge production process itself by compelling and enticing academics to work with short timelines and with an eye to profitability (rather than pursuing any and all interesting avenues of research that emerge), by introducing more competition and secrecy into academic research, and by enabling, if not encouraging, dishonesty and even fraud in research. Our universities are also becoming more business-like in terms of how they deal with the knowledge that is produced in them. Rather than freely sharing research results and/or products with anyone who wishes to access or use them, universities are making more and more knowledge available only to those individuals and organizations that are able and willing to pay. Should such knowledge be used without payment, universities can, and have, sued (Bollier, 2002; Washburn, 2005; Schafer, 2008).

Universities' involvement in the privatization of knowledge is producing additional changes in their more general nature and operations, further rendering them more like private sector than public sector institutions. This shift is most clearly reflected in the erosion of collegialism and democracy in the university, as administrators centralize more power, bypass collegial structures and processes, and make more decisions in secret—often in the name of better serving corporate clients or capturing fleeting commercial opportunities. However, it is reflected in many other places as well, such as in the corporate language that is being adopted in our universities (where our presidents are "CEOs" and our students are "customers") and in the displacement of academic criteria by economic criteria in the allocation of institutional resources. Thus, for example, professors are increasingly valued and rewarded for the quantity of the money they make for their university rather than for the quality of the contributions they make to the broader society (Tudiver, 1999; Newson, 2005).[3]

Finally, more than simply leading them to operate as does business, our universities' involvement in the privatization of knowledge is also converting them into knowledge businesses in their own right. Increasingly, our universities, and the academics within them, are getting involved in lucrative entrepreneurial activities of their own, such as licensing valuable intellectual property or setting up spin-off companies, smart parks, and the like (Lacroix, 2010). And these activities are consuming more and more of their money, effort, time, and other resources at the expense of other obligations and responsibilities, such as providing affordable and high-quality education and serving a broad range of community needs. This transformation of our universities from public-serving institutions into knowledge businesses has a wide range of harmful implications that threaten the public's well-being, both now and in the future. It reduces the university's usefulness, responsiveness, and accountability to a growing number of social constituencies (as more use of, and control over, university resources are being ceded to private interests). Further, as universities and academics progressively prioritize their own and others' private interests over the public interest, our society is deprived of a reliable and disinterested source of expertise to which we can turn for help with, or advice on, important social, political, and economic issues and questions, such as the impacts of genetically modified foods or the safety of various drugs and treatments (Washburn, 2005; Turk, 2000; Woodhouse, 2009).[4]

In sum, then, there are two, rather than just one, valuable public resources being privatized—both public knowledge and public universities. And the privatization of each reinforces and advances the privatization of the other. The public university cannot be sustained when its lifeblood—public knowledge—is diminished. And the commons of knowledge cannot be sustained when there are fewer able and willing contributors to it (both within the university and elsewhere) than there are exploiters of it.

So how do we help to preserve both the commons of knowledge and our public-serving universities? It seems to me that the most effective way to accomplish these twin goals would be to prohibit academics and the university from engaging in the privatization and commercialization of knowledge, either in the service of others or on their own. Instead, all knowledge produced in the university, with either public or private funds, would have to be placed in the public domain. To prevent others from privately appropriating this knowledge, it would also need to be protected in some ways, such as through mandatory nonexclusive licences.[5]

Such a strategy would go a long way toward returning our universities to their public service mission. Among other things, it would help free up substantial institutional resources that could be spent on more broadly based and public-serving research and other activities; it would delegitimize reduced democracy, transparency, and accountability in academic governance; and it would eliminate the various conflicts of interest and abuses of the public trust that result from the university's involvement in business ventures of others and their own. This strategy would also go a long way in terms of protecting and revitalizing the commons of knowledge by restoring conditions within the university—and beyond—that promote and facilitate public knowledge production, such as open communication of research results, greater research collaboration, and lower research costs. It may also be the case that the university's withdrawal from private knowledge production would increase rather than decrease academics' access to the intellectual property held by others, such as those in the private sector. This is because requests for intellectual property exemptions for the academic community are far more likely to be accepted by companies that need not fear that the knowledge produced using their intellectual property will be privately appropriated by a competitor.

While my proposal seems to fly in the face of current government policy and popular wisdom, the time may actually be quite ripe for it. As evidence of the harms of the university's involvement in the privatization of knowledge mounts, a number of groups are becoming more concerned about it. These include students who are suffering from intolerable debt loads; academics whose access to increasingly expensive research materials is being limited; members of university departments and faculties who are being penalized for their inability or unwillingness to engage in private knowledge production; those in the private sector who are being harmed by the patent scope problem (i.e., the proliferation of excessively broad and excessively narrow patents) and by publicly subsidized competition from university businesses; and citizens who are distressed by the university's apparent willingness to sacrifice the public interest in the pursuit of private profit (see, for example, the websites of the Canadian Federation of Students and the Canadian Association of University Teachers, as well as Canadian Centre for Policy Alternatives Education Project, 2005 and Washburn, 2005). Add to this the more general concern about the erosion of the knowledge commons shared by farmers, Aboriginal people, environmentalists, health professionals, religious groups, and others, and a potentially powerful coalition to push for an end to the privatization of academic knowledge could be produced (see Shulman, 1999; Bollier, 2002; and the website of the Forum on Privatization and the Public Domain). I leave for another time discussion of how such a coalition could be formed and how its agenda might be advanced. Instead, I wish to address two potential objections to my proposal and then pose some questions to help further develop and refine it.

One potential objection to my proposal has to do with our ability to, and the requirements to, protect academic knowledge so that it may be kept in the public domain. While mandatory nonexclusive licences would protect academic knowledge from being privately appropriated once it is placed in the public domain, this knowledge is still vulnerable to private appropriation in the production stage, be it through industrial espionage, the leaking of research results to the private sector, or by being scooped from academic meetings and conferences. As well, in order to lay claim to academic knowledge in the first place, objectionable practices such as research secrecy, publication delays, and the like would have to be maintained by some academics some of the time. While some of these concerns may be easily allayed (for example, by requiring all academic conference attendees to sign some kind of nonappropriation agreement), and while some of these concerns may be exaggerated (given that, for example, this new policy is likely to diminish the industrial orientation of academic research), it is true that this strategy cannot ensure that all academic knowledge will be kept in the public domain or that it will be placed there at the optimal time. I encourage readers to consider whether this is a serious problem and, if so, how it might be resolved.

The second, and main, objection I can foresee is that this proposal is "too radical" and/or "unrealistic." Objectors are likely to call for less drastic approaches to dealing with the privatization of the university and the commons of knowledge. Thus far, however, I have not come across any satisfactory alternative. To illustrate, I address four strategies that have been advocated elsewhere and explain why I believe they should not be pursued.

The first, and most popular, alternative that people put forward is to attempt to regulate the university's involvement in the privatization of knowledge in order to minimize its harmful impacts, particularly the various scandals and conflicts of interest it has generated. For example, there have been numerous calls for policies that mandate academics' full disclosure of potential conflicts of interest, that put limitations on publication delays, that impose restrictions on corporate sponsors' abilities to shape research protocols and research papers, etc. (see, for example, Bok, 2003, chapter 8).[6] While there is nothing inherently wrong with many of these proposals, they are very problematic in that they do not acknowledge, much less do anything to resolve, the more serious problems posed by the university's involvement in intellectual property, including the skewing of the research agenda, growing managerialism and declining collegialism and institutional democracy, the erosion of the university's public service ethic, and the depletion of the knowledge commons. On the contrary, these proposals make these more serious problems invisible, which serves to perpetuate and to intensify them. I liken the strategy of regulation to cutting off the tip of the iceberg of the problems of private ownership in the university, making it more difficult for us to realize that larger problems loom beneath the surface. In providing the illusion that the problems around intellectual property in the university have been taken care of, the strategy of regulation simultaneously reinforces and legitimizes the privatization of both the commons of knowledge and our public universities (also see Krimsky, 2003).

A second alternative that has been put forward is to call for various legal documents and agreements, such as government acts related to higher education or university collective agreements, to be rewritten in ways that oblige universities and academics to prioritize public service and the public interest in all of their activities, including knowledge production and transmission. Thus, for example, authors such as Washburn (2005) and Bok (2003) propose modifying the Bayh-Dole Act[7] in the United States in order to make it more difficult for universities and academics to use their intellectual property to promote narrow, private interests and to make it easier for public officials to intervene when they do. While I do not object to this strategy—indeed, it could be used to fortify my preferred option—I think it is too soft, fuzzy, and, above all, contestable to accomplish much on its own. This is particularly the case in the current climate where business interests are increasingly equated with the public interest.

A third suggestion is to set up independent, nonprofit, third-party bodies—on institutional, local, and/or regional levels—that are responsible for all aspects of the privatization and commercialization of academic research, including the distribution of profits to universities, academics, and their corporate partners. One model Washburn (2005) offers is the Research Corporation that was set up by Frederick Cottrell in California several decades ago to ensure that neither academics nor universities were corrupted by the commercialization process. Here, again, this strategy strengthens and legitimizes the privatization of the commons of knowledge. And although it may help to diminish some aspects of the privatization of the university, it leaves others—such as increasing research costs, growing secrecy and competition, and the promotion of a private-service, as opposed to a public-service, ethic—intact.

A fourth suggestion is to vest all knowledge produced in the university with the state. It would thus be up to government to decide what to do with academic knowledge: when to place it in the public domain, when to make it available through an exclusive licence, when to commercialize it, and so forth. While this strategy might go furthest in terms of reversing the privatization of the university—given that the incentive, if not pressure, to produce industrially oriented and financially lucrative knowledge would be diminished—it is potentially quite problematic nonetheless. Not only is the state unlikely to have the resources and expertise to properly manage huge amounts of academic research, but, in the present context, where private sector priorities and representatives are deeply incorporated into public policy-making processes and bodies (Brownlee, 2005; Newson, 2005; Advisory Council on Science and Technology, 1999), the government is likely to be very aggressive in terms of privatizing and commercializing academic research to the detriment of the knowledge commons.

While I therefore also reject this option, it does raise the key questions of how academic knowledge is to be put in the public domain and who is to make those decisions. Will we have a one-size-fits-all formula such as mandatory nonexclusive licences across the board? Will we use a variety of tools that keep knowledge in the public domain? And will *any* privatization or commercialization be allowed and under what circumstances? Further, who will decide what approach to use and when? Will it be academic researchers, university administrators, local bureaucrats, citizen councils, various combinations of these? These are difficult and complex questions that we need to confront and work through. Before that, however, we must successfully build a consensus that the privatization of knowledge in Canada's universities should come to an end.

References

Advisory Council on Science and Technology. (1999). *Public investments in university research: Reaping the benefits*. Report of the Expert Panel on the Commercialization of University Research. Ottawa, ON: Industry Canada.

Bok, D. (2003). *Universities in the marketplace: The commercialization of higher education*. Princeton, NJ: Princeton University Press.

Bollier, D. (2002).*Silent theft: The private plunder of our common wealth*. New York, NY: Routledge.

Brownlee, J. (2005). *Ruling Canada: Corporate cohesion and democracy*. Halifax, NS: Fernwood Publishing.

Canadian Centre for Policy Alternatives Education Project. (2005). *Challenging McWorld second edition*. Ottawa, ON: Author.

Krimsky, S. (2003).*Science in the private interest*. Lanham, MD: Rowman and Littlefield Publishers, Inc.

Lacroix, A. (2010). *Survey of intellectual property commercialization in the higher education sector*. Ottawa, ON: Statistics Canada. Retrieved from http://www.statcan.gc.ca/bsolc/olc-cel/olc-cel?catno=88-222-X&lang=eng retrieved 23/08/2010

Mahood, S. (2005, November 15–18).*Privatized knowledge and the pharmaceutical industry*. Paper presented at Free Knowledge: Creating a Knowledge Commons in Saskatchewan Conference, University of Regina, Regina, Saskatchewan.

Mangan, K. (2010). Texas A&M system will rate professors based on their bottom-line value. *The Chronicle of Higher Education*. Retrieved from http://chronicle.com/article/Texas-A-M-system-Will-Rate/124280

Newson, J. (2005). The university on the ground: Reflections on Canadian experience. *Puerto Rico Higher Education Research and Information Centre Journal*. Retrieved from http://cedesp.cespr.org/revista

Newson, J., & Buchbinder, H. (1988). *The university means business*. Toronto, ON: Garamond Press.

Noble, D. (1993). Insider trading university style. *Our Schools/Our Selves*, 4(2), 45–52.

Polster, C. (2000). The future of the liberal university in the era of the global knowledge grab. *Higher Education*, 39(1), 19–41.

Schafer, A. (2008). The university as corporate handmaiden: Who're ya gonna trust? In J. Turk (Ed.), *Universities at risk: How politics, special interests and corporatization threaten academic integrity* (pp. 43–69). Toronto, ON: James Lorimer and Company Ltd.

Shulman, S. (1999). *Owning the future*. Boston, MA: Houghton Mifflin Company.

Tudiver, N. (1999). *Universities for sale: Resisting corporate control over Canadian higher education*. Toronto, ON: James Lorimer and Co. Ltd.

Turk, J. (2000). *The corporate campus: Commercialization and the dangers to Canada's colleges and universities*. Toronto, ON: James Lorimer and Company Ltd.

Washburn, J. (2005). *University, inc.: The corporate corruption of American higher education*. New York, NY: Basic Books.

Woodhouse, H. (2009). *Selling out: Academic freedom and the corporate market.* Montreal, QC/Kingston, ON: McGill-Queen's University Press.

Notes

1   Substantial evidence of the growth in the privatization of Canadian university research can be found in Canadian government and university publications and in the academic literature on higher education in Canada. In terms of the former, Statistics Canada's surveys of intellectual property commercialization in the higher education sector document a substantial increase in research commercialization in recent years. Various reports produced by other government departments (such as Industry Canada) and professional bodies (such as the Association of Universities and Colleges of Canada) also track increasing privatization. In addition to the privatization of university knowledge, several academics have examined the privatization of the university research process, and they have explored the origins of this development, which is a matter I do not take up here. The classic study of the origins of the privatization of university research (and of Canadian universities more generally) is Newson and Buchbinder's *The University Means Business*. Other useful resources include Tudiver's *Universities for Sale*, Turk's *The Corporate Campus*, and various publications produced by the Canadian Centre for Policy Alternative's Education Project, particularly its *Missing Pieces* series.

2   Bok (2003) elaborates on some of how this works, noting that universities have refused to share important research tools with other universities unless the latter agree to give them a share of any royalties eventually earned through inventions making use of the loaned materials. They have likewise given exclusive licenses to a single firm to develop basic discoveries well upstream from any eventual applications or useful products. By so doing, they have prevented a healthy competition to exploit the patented knowledge, hoping instead to have their university share in the monopolistic profits earned by the exclusive licensee. (p. 141)

3   A disturbing illustration of this new value system is Texas A&M University's effort to evaluate the worth of all faculty simply by calculating the difference between their salaries and the amount of money they generate through their teaching and other activities (Mangan, 2010).

4   Examples of how universities have prioritized their own interests at the expense of the public interest include their putting a chill on researchers and research that threaten their own financial interests and/or those of their corporate partners (Washburn, 2005), failing to ensure that faculty conform to the highest possible ethical and academic standards in their research (Krimsky, 2003), and engaging themselves in objectionable practices such as taking out—and attempting to renew—patents on life-saving drugs to keep profits high and participating in insider trading in public goods (Noble, 1993).

5   Note that I am not simply calling for open or free access to all academic publications produced with government funds, as is being encouraged in many

quarters, including by Canada's national research granting councils. Rather, I am suggesting that no university knowledge or product be withheld from the public domain in any way, be it through exclusive copyright, patents, trade secrets, etc.

6   Many such policies have been put into place and may be found on the websites and/or in the academic collective agreements of Canadian universities.

7   This act allows universities to patent the results of publicly funded research. It is credited with catalyzing the huge increase, since the 1980s, in the commercialization of university research in the United States. In Canada, a less publicized federal regulation, passed in the 1990s, also permits the commercialization of federally funded research with similar effect. Such a proposal could apply equally to that Canadian regulation.

PART 2

KNOWLEDGE FOR PEOPLE: EXAMPLES OF ALTERNATIVE PRAXIS

FIVE

THE CANADIAN CO-OPERATIVE MOVEMENT AND THE PROMISE OF KNOWLEDGE DEMOCRACY

Mitch Diamantopoulos

On the one hand, the world co-operative movement's democratic structures have created unprecedented opportunities for knowledge sharing. On the other hand, bureaucratization has taken its toll on movement vitality.

Introduction: Co-operation, Knowledge, and the Democratic Paradox

There is a vexing paradox at the heart of the world co-operative movement. On the one hand, its democratic structures have created unprecedented opportunities for popular learning, knowledge sharing, and skill building in economic life over the past century and a half. In keeping with this democratizing thrust, the movement's guiding principles include "voluntary and open membership," "democratic member control," "co-operative education, information and training," "co-operation among co-operatives," and "concern for community" (International Co-operative Alliance [ICA], 2013a). These principles lend further moral force to the fullest possible realization of this democratic structure's potential to further broaden membership, deepen member participation, and realize member potential in an ever-expanding movement to create alternatives to economic structures that too often exploit or exclude. These structuring principles hold out the promise of a knowledge democracy, based on a thoroughgoing practice of adult education and a commitment to developing knowledgeable and skillful members. Through this developmental movement (Diamantopoulos, 2012a), the diffusion of co-operative innovations should drive new frontiers of co-operative development.

On the other hand, bureaucratization takes its toll on movement vitality as the values, energies and movement-building knowledge, networks and skills of founding members diminish over time. As co-operatives mature and become more institutionalized, they also tend to become management-led. They retreat from movement goals—like co-operative education, new co-operative development, and building a movement culture. Instead, they favour operational goals—like building market share, efficiency, and growth. This pathology can lead to movement oligarchization, co-option, or the dissolution of member support. This is what Doug McAdam (1982) calls movement degeneration. Indeed, Peter Maaniche's "generation and a half theory" predicts the life cycle of a co-operative will be limited to only a generation and a half without educational interventions to revitalize the founding principles and energy of the co-operative's founding members (Crewe, 2001).[1] By turning away from broader involvements, support to emerging sectors, and the democratic ethos that once drove founding members, established co-operatives—and the movements they dominate—may slow innovation diffusion, place drag on movement mobilization, and delay potential new co-operative development. Although established co-operatives or sectors may be economically strong, growing, profitable, and even dominant in their markets, as their democratic vitality wanes, they cast a long shadow over wider movement potential (Diamantopoulos, 2012b).

The discussion below examines this paradox of the potential of the co-operative movement to democratize our lives but its propensity to degenerate instead. At the centre of this paradox is the leading role of adult education. The role of democratic knowledge and knowledge mobilization networks in the origins of the co-operative movement in nineteenth-century Britain illustrates this.[2] The twentieth-century cases of the Canadian provinces of Saskatchewan and Quebec are also compared to demonstrate the central importance of adult education to the take-off periods of these movements and in the subsequent degeneration or regeneration of those well-established movements. The comparison of these cases highlights the importance of continually renovating existing knowledge mobilization networks and educational intermediaries to meet the challenges that face each new wave of co-operative organization. For while the Quebec movement has invested heavily in co-operative education to meet the challenge of emerging needs and opportunities and has realized significant gains in recent decades, the Saskatchewan movement has neglected and dismantled its democratic educational infrastructure and suffered considerable setbacks (Diamantopoulos, 2011).

Rochdale and the Promise of Knowledge Democracy

The co-operative movement was an important part of the historic struggle for modern democracy. Like trade unions, co-operatives have empowered popular classes since the mid-nineteenth century (Thompson, 1966; Williams, 1962; Birchall, 1997; B. Fairbairn, 1994). Although connected to the great working class movement to secure the universal franchise, early British co-operatives reached beyond both the limited and intermittent involvements of electoral politics and the strictly instrumental objective to provide goods, services, or employment. These early co-operative associations also immersed their members in a living democratic culture that provided important new opportunities for knowledge acquisition, democratic skill building, and self-realization. These co-operatives were workbenches for democratic citizenship and social emancipation.

The historic emergence of the Rochdale co-operative in 1884 thus marks a democratic milestone. Like the abolition of slavery, the extension of the franchise to the unpropertied (and then women), or the recognition of trade unions, the democratic involvement of ordinary people in popular economic action was an important structural reform on the long road of the democratic revolution. Co-operatives further empowered working people as economic citizens. Like the vote or the union card, co-operative membership conferred a new democratic franchise: to make substantive improvements in their quality of life through direct economic action. Co-operation was a democratic alternative to remaining ignorant in economic life and thus dependent on merchants, employers, philanthropists, or the state.

This new franchise was based on collective entrepreneurship rather than electoral participation or trade union rights. But like the vote and the right to bargain collectively, winning the means for effective collective entrepreneurship hinged on the construction of new knowledge, skills, and relationships.

Members were introduced to new co-operative principles, like voluntary open membership, and new practices, like patronage refunds. Elections of directors introduced workers to business plans, financial statements, and the work of board, staff, supplier, and customer relations. Adult education was central to unleashing this new democratic potential.

The pioneers of the early co-operative movement attended very carefully to the leading role of adult education in their democratic project. Rochdale was a hub of Owenite agitations for trade union and co-operative organizing. Lectures were frequently held at the Weaver's Arms, a pub taken over by the local Owenite branch. The Pioneers may have taken their name from a trade union newspaper, *The Pioneer*. They subscribed to newspapers and journals for their members to read and offered a wide range of instructional programs. The Rochdale Pioneers introduced a fund for co-operative education, developing a library and a reading room for their members' use.

As the movement spread, adult education continued to clear its path. In 1871, a workers' co-operative launched the movement's first national newspaper, *The Co-operative News*. The National Co-operative Union formed an education committee in 1883, the same year the Women's League for the Spread of Co-operation was launched. Co-operatives provided strong support to the Workers' Educational Association, founded in 1903. By 1914, co-operative education in Britain involved over twenty thousand students a year with a budget of £113,000 (B. Fairbairn, 1994).

The co-operative movement thus re-appropriated the entrepreneurial and managerial knowledge upon which class power rested but turned it to democratic, community purposes. Much as literacy and numeracy once invested substantive meaning in the vote, or labour education gave the union card its substance and meaning on the shop floor, co-operative education made membership meaningful by democratizing economic literacy, numeracy, and agency. It extended the entrepreneurial franchise to democratic memberships of ordinary working people and unleashed a new tradition of member-driven economic action.

By broadening the class base for entrepreneurship, redefining entrepreneurship as a collective enterprise, and redirecting economic knowledge and skills in the service of democratic working class memberships, early co-operators both democratized economic power and laid a stronger foundation for a more meaningful political democracy in nineteenth-century Britain. Continuous involvements in their co-operatives built democratic skills in discussion, decision making, and group development, and cultivated confidence and commitment to expanding the frontiers of collective action in the emerging democratic culture of the era. Indeed, emerging in predemocratic Britain, Rochdale served as proof that modern democracy could work. Over the next four decades, co-operative action helped build the case for extending the vote to all adult men (B. Fairbairn, 1994). Suffragettes, working through the Women's League for the Spread of Co-operation, carried on this tradition of prefigurative democracy.

The early co-operative movement was thus a workshop for democracy, but each venture was also a workbench for building the human and social capital (Coleman, 1988) upon which wider democratic gains would be built. Indeed, the historic struggle to build co-operatives helped transform early capitalist democracy in Britain. First, by achieving a measure of economic democratization, the movement helped to level the political advantages structured by disparities of wealth, income, and economic power (Dahl, 1985). Second, it achieved a degree of cultural democratization (Trend, 1997) by levelling the political advantages structured by elite monopolization of knowledge, skills, and leadership experience. Co-operatives thus deepened democracy by levelling both economic and knowledge inequalities.

What relevance can this experience from the era of the Industrial Revolution possibly hold to the contemporary world, with its global markets, transnational corporations, instantaneous electronic communications, destabilized climate, and increasingly transient populations? While conditions have changed radically over the last century and a half, what future this divided, war-torn, and polluted planet may have today once again rests on a deepening of democracy; the rule of an informed, organized public with a clear sense of its wider interests and its ability to take organized political—and economic—action on those priorities. The level of popular intellectual, ethical, and cultural development will drive the quality of our democracy, the strength of democratic publics to overcome vested interests, and the overall quality of democratic decisions. By producing and widely distributing popular economic knowledge and the democratic skills necessary to effective co-operative action, and re-appropriating expert entrepreneurial, managerial, financial, and technical knowledge in the process, the co-operative movement continues to extend the horizon, and capacity, for democratic action. It continues to deepen democracy.

In its second century, the role of co-operative education thus once again remains central to this movement's potential. For co-operative development remains as much an adult education struggle to overcome popular cognitive and cultural dependency on ruling elites as it is an instrumental struggle against an exploitative political economy. As Raymond Williams (1962) has argued, "what we call society is not only a network of political and economic arrangements, but also a process of learning and communication" (p. 11). Indeed, every new wave of co-operative development requires attentiveness to the importance of democratic "learning and communication" if its campaigns are to prove successful and durable.

Who Owns Economic Knowledge?
The Elite versus Democratic Models

It is both peculiar and presumptuous to suggest that all economies everywhere have not always also been "knowledge economies" (MacPherson, 2010). Certainly, both the development of popular economic knowledge and the re-appropriation of expert knowledge have played leading roles in the constitution and progress of the world co-operative movement since the nineteenth century. In reality, the modern co-operative movement is fundamentally rooted in a political struggle over who defines, owns, produces, and distributes economic knowledge, and for whose purposes. In other words, it is a knowledge struggle for popular economic literacy, authority, and agency. Brett Fairbairn (1994) argues, for example, that the early Rochdale co-operatives were the product of decades of education, organization, and action across a wide-ranging social movement family. They expressed the emergent needs, aspirations, and capacities of the English working class:

> It is...reasonable to say that the forces of poverty and need inspired the formation of the Rochdale co-operative. But they did so somewhat indirectly, mediated by the agency of idealism and critical social thought, and by the activists of Owenism, Chartism, and other social movements. The Rochdale Pioneers did not rise spontaneously from need, but were organized consciously by thinkers, activists, and leaders who functioned within a network of ideas and institutions. The same can probably be said of all successful co-operatives in all times and places: they arise from need— when some activists, institutions or agencies consciously promote and organize them. (p. 4)

The global diffusion of co-operative innovations over the last century and a half reflects a similar history of social learning and social innovation, as proponents studied, discussed, debated, and ultimately adopted, adapted, and reinvented co-operative models from elsewhere. Dispersed memberships

often relied on knowledge sharing and bridging social capital—social movement networks, information exchange, and norms of reciprocity (Coleman,
1988)—to build their businesses. Although this exchange is most clearly
expressed through the formal processes of sectoral federations or in the
pages of the movement press, informal cross-movement and peer-to-peer
learning have also always overlapped these structures. Collective entrepreneurship thus builds on these popular vehicles for knowledge production
and knowledge sharing.

This democratization of knowledge embodies a fundamentally different
approach than the sociology of knowledge in capitalist entrepreneurship.
For a co-operative is both the construction of an economic enterprise and
the intellectual, ethical, and cultural achievement of a democratic community. A co-operative organizing campaign is thus an insurgency against the
cultural hegemony of established economic power and investors' near-exclu-
sive claims to authority and action in economic matters. It may be sponsored
by the church or state, by farmers' movements or trade unions, socialists
or nationalists. But co-operation is always based on the empowerment of
those presently excluded from economic power and the appropriation of the
expertise they need to exercise that entrepreneurial franchise. It is always,
therefore, a struggle over knowledge and skills, as well as raw market power.

Since Rochdale, the diffusion of movement innovations has circled the
globe through correspondence, conferences, speaking tours, movement publications, study tours, and a diversity of educational intermediaries (Birchall,
1997). The world movement's achievements now reach into diverse sectors
in eighty-five countries. In the Canadian credit union sector alone, one out
of every three Canadians now belongs to a credit union. Over its first century, this national sector has amassed $209 billion in assets (Credit Union
Central of Canada, 2008; Statistics Canada, 2008). From credit to hous-
ing, retail, and manufacturing, world co-operation straddles varied sectors
of socio-economic production and service. Organizational structures also
range widely, from single membership co-operatives of producers, workers,
or consumers to multi-stakeholder co-operatives. It is a continually adapting
and evolving movement that has realized vast global scope and scale. The
pooling of knowledge is central to its successes.

Today's world co-operative movement employs over one hundred million
people, sustaining over 20 per cent more jobs than the combined workforce
of the entire multinational corporate sector (ICA, 2013b). But co-operatives do more than create jobs. Over eight hundred million members belong
to a co-operative worldwide (Restakis, 2010). Indeed, the United Nations

estimates co-operatives help secure the livelihoods of nearly three billion people, half the world's population (ICA, 2013b). It is the invisible giant of the global economy.

It is on the basis of this considerable leverage that the International Labour Organization (ILO) has called on governments to promote co-operative development to meet popular needs for income and decent work (ILO, 2002) and the United Nations declared 2012 the International Year of Co-operatives. However, democratic bodies' preference for co-operatives in international development reflects more than its proven performance and adaptability across borders and socio-economic sectors; it also reflects its democratic structures and developmental potential for building the capabilities of disadvantaged and marginalized populations, including advancing women's equality (United Nations, 1995). These are tributes to its democratizing role in levelling inequalities of knowledge, skill, and experience.

In twentieth-century Canada, for example, different movements developed varied means to build up local knowledge and to share that knowledge across movement networks—from the study circles of the Antigonish Movement (MacPherson, 1979), to the Desjardins Movement's parish network in Quebec (Poulin, 2000; Rudin, 1990; B. Fairbairn, 2000; Lévesque, 1990), to the rural committee network knitted together by Saskatchewan Wheat Pool field men (B. Fairbairn, 1989; MacPherson, 1987, 2007; G. Fairbairn, 1984; Kristjanson, Baker, & Everson, 1964), to the many varied contributions of the early movement presses (Birchall, 1997; Brown, 1973; G. Fairbairn, 1984; Diamantopoulos, 2012c, 2014; B. Fairbairn, 1994; Lipset, 1959; MacPherson, 1979, 2007; Poulin, 2000; Campbell, 1983). But the diffusion of co-operative innovations everywhere relied on some form of mobilizing network for co-operative learning and communication.

This democratic model of co-operative knowledge sharing through movement networks rests on a different knowledge ethic than the elite model of knowledge ownership, which governs investor-led development. For investors, knowledge is a form of private property rather than a mechanism of democratic empowerment. Patents, licences, and industry knowledge and expertise are competitive advantages that help establish greater market share and return on investment. Knowledge capitalism thus relies on heavily protected private concentrations of expert knowledge. It largely confines knowledge and learning opportunities to an elite cadre of wealthy directors, managers, professionals, and technical experts. The research and development budget of General Motors is greater than that of most countries, including Sweden, Norway, Australia, and Belgium (Organisation for

Economic Co-operation and Development, 1984) because knowledge domi-nance is an important competitive advantage.

The currency of terms such as "knowledge economy" and "knowledge industries" reflects the importance of corporate control in this dominant, instrumental conception of "knowledge." Confining proprietary knowledge to a small group of well-paid executives and shop-floor deskilling enabled capitalist firms to avoid "training the competition" in the twentieth century. In this corporate knowledge hierarchy, innovations must be commercialized and profits from their diffusion captured by the firm. Learning and commu-nication beyond the proprietary network that threatens corporate control or profits must be curtailed, contained, and even legally prosecuted.

Knowledge capitalism distributes knowledge, skills, and leadership unequally, creating a polarized society of knowledge haves and have-nots. Owners, professionals, and managers monopolize the strategic, analytic, and planning functions in their working lives. Working people are often confined to tasks that do not prepare them adequately for democratic citizenship—or popular economic action. Others are excluded from the workforce altogether. This elite model of knowledge mobilization in the firm also has clear impli-cations for the broader democratic functioning of society. Knowledge pri-vatization and the stratification of the population into information classes threaten to reverse the democratic levelling achieved by the vote, public schooling, trade unions, and by early co-operatives' efforts to popularize entrepreneurial and democratic know-how. Just as capitalist society divides rich and poor, it also structures cultural inequalities in the distribution of knowledge, skills, and confidence. Dominant-class appropriation of knowl-edge and skills provides the already privileged with inordinate advantage over the information-poor; undermines popular abilities and their confi-dence to participate in democratic life, including collective entrepreneurship; and makes a mockery of the democratic ideal of equal citizenship.

In contrast to the elite model of knowledge capitalism—and the profes-sional knowledge monopolies it fosters, co-operative enterprise is based on an ideal of knowledge democracy—in which co-operative innovations are viewed as pool goods that deserve to be diffused through a movement commons. Of course, co-operatives also compete in the marketplace and they often adopt corporate managerial practices, including the protection of proprietary knowledge. However, the democratic structure of co-opera-tives, based on open and voluntary membership, necessarily extends pop-ular knowledge and skill development. Standing for democratic election extends members' ability to learn the business, including basic financial, management, and democratic board practices. These involvements build their human and social capital (Coleman, 1988) for escalating orders of movement involvement. In contrast to investor-owned firms that limit ownership and knowledge to small, already privileged elites, the democratic structure of co-operatives extends ownership, the entrepreneurial franchise, and the pool of knowledge and skills—often to a broad membership group of relatively modest means. Rather than privatizing knowledge, the co-operative movement structures a sharing of economic knowledge, skills, and experiences through membership governance and often through federated structures and the application of the principle of co-operation among co-operatives. The formation and governance of these co-operative associations also diffuses democratic know-how–further distinguishing the model from shareholder-driven firms.

Building a Movement Culture:
Adult Education for Economic Action in Canada

Ever since the Rochdale co-ops emerged from the great movements, debates, and movement presses of England's Industrial Revolution, activists around the world have adapted and reinvented popular knowledge mobilization networks—like the pub, library, reading room, lecture series, and educational fund—to carry out co-operative education and spread co-operative innovations. Co-operative history clearly shows that the communication channels of a wider social movement family were important to seeding and supporting the emergent culture of co-operative innovation against the dominant culture of the day. The first co-operative movement in England benefitted from exposure in the alternative press of early modernity. Examples include William King's magazine *The Co-operator* (Birchall, 1997) and later *The Co-operative News* (B. Fairbairn, 1994). Similarly, the worker-owned newspaper, *L'Artisan*, played a leading role in popularizing worker co-operatives in France (Birchall, 1997). In the 1920s, British weeklies such as *The Eye Witness*, *The New Witness*, and *G.K.'s Weekly* preached the Catholic theology of Distributism, a third-way model based on small, distributed property (Matthews, 1999). Similarly, the editorial agitations of the *Grain Growers Guide* (and later *The Progressive* and *The Western Producer*) were a leading element in the cultural revolution that drove the rise of the great Prairie wheat pools in Saskatchewan in the early years of the twentieth century (Brown, 1973; Diamantopoulos, 2012c; Knutilla, 1994; MacPherson, 1979, 2007).

The Extension Bulletin (now *The Maritime Co-operator*) helped mobilize the Antigonish Movement (Matthews, 1999).

It is not typical for co-operatives to evolve spontaneously in Canada (Hammond Ketilson, Fulton, Fairbairn, & Bold, 1992). Instead, they have been backed by institutional actors with resources, communication channels, and policy leverage. The Desjardins Movement was organized through Catholic Church parishes in early-twentieth-century Quebec. The Antigonish Movement was organized through university, church, and adult education networks. And the Prairie wheat pools were organized through the networks, narratives, and organizations built up by the activists of the farmers' movement. Without well-focused and well-funded campaigns, co-operative movements are unlikely to countervail effectively the cultural monopoly that the investor-led model tends to hold over popular thought and action.

This enduring focus on co-operative education reflects movements' need to go beyond their already existing base, both to build the economic power of their federations and extend the reach of their ideals: to identify and engage constituencies of need and opportunity; to communicate the benefits of the model to new potential adopters; to ensure intergenerational succession; to offset the churn of failed co-operatives; and to protect against the pathologies of movement degeneration.[3] Recent studies have emphasized the continued contemporary importance of educational efforts to foster popular economic literacy and support emerging proponents (National Task Force on Co-operative Development [NTFCD], 1984; Hammond Ketilson et al., 1992; Fairbairn, Fulton, Hammond Ketilson, Krebs, & Goldblatt, 1993).

The cases of Canada's leading co-operative provinces further illustrate the central importance of adult education. Both the Quebec and Saskatchewan movements thrived through the first eight decades of the twentieth century. In Saskatchewan, a strong, broad-based, adult education infrastructure was neglected and then gradually dismantled in the globalization era. Established sector leadership was focused on consolidating established sectors in the face of rural decline, market deregulation, and new competitors. From 1985 to 2005, new co-operative start-ups grew by an anemic 11 per cent—a clear symptom of movement degeneration, and a generation lost to co-operation.

In Quebec, by contrast, its knowledge mobilization network was widened and modernized, and substantial new investments were made in co-operative innovation, research, and education. From 1985 to 2005, new co-operative start-ups in Quebec grew by 152 per cent (Co-operatives Secretariat, 1986, 2006). The movement exhibited a new vitality, emerging as a global growth pole for the co-op movement and a magnet for idealist youth. While reducing the complex divergence of these movements to the different emphasis each placed on adult education alone would be a mistake, examination of these contrasting cases does illustrate the continued importance of knowledge mobilization networks in the globalization age.

Demobilizing the Movement in Saskatchewan

From the very origins of the Prairie campaign to tackle the grain trade, farm movement leaders like E. A. Partridge understood the importance of communication channels, compelling stories, and quality information. Partridge lobbied the Territorial Grain Growers Association (TGGA) tirelessly to establish a newspaper in the movement's early days. The *Grain Growers Guide* created an important forum for farmers. It criticized vested interests, built a strong ideological foundation for left-populism, and spread the pooling concept across the Prairies. The TGGA also organized local meetings to establish and popularize the farmers' voice and agenda (Knutilla, 1994). As the American pool organizer and advocate Aaron Sapiro toured the West to preach the pool gospel, he found throngs of well-informed *Guide* subscribers in his audience. A key tool in the TGGA repertoire, the *Guide* supported on-the-ground activism; organized a persuasive, consistent, and insistent agrarian voice; and led campaigns for farmer control. It helped forge a shared definition of farmers' problems, facilitate farmer-to-farmer dialogue, and built a sense of shared interests, collective identity, and common purpose. If the TGGA would become the new province's "farmers' parliament," then the *Guide* was their bible (Brown, 1973). Like the *Guide*, *The Progressive* (later *The Western Producer*) and *The Co-operative Consumer* all advanced the cultural frontier for co-operative development in Saskatchewan (Diamantopoulos, 2012c).

Against the American pragmatist influence, the agrarian press was also a conduit for the more modern, radical traditions emerging in Europe and imported by immigrants from England, Germany, and Scandinavia. By profiling new forms of co-operative development, the *Guide* also promoted buying clubs, stores, and silo construction co-operatives (MacPherson, 2007). The *Guide* spurred settler innovation, a wider agrarian press tradition, and a more vibrant intellectual and democratic life on the Prairies. In the forties, Lipset (1959) found a larger proportion of lay social scientists in Saskatchewan than any other area he visited, noting farmers were exceedingly well-read, with the average farmer he visited subscribing to three or four farm weeklies. The agrarian press established a greater capacity for rational autonomy for farmers, otherwise isolated by geography and climate and dominated by the colonial, partisan, and commercial press. By democratizing Prairie culture, the farm movement and its alternative press made economic and political democratization meaningful, attractive, and therefore possible.

During the Great Depression, it fell to the Pool's field men to form a new mobilizing network for renewal. They helped sell *Western Producer* subscriptions (G. Fairbairn, 1984) and insurance mutual policies. They helped build credit unions and organize co-operative stores (MacPherson, 2007). Brett Fairbairn (2005) argues "the Pool staff of the 1930–40s was likely the most important group of community economic developers the province has ever seen" (p. 22). But a great deal of the field men's work in the thirties and forties was educational and cultural work. They staged film nights[4] and helped organize recreational facilities like rinks, creating common projects and gathering places for isolated neighbours. Pool elevator agents also managed a travelling library for the widely dispersed farm community. These cultural interventions built awareness of the consumer co-operative and credit union models, and deepened commitment to a co-operative social project. Membership overlap with the social gospel movement and the socialist Co-operative Commonwealth Federation party also provided important validation, communication channels, and mobilizing networks for early agrarian co-operation.

However, with urbanization, secularization, and the rise of consumer culture, the co-operative movement's traditional outreach capacity was reduced. Significant efforts were taken to reposition co-operation and rebuild the movement on sustainable modern foundations. These included investments in study groups (Welton, 1986), public relations clubs, membership development, and the creation of the Western Co-operative College (later the Co-operative College of Canada) to deliver sector-wide extension education and incubate movement leadership (Crewe, 2001).

In the post-war boom of the fifties, there was an ambitious expansion of adult education networks. New retail stores and credit unions needed training and assistance in accounting, management, and marketing. New boards and managers needed training. The consumer wholesale federation organized regional education federations. Their paid field men studied co-operative principles and adult education and group development methods at the Co-operative College of Canada in Saskatoon. They assisted local boards and women's guilds in their districts and worked with Pool field men to staff co-operative schools for young people and other district activities. University extension also offered credit courses to the public based on the

Co-operative College certificate program. It was the "golden age" of co-operative education in Saskatchewan (Chapman, 2012).

In the field, as the retail stores and credit unions grew and developed their own field staff, education and development efforts became fragmented. Overlapping districts meant field men from the Wheat Pool, the Credit Union League, Federated Co-operatives, and the Co-operative Union of Saskatchewan worked overlapping territories but were unable to effectively coordinate regional development support. Centralization within sectors also encouraged a technical focus on area specialists. With the addition of field staff from the provincial government, co-operative education became increasingly incoherent in the early sixties (Kristjanson et al., 1964).

The fieldworkers' era was drawing to a close. It was still possible for researchers to interview twenty-three government field men, sixteen Wheat Pool field men, fourteen Co-operative Union field men, ten Federated Co-operatives field men, and four Credit Union League field men by 1964. But their ranks would be culled and their mandate refocused from education and development to commercial sales and service over the decades ahead. Leaders had "become more concerned with organizational maintenance ... than with creating a sustained co-operative movement" (Kristjanson et al., 1964, p. 67).

As increasing farm size liquidated the movement's historic agrarian base and drove rural depopulation, Saskatchewan co-operatives moved to centralize and consolidate operations. There was a new vocational emphasis on education, specialist training was brought in-house, and sector commitments to movement building diminished. Outreach and education were gradually reduced to the marketing activities of individual co-operatives, centrals, and federations. In 1982, The Co-operative Consumer ceased publication; in 1987, both the Co-operative College of Canada (CCC) and the provincial Department of Co-operation and Co-operative Development (DCCD) were wound down;[5] and, in a prelude to the privatization of the Saskatchewan Wheat Pool itself, the Pool next orphaned The Western Producer.

In 2013, there is no equivalent of the crusading Guide or early Western Producer. There is no formal adult education capacity like that which the Co-operative College once organized. There are no women's guilds. And there is no network of co-operative fieldworkers. This broad-based educational and cultural retrenchment left the Saskatchewan movement with neither capacity nor a strategy for meaningful cultural renewal or expansion. Co-operative movement outreach and promotion activities have been largely reduced to tokenism: an annual summer youth program, Co-operative Week events in Saskatoon and Regina, and an annual golf fundraiser. In this vacuum, community leaders and "movement ambassadors" of the past, such as clergy, teachers, social workers, the unions, and the student movement, no longer preach the "old-time religion" of Prairie co-operation. The co-operatives branch of government is now virtually nonexistent.

The lack of technical assistance for new co-operatives is a key failing. While some business development services in Saskatchewan are somewhat useful to co-operative proponents, the fundamental assumption—apparently shared by sector and state leadership—is consistent with a laissez-faire approach to co-operative finance, program, and policy support: co-operatives have the same needs as other businesses and do not need distinct supports. As a result, new co-operative proponents are frequently unsure how to proceed or where to seek assistance.

Related is a lag in formal co-operative research in the region. Although Prairie sociology, since the landmark publication of *Agrarian Socialism* in 1955, has recognized the importance of co-operatives, co-operative education was not traditionally anchored in universities. It was first rooted in farmers' movements, the agrarian press, Wheat Pool structures, and youth groups and women's guilds. Later, it was strengthened through training retreats for field men, directors, and managers at the Co-operative College of Canada in Saskatoon (Crewe, 2001). Formal academic research on the movement arrived late to Saskatchewan. This reflected late settlement of the Prairies, its small population base, its late-blooming university sector, and the University of Saskatchewan's early emphasis on extension services to farm communities. The development of significant research capacity was delayed until the formation of the Centre for the Study of Co-operatives at the University of Saskatchewan in 1984.

This research centre contributed significantly to co-operative development strategy at the federal level (Hammond Ketilson et al., 1992; Fairbairn et al., 1993) and provided an important new platform for the development of co-operative research and curricula. Yet, from its first conference on worker co-operatives in 1985, there was clearly much work to be done. Bureaucratic inertia and entrenched attitudes blocked new sector development. Conference momentum dissipated as the dark clouds of agricultural decline shifted the political culture in a more conservative and survivalist direction. Despite its small size and relative youth, the centre nonetheless raised the profile of co-operatives and deepened reflection on the promise and perils of Prairie co-operation. Although the epic project of rethinking co-operation in a post-agrarian Saskatchewan is still in its early days, this forum provides an important venue for scholarly inquiry, training of young scholars, critical dialogue, and movement regeneration.

Remobilizing the Movement in Quebec
There is a strong tradition of co-operative campaigning in Quebec, reaching back to the autonomous mutual societies of the working class that had provided fire and life insurance since 1830 (Vaillancourt, 2009; Girard, 1999) and the early worker co-operatives of Montreal and Quebec City from 1865 (Bridault & Lafrenière, 1989; Girard, 1999). These preceded Alphonse Desjardin's journalism and public speaking tours to build the *caisse* movement at the turn of the twentieth century. However, it was Desjardin's campaign that laid the foundation for the province-wide achievements to follow by mobilizing church networks for co-operative credit. As Brett Fairbairn (2000) argues, this mobilization rested heavily on the clergy:

> *The clergy...were essential to the spread of...Desjardins' co-operatives. Priests assembled groups of parishioners to speak about the merits of economic co-operation; they spoke to young men and community leaders, urging them to join; often they served as secretaries, managers, and book-keepers for new co-operatives—free of charge, of course....The social role of the clergy in the co-operatives was critical to their success, for the clergy brought both skills and legitimacy to the new organizations. As educated men who were (or were supposed to be) impartial in community affairs, above all family and factional divisions, priests brought trust: today we would say they reduced the "transaction costs," the uncertainties and suspicions of forming co-operatives. In a larger sense, they conferred a blessing on the co-operative movement, suggesting that it was about a higher purpose, something more noble than a conventional business in which a priest would rarely have taken part. (p. 19)*

Desjardins organized the *caisses* parish by parish. He "did not like to found a *caisse* in a parish without the explicit support of the parish priest, and very much hoped that a priest would participate in the administration, and if necessary, management of the organization" (Poulin, 2000, p. 35). By 1920, priests were the chairmen of 116 of the 160 *caisses* and leaders in 140 (Lévesque, 1990).

Desjardins thus co-opted the Catholic Church network—the province's most important medium of mass communication at the time—but he also made substantial use of the popular press. He enlisted a young priest to contribute regularly to Quebec City publications *La Verité* and *L'Action Catholique*. When Henri Bourassa launched *Le Devoir* in 1910, it editorialized for the *caisse* movement (Poulin, 2000).

Similarly, as church rule in Quebec was challenged through the fifties, George-Henri Lévesque leveraged the increasing importance of higher education to reposition and advance the co-operative movement. As the first director of Laval's School of Social Sciences, Lévesque had organized the *Conseil supérieur de la coopération* as an apex organization to unify the sector in 1939. He edited its new magazine *Ensemble* to strengthen its collective voice (Campbell, 1983).[6] Through the stream of occasional papers, research reports, editions of *Ensemble*, conferences, and, of course, the graduation of his students at Laval, Father Lévesque helped renovate and reinvigorate the movement. Lévesque's curriculum vitae cites forty-eight publications, most in nonacademic journals. About a third deal with Quebec's co-operative movement (Campbell, 1983). The institutionalization of academic research on co-operatives in Quebec thus preceded the Saskatchewan effort by nearly half a century.

This modernization of co-operative research and education left an important legacy. Rather than being marginalized as part of the discredited, church-based *ancien régime* during the Quiet Revolution, Lévesque's manoeuvres rescued the movement's continuing relevance and lent it the institutional support it needed to modernize and expand on new, nondenominational foundations. Indeed, the role of Laval as a "dialogue site" for the movement in the throes of the Quiet Revolution forged a powerful affinity between the academy and co-operation in Quebec.

This movement-academy rapprochement had four important implications. First, co-operative development became central to Quebec social science and the study of social innovation. In the post-eighties period, academics like Benoît Tremblay at *École des hautes études commerciales* (HEC) played a central role in implementing new development mechanisms. The journal *Co-opératives et développement* (later, *Revue Économie et Solidarités*); research alliances like the *Centre international de recherches et d'information sur l'économie publique, sociale et coopérative* (CIRIEC-Canada), the *Centre de recherche sur les innovations sociales* (CRISES), the *Alliance de recherche université-communauté en économie sociale* (ARUC-ES), and the *Réseau québécois de recherche partenariale en économie sociale* (RQRP-ES); institutions like the *Institut de recherche et d'éducation pour les coopératives et les mutuelles de l'Université de Sherbrooke* (IRECUS); and research chairs dedicated to the study of the field all reflect an abiding conviction that collective enterprise is an important feature of the Quebec political economy. The *Conseil québécois de la co-opération et de la mutualité* (CQCM, formerly the CCQ) hired an in-house research director to further strengthen these linkages. Through movement publications and frequent fora, this dense network of social scientific and business researchers overlaps with movement leaders, policy makers, and activist circles. The result is a highly expert, innovative, and reflexive movement culture that enjoys significant credibility and influence with policy makers.

Research has also played an important historic role in driving Quebec's co-operative knowledge mobilization networks. From Desjardins's trans-Atlantic correspondence, which guided the launch of the *caisse populaire* movement at the turn of the twentieth century, to Lévesque's role in modernizing co-operation through the Quiet Revolution, research has played a formative role at key moments in the constitution of the movement. The jobs crisis in the eighties spurred the latest wave of research activity. The development of the *Coopératives de développement régional* (CDR) network by Benoît Tremblay, and his secondment from HEC to oversee its rollout provides only one glimpse into Quebec's tradition of engaged research at the service of co-operation. More recently, two other HEC professors led a study tour to Europe (Côté & Vézina, 2001). Cosponsored by the sector and the state, it provided leadership ranks with important information and education on options for movement and policy modernization. It spurred innovation adoption in Quebec's movement and policy circles, a strategic intervention in the course of subsequent developments.

Second, the *"concertation"* of co-operatively focused academic energies created important conditions for new educational innovations: modern curricula, in-service programs, and a vast literature in support of Quebec's co-operative development personnel in the field. Opportunities for professional specialization and employment in co-operative development are significant.

Third, the co-operativization of bookstores at Quebec's CEGEPs and universities demonstrates the practical benefits of membership to the total student body. Students can participate as members, elected directors, and staff. This co-operative presence on campus has raised the profile and prestige of the model and provided youth with a ladder of escalating involvement as they prepare to enter the workforce. Opportunities for experiential learning are reinforced by student co-operative bids on campus concessions and by provincial program support to summer student employment co-operatives. The co-operative presence in the college years raises Quebec youth's

familiarity with co-operative enterprise, highlights the rewards of co-operative membership, and encourages careers in the co-operative sector, including specialization in co-operative development.

Finally, each of Quebec's eleven government-funded CDRs has a full-time
staff person to promote co-operative development in their region. They make
presentations in district high schools, facilitate co-operative week activities,
organize co-operative youth programs like summer camps, and publish CDR
magazines for regional distribution.

The lynchpin of Quebec's technical assistance delivery system of CDRs,
itself a product of the CCQ consultations, is the regional outreach and education function. Over sixty employees staff the province-wide network.
Similar to the Co-operative Development Agencies in the United Kingdom
and *boutiques de gestion* in France in the early eighties (Cornforth, Thomas,
Lewis, & Spear, 1988; Tremblay, 1985), its staff work with proponents on
feasibility and business plans and deliver after-care to new co-operatives.
The network is a decentralized innovation dissemination system through
which new models and applications can be tested, refined, and systematically rolled out province-wide. This network is the hub of the movement's
development system. It has stimulated record sector growth and is considered one of the world's best co-operative development systems. Over fifteen
years, the CDR network assisted over one thousand new co-operatives and
created or maintained over eleven thousand co-operative jobs (*Fédération des
coopératives de développement régional du Québec*, 2010).

Beyond creating new co-ops and new jobs, Quebec's regionalization strategy has also breathed new movement vitality into existing co-operatives. By
anchoring a sense of civic purpose, the CDRs have helped co-operators renew
their historic leadership role at the community level and regain the regional
development initiative. Like the Wheat Pool field men of the thirties and
forties, who once organized countless new credit unions and retail stores,
and sold co-operative insurance policies and *Western Producer* subscriptions
in Saskatchewan, the CDRs do not simply place technical assistance at the
service of struggling new co-ops. They help to build a movement culture.
The CDR network enlists local co-operators as grassroots ambassadors at the
regional level, drives community referrals, and encourages member co-operatives to provide credit, supplier, and customer support to emerging co-ops,
as well as to do business with each other. In other words, this development
mechanism makes the principle of "co-operation among co-operatives" more
than hollow rhetoric; it makes it a prudent business-building, sector-build-
ing, and community economic development strategy. It is an adult education

mechanism that involves, educates, and mobilizes co-operative staff and directors region by region.

Clearly, an aggressive adult education movement has driven the regeneration of Quebec's movement. It has included investments in academic and professional specialization in co-operative development; the creation of immersion experiences in co-operative membership and development through summer co-operative employment programs and the province-wide network of co-operative bookstores on CEGEP and university campuses; and the creation of new centres of regional development activity through the CDR network. However, it is also worth noting that from 1990 to 1992, CCQ President Claude Béland challenged a stagnant and gridlocked co-operative sector by stimulating a series of regional discussions to animate and involve the movement base—*les États generaux de la coopération*. Many innovations emerged from that process, including a 1993 conference on co-operative education that led, in turn, to the creation of an educational foundation and subsequent conferences on this theme.

From Innovation Diffusion to Dissemination

This very brief survey reveals a major conceptual and strategic difference between the Quebec and Saskatchewan models since 1980. In Saskatchewan, once vigorous and extensive knowledge mobilization networks have been eroded and dismantled, as the province's traditionally farmer-led co-operative sector was caught up in a vicious, long-range cycle of rural decline and agrarian movement degeneration. The result is the loss of crucial educational infrastructure but also movement memory, skills, and knowledge— what George Keen once called "associative intelligence" (MacPherson, 1979, p. 28). By contrast, in Quebec, traditional networks have been regrouped, repaired, renovated, and expanded with the support of the *Confédération des syndicats nationaux* (Confederation of National Labour Unions [CSN]) trade union federation, community movements, and the provincial state. Modernization of research and educational infrastructure now drives movement dynamism and social innovation.

In Saskatchewan, state and sector personnel have typically responded to proponents' inquiries from the field (Co-operatives Directorate, 1997; McCarthy, 1985). This reactive model discounts the active role of adult education. By contrast, Quebec's development system provides comprehensive promotion and support to new co-operatives—reaching out in systematic and powerful ways to youth and to regional partners. Sector and state personnel work closely, often with social movement partners, to stimulate demand, promote new models and applications, and plan campaigns province-wide. The ever-widening range of services and incentives to co-operative start-ups in Quebec reflects a responsive and proactive model that is sensitized to frontline needs by active educational engagement.

Diffusion and Reaction: The Saskatchewan Model

Saskatchewan's inquiry-driven approach (Co-operatives Directorate, 1997; McCarthy, 1985) assumes co-operatives emerge spontaneously and need only minimal support. The governing assumptions are that good ideas spread; when they match people's needs, they are adopted; and, as they proceed to adopt the innovation, some assistance with bylaws or referrals may be necessary from a responsive agency. This model relies on a semi-automatic diffusion process and discounts the facts that basic knowledge of co-operative models may be lacking to potential proponents; co-operative proponents are more likely to come from nonbusiness backgrounds; knowledge, skills, and experience in democratic governance may also be lacking; and founding members face a "hostile environment," including lawyers, accountants, and bankers for whom the investor-owned firm is the presumptive ideal.

The laissez-faire emphasis on self-help and voluntarism in Saskatchewan has nostalgic resonance with rugged frontier individualism and the pioneering ethos of the co-operative movement. It also justifies sector and state managers' decisions to strip "expendable" movement education and development capacity over the years. However, the history of Saskatchewan co-operatives does not support "common sense" interpretations that people simply pull themselves up "by their bootstraps." In fact, the early co-operative movements relied on vigorous knowledge mobilizations. Leadership invested heavily in movement organizations (the TGGA, and then the United Farmers of Canada [Saskatchewan section]); the agrarian and co-operative press (*The Guide, The Progressive, The Western Producer,* and *The Co-operative Consumer*); parent co-operatives (the Saskatchewan Wheat Pool); apex organizations (the Co-operative Union of Canada, the Saskatchewan Conference of Trading Associations, the Canadian Co-operative Association–Saskatchewan Region, and the Saskatchewan Co-operative Association [SCA]); and educational intermediaries (study groups, women's co-operative guilds, field men, youth camps, co-operative summer schools, and the Western Co-operative College, later the Co-operative College of Canada).

As Hammond Ketilson et al. (1992) explain, "every major co-operative movement in Canada today was sponsored originally by some larger
social movement and received educational and organizational assistance
from established agencies possessing staff and other resources" (p. i). As
Maaniche's generation and a half theory suggests (Crewe, 2001), the contemporary misunderstanding of how new co-operatives develop reflects the
decay of institutional memory and movement know-how in the command-
ing heights of Saskatchewan's established sectors. Ian MacPherson (1987)
suggests arrested co-operative development reflects a "loss of organizing
skills." Without educational interventions, our "understanding of how
co-operative entrepreneurship, building on context and networks, worked
in the past" simply decays over time (p. 10). The failure to preserve and pass
along the know-how of founding generations thus erodes the movement's
associative intelligence.

Jared Diamond (2005) refers to the perceptual trap that makes the
degeneration of movements appear normal as "landscape amnesia." In a
slow-moving crisis, he argues, there is a creep in what we perceive as normal.
We gradually forget how fundamentally things have changed over time. An
example of this perceptual trap is the present-day notion in Saskatchewan
that co-operatives develop more or less spontaneously, based on need alone.
This implies considerable forgetting of movement history, such as the ener-
getic role of farm movement organizations in campaigning for the Wheat
Pool; the role of the Wheat Pool field men in stimulating grassroots action
to form retail stores, credit unions, and build insurance mutualism in the
thirties and forties; and the role of farm, labour, and co-operative movement leaders in the community clinic campaign in the sixties (Rands, 1994).
Landscape amnesia enables us to forget the active educational, cultural,
and development policies that once built up, broadened out, and sustained
a vibrant movement culture. Instead, movement disengagement, coordination failure, and degeneration appear normal.[7]

Crucial elements of the Saskatchewan mobilizing network have been systematically dismantled over the years. Some have been wound down (field-
men networks, the agrarian and co-operative press, the women's guilds,
and the Co-operative College), while others have been under-resourced
(Co-operatives Branch and the SCA). The co-operative development system has thus fallen into a state of disrepair. In the globalization age, it has
been unable to regenerate the movement. Start-ups are in steep decline, the
movement shows symptoms of stagnation, and once active members retire
into fatalistic resignation.

The "coordination failure" in co-operative development in Saskatchewan thus reflects an underlying crisis in how we think about co-operative development. History shows that new co-operative development requires structured intervention and an extraordinary marshalling of education, organization, and support. Infrastructure that has been pared back and dismantled over the years has come at a price to current development capacity. Restoring it will require movement reinvestment. Comparative experience in Quebec supports this interpretation.

Dissemination and Accompaniment: The Quebec Model
Co-operators in Quebec place less faith in the "invisible hand" to guide individuals to the co-operative model. The Quebec model is based on planned innovation dissemination through continuous, aggressive, and comprehensive adult education campaigns. Its agents do not merely stand at the ready to assist proponents as they step forward. The CDR network organizes ongoing outreach to youth, co-operatives, *caisses populaire*, other development agencies, and the general public in their development zone. Targeted campaigns for specific models and applications reinforce the core education and promotion program. Through ongoing educational campaigns, the CDRs stimulate inquiries and start-ups; broaden the base for co-operative innovation adoption; accelerate the innovation-adoption process; and cultivate a business culture in which co-operatives are a visible, credible, and compelling option. Robust technical assistance makes the co-operative option more attractive and increases prospects for its successful adoption. New legal models, tax incentives, and targeted co-operative financing pools have been informed by this collaborative development culture, effectively addressing working people's lack of capital and risk aversion.

The Quebec approach relies on concerted action or *"concertation."* Movement organizations, state agencies, sector federations, co-operative support organizations, unions, and solidarity finance instruments all play key roles.[8] Planned dissemination campaigns have driven the growth of several emerging sectors, including worker co-operatives, worker-shareholder co-operatives, solidarity co-operatives, funeral co-operatives, ambulance co-operatives, and proximity-service conversions.[9] The state and sector have developed a joint campaign for co-operative retirement succession, including a strategy, training modules, background materials, promotional materials, and guidelines for this new form of intervention. Each CDR also develops its own dissemination strategies based on the structure of need and opportunity in its region. Overall, the fundamental advantage of the

Quebec model is that it is based on a strategic, active, and targeted approach to co-operative development and a commitment to constant campaigning. It thus recalls the historic role of similar grassroots education and organizing efforts in the movement's formative stages.

In Quebec, traditional development mechanisms have not simply been wound down or defunded as they failed to meet new needs. As job creation and regional development capacity became urgent priorities in the early eighties, the development system was reinvented, with intensive research guiding the renovation and scaling up of institutional intermediaries like the CDR network and solidarity finance networks (developed since the eighties to finance co-operative and social economy enterprises). Movement leaders also built a modernized adult education infrastructure, expanding development through new institutional means. By bringing together expert staff and grassroots co-operators in the CDRs, this strategy fuses traditional movement knowledge, skills, and networks with modern technical expertise and wider movement and state resources. This modern development network assembles a permanent research and educational infrastructure for continuous innovation dissemination. It drives co-operative start-ups and a vibrant movement culture.

Conclusion: Education Is the Future

From Rochdale to Quebec to Saskatchewan and around the world, co-operative movements have harnessed infinitely flexible means to solve the problems of diverse constituencies. Co-operation was the medium and the message of these great chains of learning and communication. Its innovations were freely shared, diffused, replicated, and adapted. The movements' achievements were thus built on a knowledge commons. Unlike the stock market, which has driven investor-led development and a privatization of the world under the rubric of globalization, this co-operative knowledge nexus has both driven the expansion of co-operation and a profound democratization of the world. Yet co-operative movements frequently fail to fulfill their full potential. Often their failure to coordinate movement expansion may be based in the neglect of their educational and cultural infrastructure. The consequence is the degeneration of the movement and a high opportunity cost in lost human potential.

As outlier cases of extreme movement degeneration and regeneration with radically diverging consequences for the range and scope of democratic economic action, the cases of Saskatchewan and Quebec provide valuable lessons on the promise of educational innovation and the perils of its neglect. Saskatchewan's relative failure to develop new co-operatives at the turn of the twenty-first century is one index of movement degeneration and its broad-based retreat from adult education and knowledge mobilization networks. As Maaniche's generation and a half theory argues, co-operative movements tend to degenerate as the energy, ideology, and influence of founding members dissipate over time (Crewe, 2001). Moreover, the erosion of member participation, founding principles, and associational vitality is often matched by increasing market pressures, growing management power, and the dominance of business objectives. As institutions mature, social objectives and the democratic movement ethos can be subordinated to market pragmatism.[10] While the co-operative may enjoy great business success, its democratic life may erode and the wider movement culture may degenerate. As the Quebec case demonstrates, educational interventions, such as new sector campaigns, are thus required to sustain movement values and momentum against the pressures of institutionalization. Using the number of new co-operative start-ups as the main measure of movement regeneration, this chapter finds that the Quebec movement very successfully intervened against degeneration in the globalization era. The Saskatchewan movement did not. Different conceptual and practical approaches to adult education and the mobilization of co-operative knowledge networks were important elements of these diverging paths.

This cross-case comparative study thus illustrates that as a democratic movement, co-operation crucially depends on cultivating and supporting well-informed, engaged, and skilled groups of founders and members. For co-operation is an educational, as well as a narrowly "economic," project. The alternative to mobilizing knowledge for the democratic mutualization of socio-economic life is to demobilize that knowledge, deskill emerging publics, and open the door to a process of creeping cultural demutualization. Educational and cultural retrenchment may create drag on a movement's development potential, stall start-ups, prefigure formal demutualizations, and contribute more generally to the stealth privatization of economic life and the erosion of democratic culture. Conversely, strategic investments in co-operative education can unleash that untapped potential, drive the penetration of new sectors, and help sustain a viable co-operative economy and build a more substantively democratic society.

References

Argue, G. (1992). *The department of co-operation and co-operative development, 1944 to 1987* (Unpublished master's thesis). University of Regina, Regina, Saskatchewan.

Benello, G. (1982). Building support systems for worker co-operatives. *Clinical Sociology Review*, 1, 125–133.

Birchall, J. (1997). *The international co-operative movement*. Vancouver, BC: University of British Columbia Press.

Bridault, A., & Lafrenière, G. (1989). Social history of worker co-operatives in Québec. In J. Quarter & G. Melnyk (Eds.), *Partners in enterprise: The worker ownership phenomenon* (pp. 161–174). Montreal, QC: Black Rose Books.

Brown, L. (1973). The progressive tradition in Saskatchewan. In D. I. Roussopoulos (Ed.), *Canada and radical social change* (pp. 62–87). Montreal, QC: Black Rose Books.

Campbell, D. F. (1983). *Beginnings: Essays on the history of Canadian sociology*. Port Credit, ON: The Scribblers' Press.

Chapman, H. E. (2012). *Sharing my life: Building the co-operative movement*. Saskatoon, SK: Centre for the Study of Co-operatives.

Coleman, J. S. (1988). Social capital in the creation of human capital. *The American Journal of Sociology*, 94, S95–S120.

Co-operatives Directorate. (1997). *Support for the development of co-operatives: Discussion paper*. Regina, SK: Saskatchewan Economic and Co-operative Development.

Co-operatives Secretariat. (1986). *Co-operation in Canada*. Ottawa, ON: Author.

Co-operatives Secretariat. (1994, 2004, 2006). *Co-operatives in Canada*. Ottawa, ON: Author.

Cornforth, C., Thomas, A., Lewis, J., & Spear, R. (1988). *Developing successful worker co-operatives*. London, UK: SAGE.

Côté, D., & Vézina, M. (2001). The co-operative movement: European experiences. In E. A. Lindquist & J. Restakis (Eds.), *The co-op alternative: Civil society and the future of public services* (pp. 52–76). Ottawa, ON: Institute of Public Administration of Canada and the Canadian Co-operative Association.

Credit Union Central of Canada. (2008, April). *Fourth quarter 2007. System results*. Retrieved from http://www.cucentral.ca/4thq07_revised_29april08

Crewe, J. (2001). *"An educational institute of untold value": The evolution of the Co-operative College of Canada 1953–1987*. Saskatoon, SK: Centre for the Study of Co-operatives.

Dahl, R. (1985). *A preface to economic democracy*. Berkeley, CA: University of California Press.

Diamantopoulos, M. (2011). Co-operative development gap in Québec and Saskatchewan from 1980 to 2010: A tale of two movements. *Canadian Journal of Non-Profit and Social Economy Research*, 3(1), 6–24.

Diamantopoulos, M. (2012a). The developmental movement model: A contribution to the social movement approach to co-operative development. *Journal of Co-operative Studies*, 45(2), 42–56.

Diamantopoulos, M. (2012b). Breaking out of co-operation's 'iron cage': From movement degeneration to building a developmental movement. *Annals of Public and Co-operative Economics*, 83(2), 197–212.

Diamantopoulos, M. (2012c). The foundations of agrarian socialism: Co-operative economic action in Saskatchewan, 1905–1960. *Prairie Forum Journal of Co-operative Studies*, 45(2), 103–150.

Diamantopoulos, M. (2014, Summer). On breaking a wild young colt: Associative intelligence, alternative journalism and the cultural mutualization of the Canadian Prairies. *Journal of Co-operative Studies*, 39–55.

Diamond, J. (2005). *Collapse: How societies chose to fail or succeed*. New York, NY: Viking.

DiMaggio, P., & Powell, W. (2004). The iron cage revisited: Institutional isomorphism and collective rationality in organizational fields. In F. Dobbin (Ed.), *The new economic sociology: A reader* (pp. 111–134). Princeton, NJ: Princeton University Press.

Fairbairn, B. (1989). *Building a dream: The co-operative retailing system in western Canada, 1928–1988*. Saskatoon, SK: Western Producer Prairie Books.

Fairbairn, B. (1994). *The meaning of Rochdale*. Saskatoon, SK: Centre for the Study of Co-operatives, University of Saskatchewan.

Fairbairn, B. (2000). Raiffeisen and Desjardins: Co-operative leadership, identity and memory. In B. Fairbairn, I. MacPherson, & N. Russell (Eds.), *Canadian co-operatives in the year 2000: Memory, mutual aid and the millennium* (pp. 13–27). Saskatoon, SK: Centre for the Study of Co-operatives.

Fairbairn, B. (2005). *Canada's co-operative province: Individualism and mutualism in a settler society, 1905–2005*. Saskatoon, SK: Centre for the Study of Co-operatives.

Fairbairn, B., Fulton, M., Hammond Ketilson, L., Krebs, P., & Goldblatt, M. (1993). *Co-operative enterprise in Canada: An action plan*. Saskatoon, SK: Centre for the Study of Co-operatives, University of Saskatchewan.

Fairbairn, G. (1984). *From Prairie roots: The remarkable story of the Saskatchewan Wheat Pool*. Saskatoon, SK: Western Producer Prairie Books.

Fédération des coopératives de développement régional du Québec. (2010). *Portrait*. Retrieved from http://www.fcdrq.coop/index.php?id=41

Girard, J.-P. (1999). *An identity to be asserted, a gap to be filled: Historical overview of the co-operative movement in French Canada: 1850–2000*. Montreal, QC: Chaire de coopération Guy-Bernier/Université du Québec à Montréal.

Halladay, A., & Peile, C. (1988). *The future of worker co-operatives in hostile environments: Some reflections from down under*. Saskatoon, SK: Centre for the Study of Co-operatives.

Hammond Ketilson, L., Fulton, M., Fairbairn, B., & Bold, J. (1992). *Climate for co-operative community development: Report to the Federal/Provincial Task Force on the Role of Co-operatives and Government in Community Development*. Saskatoon, SK: Centre for the Study of Co-operatives, University of Saskatchewan.

International Co-operative Alliance (ICA). (2013a). *Statement on the co-operative identity*. Retrieved from http://www.ica.coop/coop/principles.html

International Co-operative Alliance (ICA). (2013b). *Statistical information on the co-operative movement.* Retrieved from http://www.ica.coop/members/member-stats.html

International Labour Organization (ILO). (2002). R193 *Promotion of cooperatives recommendation.* Retrieved from http://www.ilo.org/ilolex/english/recdisp1.html

Jacoby, R. (1975). *Social amnesia: A critique of contemporary psychology from Adler to Laing.* Boston, MA: Beacon Press.

Knutilla, M. (1994). *That man Partridge: E. A. Partridge, his thoughts and times.* Regina, SK: Canadian Plains Research Centre, University of Regina.

Kristjanson, L. F., Baker, W., & Everson, F. C. (1964). *An evaluation of the educational activities of co-operatives in Saskatchewan.* Saskatoon, SK: Centre for Community Studies.

Lévesque, B. (1990). State intervention and the development of co-operatives (old and new) in Quebec, 1968–1988. *Studies in Political Economy, 31,* 107–139.

Lewis, M. (2005). Common ground: CED and the social economy–sorting out the basics. *Making Waves, 15*(1), 7–11.

Lipset, S. (1959). *Agrarian socialism: The Co-operative Commonwealth Federation in Saskatchewan, a study in political sociology.* Berkeley, CA: University of California Press.

MacPherson, I. (1979). *Each for all: A history of the co-operative movement in English Canada, 1900–1945.* Toronto, ON: Macmillan of Canada.

MacPherson, I. (1987). "Better tractors for less money": The establishment of Canadian Co-operative Implements Limited. *Manitoba History, 13.* Retrieved from http://www.mhs.mb.ca/docs/mb_history/13/coopimplements.shtml

MacPherson, I. (2007). *One path to co-op studies–a selection of papers and presentations.* Victoria, BC: New Rochdale Press.

MacPherson, I. (2010). *Knowledge, research and the people-centred economy.* Ottawa, ON: 2010 National Summit on the People-Centred Economy.

Matthews, R. (1999). *Jobs of our own: Building a stakeholder society.* London, UK: Pluto Press.

McAdam, D. (1982). *Political process and the development of black insurgency, 1930–1970.* Chicago, IL: University of Chicago Press.

McCarthy, S. (Ed.). (1985). *Employment co-operatives: An investment in innovation, conference proceedings.* Saskatoon, SK: Centre for the Study of Co-operatives.

National Task Force on Co-operative Development (NTFCD). (1984). *A Co-operative development strategy for Canada: Report of the National Task Force on Co-operative Development.* Ottawa, ON: Government of Canada.

Organisation for Economic Co-operation and Development (OECD). (1984). *OECD science and technology indicators.* Paris, France: Author.

Poulin, P. (2000). The origins of savings and credit co-operatives in North America: The work of Alphonse and Dorimène Desjardins. In B. Fairbairn, I. MacPherson, & N. Russell (Eds.), *Canadian co-operatives in the year 2000: Memory, mutual aid and the millennium* (pp. 28–39). Saskatoon, SK: Centre for the Study of Co-operatives.

Rands, S. (1994). *Privilege and policy: A history of community clinics in Saskatchewan*. Saskatoon, SK: Community Health Co-operative Federation.

Restakis, J. (2010). *Humanizing the economy: Co-operatives in the age of capital*. Gabriola Island, BC: New Society Publishers.

Rogers, E. (1995). *Diffusion of innovations*. New York, NY: Free Press.

Rudin, R. (1990). *In whose interest? Quebec's caisses populaires, 1900–1945*. Montreal, QC: McGill-Queen's University Press.

Statistics Canada. (2008). *Population by year, by province and territory*. Retrieved from http://www40.statcan.gc.ca/l01/cst01/demo02a-eng.htm

Thompson, E. P. (1966). *The making of the English working class*. New York, NY: Vintage Books.

Tremblay, B. (1985). Contribution of the Ministry of Industry and Commerce of Québec to the establishment and development of workers' co-operatives. In S. McCarthy (Ed.), *Employment co-operatives: An investment in innovation, conference proceedings* (pp. 144–151). Saskatoon, SK: Centre for the Study of Co-operatives.

Trend, D. (1997). *Cultural democracy: Politics, media new technology*. Albany, NY: State University of New York.

United Nations. (1995). *Contribution of the co-operative movement to the advancement of women*. Geneva, Switzerland: United Nations Department for Policy Coordination and Sustainable Development with the International Co-operative Alliance.

Vaillancourt, Y. (2009). The social economy in Quebec and Canada: Configurations past and present. In J. J. McMurtry (Ed.), *Living economics: Canadian perspectives on the social economy, co-operatives, and community economic development* (pp. 57–104). Toronto, ON: Edmond Montgomery Publications.

Vanek, J. (1971). *The participatory economy: An evolutionary hypothesis and a strategy for development*. Ithaca, NY: Cornell University Press.

Welton, M. (1986, Fall). Conflicting visions, divergent strategies: Watson Thomson and the Cold War politics of adult education in Saskatchewan, 1944–6. *Labour/ Le Travail*, 18, 111–138.

Williams, R. (1962). *Culture and society: 1780–1950*. New York, NY: Columbia University Press.

Notes

1   Maaniche's theory underpinned significant innovations in co-operative adult education in Saskatchewan in the forties and fifties (Crewe, 2001, p. 12). It suggests that, like corporate boards, movements, too, need succession planning.

2   While there were precursors to the Rochdale co-operatives, the development of these principles are commonly recognized as the most important foundation, and impetus, to the modern co-operative movement (Birchall, 1997; Fairbairn, 1994).

3   McAdam (1982, pp. 55–56) argues that formalizing social movement
     organizations, while crucial to sustained insurgency, also represents new
     movement dilemmas that can lead to degeneration from within. There are
     three such degenerative processes. First, in oligarchization, a class of leaders
     or managers may emerge who value sustaining the organization over the
     achievement of movement goals. Second, in co-optation, reliance on external
     support can divert insurgents from movement goals toward compromises with
     sponsors. Third, in the dissolution of indigenous support, formal movement
     organizations often overextend themselves into lobbying and alliance building
     and gradually lose the trust of their core constituency. This process may
     combine with processes of oligarchization and co-optation. The result is a
     powerful degenerative spiral of activist disenchantment and disengagement.

4   The Prairie tradition of showing movies was part of a strategy to boost the
     circulation of *The Western Producer*. Field men offered free admission to
     families with paid subscriptions. In fact, pool field men signed up 5,393
     subscribers to launch *The Western Producer*. One winter, field men were
     directed to devote a full two weeks to a single-minded drive to build the
     subscriber base (G. Fairbairn, 1984).

5   The wind down of Saskatchewan's DCCD provides a stark example of the
     rollback of economic pluralism and the consolidation of investor-owned
     firm hegemony in the eighties (Argue, 1992). Early in their second term, the
     Devine Tories formally disbanded the DCCD, reducing it to a branch in the
     Department of Economic Diversification and Trade. Where the DCCD had
     brought together a focused workforce of seventy-eight in 1982, by 1987, only
     thirty-five staff remained. Twenty-two were reassigned to the Department
     of Tourism, Small Business and Co-operatives and thirteen went to the
     Department of Consumer and Commercial Affairs (pp. 122–123). Since
     taking power in 1982, the Devine regime had cut the number of personnel
     dealing with co-operatives by more than half. In the new "common sense"
     of neoconservatism, co-operatives were like any other business and would
     not receive state favouritism; the influence of these remaining co-operative
     specialists was therefore diminished, dispersed, and diluted. This muscular
     assertion of exclusive investor authority sent a clear message to the public:
     the economy is no place for democratic social action. In short, the very idea of
     entrepreneurship itself was privatized in the neoliberal age.

6   This was no small achievement. Desjardins had gone to his grave in 1920,
     unsuccessful in his efforts to persuade the 138 *caisses* then in operation to
     form a second-tier federation to deliver financial and technical services to its
     branches (Poulin, 2000).

7   Jacoby (1975) argues there is a "general loss of memory" that he calls "social
     amnesia—memory driven out of mind by the social and economic dynamic of
     this society ... a forgetting and repression of the human and social activity that
     makes and can remake society." He argues

         the syndrome is a general one. In brief, society has lost its memory, and
         with it, its mind. The inability or refusal to think back takes its toll in

*the inability to think. The loss of memory assumes a multitude of forms,
from a "radical" empiricism and positivism that unloads past thought like
so much "intellectual baggage" to hip theories that salute the giants and
geniuses of the past as unfortunates born too soon. The latter ... in the
impatience to contrive new and novel theories hustle through the past
as if it were the junk yard of wrecked ideas. "In every era," wrote Walter
Benjamin, "the attempt must be made to wrest tradition away from a
conformism that is about to overcome it." (pp. 3–4).*

8   The conversion of many of Quebec's investor-owned ambulance firms to union-
led worker ownership provides an illustration. Without the mobilizing leverage
of the CSN, which was open to the co-operative model and to collaborating with
the co-operative movement (and vice versa), it is very doubtful that individual
groups of emergency medical services (EMS) workers would have been able or
willing to decide to adopt this innovation strategy in 1988. Moreover, the CSN
itself did not even come into existence until 1960, as an expression of that
broad-based social movement known as the Quiet Revolution. By establishing
a credit union in 1971, it built its financial know-how and capacity to launch
an in-house technical assistance unit for worker co-operatives in 1987 and a
labour-sponsored investment fund in 1996. Over three and a half decades, the
trade union put in place the mechanisms that were also necessary conditions
for successful innovation adoption by the EMS workers.

Other crucial development mechanisms included a parallel chain of
innovations within the state apparatus. This innovation chain included the
formation of a co-operatives branch in 1963; the introduction of co-operative
development subsidies in 1976; the creation of a system of development
groups and a crown corporation to finance co-operatives in 1979; the creation
of an act enabling the formation of worker-shareholder co-operatives in 1983;
and the creation of the CDR network and an enabling policy framework,
including tax incentives for worker buy-outs, in 1985.

This chain of movement and public policy innovations transformed the
climate for co-operative conversion, overcoming crucial barriers to subsequent
innovation adoption. Moreover, the coordination of these disparate elements
into a coherent development system (Lewis, 2004) rested on a mobilizing
network that encompassed, and brought into strategic alignment, the
CSN, the CCQ (later the CQCM), and the state. A series of conferences and
summits helped to integrate these efforts across popular sectors and the state
apparatus.

The ambulance buyouts are cases of *contingent innovation decision making*,
"choices to adopt or reject that can be made only after a prior innovation-
decision" (Rogers, 1995, p. 30). The effective diffusion of this innovation,
therefore, rested on the structures of the state and labour and co-operative
movements' prior innovation decisions. In particular, the conversion of the
EMS personnel from wage labourers to member owners depended on the
commitment of the CSN to develop a technical assistance unit and solidarity

finance fund. The CSN's move to establish these development mechanisms, in turn, needs to be understood as a response partially conditioned by two prior innovation decisions. The first enabling innovation decision was its involvement in the founding of its *caisse d'économie*. This institution was able to provide financing to the emerging co-operatives. It also built the CSN leadership's confidence in increased involvement in economic development innovation. The prior innovation decision of its rival federation, the QFL, to launch the Solidarity Fund in 1983, further reinforced this commitment to innovate.

The possibility of the ambulance sector co-operativization campaign also depended on broader state and co-operative sector innovations. Specifically, it hinged on the development of the regional development co-operative network and other policy reforms pushed forward by the provincial apex organization, now known as the CQCM. These movement structures and development mechanisms, themselves impressive examples of social innovation, effectively defined the viability, and even the possibility of co-operative innovation diffusion, in the ambulance sector. With this strong movement and technical assistance mobilization, a substantial share of Quebec's EMS services are now delivered by worker co-operatives.

9   For example, in 2003, Quebec was the home to four community clinics, six ambulance co-ops, fifty homecare co-ops, twenty-six funeral co-ops, and four farmers market co-ops. None of these sectors even existed a decade earlier (Co-operatives Secretariat, 1994, 2004).

10 Co-operatives often face incredible pressures to institutional isomorphism (DiMaggio & Powell, 2004, pp. 111–134), i.e., to conform to the hegemonic, investor-owned firm model or to at least downplay the co-operative difference. Indeed, the investor-led development model creates a "hostile environment" (Halladay & Peile, 1988; Vanek, 1971; Benello, 1982) for co-operative innovation, pressuring assimilation into the dominant corporate culture. While state-funding criteria and dependency can steer political protest movement energies in ways that undermine movement autonomy and self-determination, co-operative movements are often challenged by the power of market values. Pressures to mimic corporate sector practices can reinforce degenerative tendencies toward traditional corporate managerialism (oligarchization), a price-point orientation to members as customers (dissolution of member support), and a favouring of traditional, bottom-line, business-focused approaches over member-driven, democratic governance (co-optation).

SIX

LIBERATING OUR PUBLIC AIRWAVES: SOUNDING OFF!

Marian van der Zon

Using numerous forms of media and expression creates collaborations that strengthen our attempts to spread knowledge in grassroots ways.

R adio has an incredible capacity to open spaces for creativity, a potential that encompasses community, knowledge, and resistance. Around the world, communities are rising up, taking media production into their own hands, speaking out, and liberating the airwaves. Perhaps this is because when we look to corporate and commercial media models, we are not met with the diversity of voices and identities that are represented in our population. Instead, our mediascape overflows with redundant messages and information that is tailored to encourage consumption and perpetuate dominant ideologies—it is a very particular set of values that are reflected in standard programming. In Canada, the Canadian Radio-television and Telecommunications Commission (CRTC) exists as the regulating body of our "public airwaves."[1] The CRTC is mandated to regulate our "public airwaves" in the "public interest." However, when granting licences, the CRTC has long favoured corporate and commercial radio stations[2] over autonomous alternatives.[3] This even applies to content,[4] demonstrating that our "public airwaves" are not truly public at all. Only a few voices are heard and thus many communities are finding their own locally empowered approaches to ensure that community knowledge is valued and heard. They are actively engaged in making their own meaning. While we have been told that "radio is dead" for over a decade, certain types of radio continue to flourish in small communities across Canada and around the world, because it is an inexpensive form of media and one that can be even more easily accessed on the receiving end. Additionally, getting involved in radio projects, be they unlicensed or low power, allows communities to flourish, individuals to be empowered, and diverse knowledges to be freed.[5] This chapter focuses on examples of unlicensed and low-power radio projects, projects that allow us to question and challenge the status quo, creating our own realities.

Unlicensed radio has been with us a long time.[6] The term "pirate radio" originates from unlicensed radio being used on ships in international waters to escape countries' regulatory sanctions. Radio Caroline is likely the most well-known example of ship-to-shore pirate radio communication, beginning in 1964, and is mostly known for its broadcast of what was then considered risqué music—the rock and roll of the Rolling Stones and the Beatles. The Voice of Peace, a station active off the Israeli coast in the 1970s, was likewise known for its broadcast of rock and roll music and the station founder's stated attempt to "foster understanding between the Arabs and the Jews through the international medium of music."[7] In this example, the genre of music moved beyond rock and roll into protest folk music.

The term "pirate radio" may have originated with radio stations being located offshore, but it quickly became used by unlicensed radio practitioners on land. Also during the 1970s, Radio Alice emerged in Italy as a notable example. This station was dramatically different in terms of its politicized content and organizational mandate. Radio Alice embraced the Autonomia movement and anarchist politics, envisioning the station as autonomous from government and private economic models, freely discussing politics over the air and using techniques such as uncensored talk radio, where participants might call in from behind protest lines, with strategic reports, rants, or humour. The Italian state deemed this to be overly threatening, imprisoned the operators, and shut the station down.[8] When the status quo is overtly threatened, regulatory measures often follow in order to censor any potentially radical messages.

Pirate radio remains alive and well in contemporary times, both internationally and in Canada. Many unlicensed radio practitioners may not choose the term "pirate radio," instead using "free radio," or the less political term, "unlicensed radio."[9] Regardless of the label used, unlicensed radio provides greater freedom in how a radio station is set up, organized, and used, including the content. In Canada, this far surpasses the possibilities afforded to us by commercial radio or public radio, such as through the CBC, and it also surpasses the possibilities of campus and community radio. Having been personally involved in radio for over ten years, including public radio and numerous campus and community stations,[10] I have also been directly and indirectly (through extensive research) part of pirate radio stations across Canada, and part of the following argument draws from personal experience.[11] I have recently returned to campus and community radio, and begun producing and hosting a spoken word show, *Be the Media*, on my local station, CHLY 101.7FM in Nanaimo, British Columbia. While this station, like many campus and community radio stations, does afford greater freedoms in terms of show content and individuals accessing the airwaves, hosting the show has brought to mind many of the formalities that do not exist in pirate radio. Scheduled station identifications, promos, language considerations, Canadian content considerations, time considerations, and fund-drive obligations were all necessary from the onset of this show. Sheila Nopper, a current radio pirate and former campus and community radio host and producer, effectively outlines numerous restrictions presented by our most accessible public radio, campus, and community stations.[12] She documents the limitations I have noted above in detail but also delves into the organizational problems and show-structure limitations that she has been up against in campus and community radio—limitations that have been freed up in her experiences with pirate radio.

Radio can be an incredible tool for disseminating knowledge. While many of our commercial and public radio stations exemplify the limitations of who gets to speak over our public airwaves, low-power radio can easily break this mold. Low-power radio is low wattage and therefore has a small broadcast range—listeners may be able to tune in from ten feet to ten kilometres. It often refers to narrowcasting rather then broadcasting and focuses on building specific communities and participation in the production of media. These stations are often unlicensed and tend to fly beneath the radar of regulatory bodies due to their small narrowcast range.[13] Numerous examples abound. Tetsuo Kogawa used low-power radio in Tokyo during the 1980s to create community, for example. This is a common goal of low-power radio practitioners. While he was only using one- or two-watt stations, providing a listening range of around three blocks, given the density of Tokyo, this translated to potentially connecting with ten thousand people. His low-power transmissions became so popular that ten companies, including Mitsubishi, Panasonic, Hitachi, and Sony, began to manufacture transmitters.[14]

From Radio Zomorana in Merida, Venezuela, which helped to mobilize people in the revolution of 2002,[15] to Radio Libertad in Guerrero, Mexico, an example of cross-country media solidarity,[16] to Radio Planton in Oaxaca, Mexico, an example of grassroots citizens occupying national media stations,[17] to the Free Radio Movement spearheaded by Mbanna Kantanko in the ghetto in Springfield, Illinois,[18] the examples of individuals using low-power and unlicensed radio to organize, create alliances, and disseminate knowledge surround us.

In Canada, unlicensed radio has historically and is currently used for purposes of building community, protest, maintaining language and culture in Indigenous communities, and for festivals and sound art.[19] While in all cases, pirate radio can be used to free knowledge and information, and to empower and create communities,[20] the use of it in protest situations provides a particularly powerful example. Here pirate radio can be used to provide tactical information or broadcast knowledge from perspectives seldom heard. During the 1999 protest in Seattle against the World Trade Organization, we saw numerous examples of collaboration and grassroots action. Using stickers and flyers to spread the word about radio broadcasts, people could receive information in a number of ways. One protestor had a small suitcase radio and used an umbrella as an antenna. While this may have only reached a few blocks, it was enough to transmit outside of the protest zone, which, in turn, could be picked up by Y2WTKO, which rebroadcast out of a tree on the Olympic peninsula, only to be picked up and rebroadcast by other radio and television broadcasters.[21] Radio Free Seattle linked up with Radio X to stream over the Internet. It is this combination of low-power radio piggy-backing combined with other forms of media, like Internet streaming and street art, that allow information and knowledge to spread through activist communities and beyond into the mainstream. This is only one example of unlicensed radio being used for protest purposes. In Montreal, in 2003, Radio Taktic was used to raise awareness of homeless issues at a tent city and Rock the WTO Radio was used during the World Trade Organization's mini-ministerial meetings to provide alternative information.[22]

In all of these radio examples, the building of community, valuing of Traditional Knowledge,[23] and resistance to domination are recurring themes. Part of the strength of low-power radio is that it can be organized for numerous purposes and in many forms, and yet it can quickly change and evolve as the circumstances require.

Small Strides: Empowering Media Production One Watt at a Time

Having personally founded a pirate radio station in 2003, and since having run this station, it is clear that unlicensed radio, in fact, the same station, can be used in various ways. Because this station, known as Temporary Autonomous Radio (TAR), is not permanent or fixed to a specific frequency, it has greater flexibility and has been used by numerous people who have had different goals in mind. In every case, however, community building and knowledge dissemination have been key. The name, "Temporary Autonomous Radio," was inspired by Hakim Bey's concept of Temporary Autonomous Zones. These zones of autonomy require three primary elements: first, they must be freely chosen, providing an intentional affinity group; second, they must include the element of festival, fun, and celebration, in a spontaneous manner; and finally, they must have a particular mindset. Here Bey borrows the term "psychic nomadism" from Gilles Deleuze and Felix Guattari to depict a traveller who is adventurous, mobile, and active. All of these elements fit TAR perfectly and the name stuck.[24]

Since its inception, TAR has been used for pirate parties (where friends and affinity groups gather to take over the airwaves); workshops (where TAR is used as an example of how accessible the technology can be); music festivals (where TAR has hosted 9–14 live bands and numerous social justice interviews, taking over the airwaves of a city for a day).[25] It has also been used to add a radio element to preplanned events, provide an avenue for children to use radio (from hosting to using the technology), provide an environment that is conducive to learning (particularly for women),[26] and stage radio theatre (*Desire & Machines: Auralizing Community*).[27] TAR has been used as a hands-on component at radio conferences (National Campus and Community Radio Association Conference), and it has been lent out to others for their own projects (Cj Your Dj of CSSH, Shh, Rez Pirate Radio, 100.1FM, in the Cowichan Valley).

For example, in June 2010, the National Campus and Community Radio Association (NCRA) conference was held on Gabriola Island, British Columbia. Gabriola Island has been in the process of applying for a low-power community radio licence since 2002. (This speaks to the various barriers of securing a licence in Canada; it requires considerable expense, expertise, and time.)[28] Because Gabriola Island's radio station, CKGI, was not yet on air, I was asked to step in and provide a temporary radio station for the event. Using TAR's technical gear provided an easy solution, only requiring three hours to set up the station, troubleshoot, and stay on air for a full week throughout the conference. Conference organizers had secured a temporary licence for the broadcast. On my part, it was yet another opportunity to use TAR to build community and disseminate the proceedings and interviews that surrounded the conference. It was also a clear indicator of how easily one can use unlicensed radio, or the gear of an unlicensed station, to free knowledge.

This theme continued through the summer of 2010. After using TAR for the NCRA conference on Gabriola Island, it languished in a cardboard box for a few weeks. A friend, Cj Your Dj, asked to borrow all of the station's equipment so she could set up a pirate radio station, CSSH, Shh, Rez Pirate Radio, 100.1FM, in the Cowichan Valley, British Columbia, with the intention of bridging communication between "native and non-native entities."[29] Additionally, she wanted to bring Native issues and musical talent out to the community.[30] Here is an example of a radio station that worked to maintain Indigenous Traditional Knowledge and create new forms of local knowledge by moving across communities and culture.

Because all of TAR's equipment was available, I was excited to loan it out to Cj. On a hot summer day in July, I arrived to help her set up the station. Cj had a nephew come by to attach the antenna onto the roof, we set up the transmitter in the attic of the home, and the on-air booth was located in the living room. After troubleshooting and checking the range, I left. Cj then proceeded to run the station for the next two months, consistently three to four days per week. She played Indigenous music, but even more, she spent considerable time interviewing Elders on the reserve with the intention of maintaining Traditional Knowledge. Cj Your Dj, states:

> I wooed the Elders by attending their lunches, giving a presentation (a couple of times), and spending time with them to get to know their concerns. I got to know and love many of them, and they got to expect me at their lunches. I was just getting to the point of winning their trust when summer ended. I did get to present a few interviews on my radio station near the end of summer, and found that one hour was usually never enough time. I found the interviews that I did get, to be serious, provocative, and highly emotional, and so—yes, very successful.[31]

For Cj, one of the highlights of the experience she describes is that "[I] inspired many people to want to do something or learn something more. I especially appreciated the interest of the younger listeners; seeing their faces light up with the idea of new possibilities was a great treasure."[32] Using pirate radio was motivating for her. It allowed her to build community connections and spearhead a project. Even those peripherally involved in the project were excited by the ease in which they could access the microphone. It is extremely time-consuming to run a radio station and in this way limited—Cj did not have the time to continue the station into the fall. She has since gone on to use other forms of media to promote Native music.[33]

Unlicensed radio has often been used in Indigenous communities in Canada.[34] Neskie Manuel of Secwepemc Radio on the Neskonlith Reserve states:

> We did not get a license from the CRTC when starting because of our position that as aboriginal people we did not give up our right to make use of the electromagnetic spectrum to carry on our traditions, language and culture. Operating this radio station is an expression of who we are as a people; it is the modern version of the campfire where people would share stories.[35]

Manuel speaks from a position where he and his community chose to embrace their sovereign rights, in this case through the use of radio, in order to maintain story, culture, and tradition. Using low-power radio to emancipate knowledge can be crucial in forming and maintaining identity. It is, perhaps, in emancipating knowledge that we emancipate ourselves.

For myself, using pirate radio has been a way to understand the importance of keeping knowledge, and access to the media, free. The various participants that have been involved in TAR over the years have confirmed this. Many have spoken about the empowerment they have felt from the experience, and many have continued to speak out and remain active in their lives, through a number of leadership and media avenues.

I have witnessed this in my own life. It may have begun by getting behind the microphone to rant, inform, and invite others into conversations around social justice issues, but it has now permeated into many aspects of my life. Writing and performing music have become increasingly important for me,[36] and writing lyrics that contain a political message or share knowledge is common. My personal is political, and this allows me to connect and create community in many ways.

Using numerous forms of media and expression creates collaborations that strengthen our attempts to spread knowledge in grassroots ways. These networks or rhizomes continue to spread in ways that are often not transparent at first but continue to grow nevertheless. For example, working on the anthology, *Islands of Resistance: Pirate Radio in Canada*, the three editors, Andrea Langlois, Ron Sakolsky, and I, made a conscious attempt to link numerous forms of media together. For example, artists' work was used throughout the anthology. The book was published copyleft,[37] in order to make it accessible. Within three months of publication, the PDF could be downloaded from the website for free.[38] The website was used to host audio from many of the pirate radio stations documented in the book and it remains live, with plans to incorporate the many stories that continue to come in, post-publication.[39] Using numerous forms of media to bring people in has allowed for a stronger network, one that continues to grow. This, in turn, leads to more emancipated knowledge, as people and communities, across media forms, continue to connect.

This expands our networks, allowing our communities to become global and yet smaller simultaneously. We begin to know the people involved with a particular issue, but also to see that these issues are interconnected, and each node leads to further knowledge. Even in my teaching work in the Media Studies and Women's Studies departments at Vancouver Island University, I actively seek out online course material, specifically copyleft and creative commons sources, because it is more accessible to students, particularly those who have limited access to resources. With rising tuition costs, earning a degree becomes increasingly challenging for low-income students. While there are many ways to obtain knowledge—in media, for example, many skills can be self-taught—it is still a degree that many employers are looking for. A degree does not guarantee these abilities, as the competency of a D student versus an A student is dramatically different, yet it remains a standard that is valued by mainstream society. It is important to remember that there are numerous ways of achieving knowledge and competency. Self-created media projects can be one way of ensuring that learned knowledge is directly relevant to one's life goals and communities.

Talking Back

Pirate radio has, and still exists in, many manifestations—it is not naturally inclusive. In some instances, like Radio Caroline, for example, pirate radio is used to play inaccessible or noncommercial music, create celebrity status for the DJs, and a cult status in the underground for the station itself. These vanity stations can be exclusive to marginalized groups—Radio Caroline, for example, was very restrictive to women. Alternately, other pirate radio practitioners have been and are presently interested in creating spaces where marginalized voices can ring out, where organizing is done in a nonhierarchical manner, and where the doing of media production is of primary importance. The nature of a station is often very specific to the individuals running the station.

There are a number of radio stations that are run by women that push the envelope, creating spaces where women are particularly welcomed. Using pirate radio can be valuable in achieving technical prowess, disseminating knowledge, and finding confidence. For women, this can be a double-edged sword. While it is often empowering to learn and use technical skill sets, it is still commonly necessary for women to have to go above and beyond to prove what they know, over and over again in a male-dominated field. In all technical media fields, women are still a minority and assumptions must be continuously overridden.[40] Nevertheless, there are numerous examples of women running low-power radio stations internationally.

A suitcase radio station was used by femLINKpacific (Media Initiatives for Women), a women's media nongovernmental organization out of Fiji. The organization launched femTALK 89.2FM in 2004 as a mobile women's community project. It focused on women's issues, specifically the issue of HIV/AIDS, in its broadcasts to the community.[41] Suitcase radio stations have been used in numerous communities internationally. The producers of Prometheus Radio, out of the United States, use their organization to help communities build suitcase radio stations and run them independently.[42]

Women's involvement in radio is not without overt risk, depending on where the station is located. Zakia Zaki was an Afghani journalist who headed a community station, Radio Sohl (translated as Peace Radio), one of four designated women's radio stations in Afghanistan. The success of her station, highly listened to in the area, led to her high profile in the community and, in June 2007, she was murdered, sending a message that women's voices are not welcome in the public arena.[43] It is obvious that we have a long way to go before knowledge is truly emancipated. Regardless, people continue to speak out.

Margaretta D'arcy has actively run pirate radio stations in Galway, Ireland, for over a decade.[44] She focuses on running a station specifically for women, providing a resource to the airwaves, but also to technical skills and networking opportunities, elements that are often hard to come by for women. She has connected this station to the community, incorporating theatre, dance, and direct action. She has been met with both opposition and support, and she continues to link women together and share knowledge.

This book, *Free Knowledge*, was inspired by the desire to document barriers to knowledge, specifically those faced by Saskatchewan farmers. Perhaps then, it is appropriate to use an example of farming communities in Mali using low-power radio to disseminate information. Timbuktu Mobile Radio used low-power radio to spread information on how to combat plagues of locusts destroying crops. The information was broadcast in six languages (Tamacheq, Songhay, Peulh, Arabic, French, and Bambara) and informed people where they could find resources and how they might organize. Furthermore, Elders were brought in to pass on knowledge that had been historically used to combat locust plagues.[45] This low-power radio station was operated out of a suitcase radio donated by UNESCO in 2001.[46]

All of these documented examples only begin to illustrate the possibilities of liberating our public airwaves—there are many more. Given that our mainstream media market, including radio, is saturated with messages that support dominant ideologies—ideologies that are not in the best interests of communities, a diversity of voices, the pursuit of creativity, and Traditional Knowledge dissemination—these examples of resistance are increasingly important. The sheer volume of all of these examples is cause for celebration. It is these numerous forms of media solidarity, where communities continue to liberate and control their own media, that provide hope and optimism for our future. They keep our airwaves truly public, and allow all of our voices on the air, to use media for own purposes and for the needs of our own individual communities.

Notes

1   The CRTC states that our airwaves are public, yet the process of obtaining a licence requires extensive documentation (where specialized knowledge is necessary), a substantial sum of money, and agreement to follow CRTC rules regarding studio construction, procedures, language, and content. Even if autonomous and/or community stations apply for a licence, there are no guarantees of receiving one and the process takes many years. In addition, CBC radio is commonly considered to be public radio and yet few Canadians can easily get their voices on the airwaves. Even the talkback shows, as is standard in the industry, require the caller to make it through a vetting process before they are allowed on the air.

2   This applies to television licences as well.

3   In relation to television, Barbara Byers, of the Canadian Labour Congress, makes the point that commercial broadcasters have long made a profit using the public airwaves. The same point can be applied for radio. For more information, see "Review of the Over-the-Air TV Policy/examen de certains aspects du cadre reglementaire de la television en direct," held in Gatineau, Quebec, on December 1, 2006, http://www.crtc.gc.ca/fra/transcripts/2006/tb1201.htm.

4   Adbusters had its ad rejected by the CBC and Canwest Global—the
     advertisement stated the fat content in a McDonald's Big Mac, promoted Buy
     Nothing Day, and asked for an end to the use of automobiles. Adbusters took
     its case to court, demanding it should have access to the "public airwaves"
     and lost. For more information, see "Adbusters Demands Access to Airwaves,"
     January 30, 2008, http://www.adbusters.org/blogs/adbusters-blog/adbusters-
     demands-access-airwaves.html.

5   This is not guaranteed, of course. There are many low-power radio projects that
     have limiting power dynamics in place. One only has to look to many of the
     pirate radio stations broadcasting out of London, UK, to see competition and
     cliques in place (Simon Reynolds, "Rave and Jungle on UK Pirate Radio," June
     1998, http://www.furious.com/perfect/simonreynolds.html).

     This chapter focuses on the examples of low-power radio that are run by
     individuals who are aware and concerned about inclusivity. While recognizing
     that all projects have inherent limitations, this chapter focuses on the
     possibilities of creating and freeing knowledge through radio stations that
     keep power relations in mind.

     For more information on London pirate radio examples and on the push to
     move successful underground pirate stations into the commercial mainstream, see
     Alexis Wolton, "Tortugan Tower Blocks? Pirate Signals from the Margins," 2010,
     http://datacide.c8.com/tortugan-tower-blocks-pirate-signals-from-the-margins/.

6   Unlicensed radio is broadcasting a terrestrial signal without a licence (usually
     this is an FM signal). Because it is illegal, many practitioners are committing
     an overt political act, maintaining that we should have access to the airwaves.
     Getting a licence to broadcast is expensive and time-consuming. Furthermore,
     corporate commercial stations are consistently granted licences over
     community and more experimental types of broadcasting—Gabriola Island
     Radio, CKGI, for example (discussed later in this chapter), has had to battle
     Rogers Communications more then once during its application process. The
     numerous challenges of obtaining a broadcast licence is one of the reasons
     many people have moved to online radio stations. These stations do not
     require a licence and are legal (although this status is currently under debate).
     Most FM unlicensed radio practitioners are interested in terrestrial broadcasts
     because of issues of accessibility (access to computers and the Internet on both
     the broadcast and receiving end) and geography (many stations are located in
     remote areas).

7   Rick Dennis, "Confession of a Pirate Radio DJ," *Cosmic Debris Musicians Magazine*,
     September/October 1995, http://www.cvnet.net/cosmic/A_Rick21.htm.

8   Franco (Bifo) Berardi and Felix Guattari, *Thought, Friendship and Visionary
     Geography* (New York: Macmillan Publishers, 2008), 29–30; Franco Berardi,
     M. Jacquenot, and G. Vitali, *Ethereal Shadows: Communications and Power in
     Contemporary Italy* (New York: Autonomedia, 2009), 80.

9   For a more detailed discussion of the politics of language around the term
     "pirate radio," see the introduction, Andrea Langlois, Ron Sakolsky, and
     Marian van der Zon, "Setting Sail: Navigating Pirate Radio Waves in Canada,"
     in *Islands of Resistance: Pirate Radio in Canada*, ed. Andrea Langlois, Ron

Sakolsky, and Marian van der Zon (Vancouver: New Star Books, 2010), 3–14, http://islandsofresistance.ca/.

10   I have been directly involved in CFUV, CKUT, and CHLY. I have contributed radio documentary, sound art pieces, or music to the majority of campus and community stations across Canada. I have also worked freelance for CBC since 2003.

11   There is a large body of knowledge available on ethnographic research. Given the space limitations of this chapter, this research is not the focus here. Instead, space is given to documenting a number of transgressive radio examples.

12   Sheila Nopper, "Freedom Soundz: A Programmer's Journey beyond Licensed Community Radio," in *Islands of Resistance: Pirate Radio in Canada*, ed. Andrea Langlois, Ron Sakolsky, and Marian van der Zon (Vancouver: New Star Books, 2010), 51–70.

13   In Canada, if pirate radio stations are found by regulatory bodies (Industry Canada is the regulatory arm of the CRTC), practitioners are most often met with a warning and told to shut down. Note that these regulatory bodies do not actively seek out unlicensed stations but act based on complaints. For more information on the legalities of pirate radio in Canada, see Langlois, Sakolsky, and van der Zon, *Islands of Resistance*.

14   Tetsuo Kogawa, "Toward Polymorphous Radio," in *Radio Rethink: Art, Sound and Transmission*, ed. Daina Augaitis and Dan Lander (Banff, AB: Walter Philips Gallery, 1994), 286–299.

15   For more information, see Peter Lackowski, "Revolutionary Radio in Venezuela," *Upside Down World: Covering Activism and Politics in Latin America*, June 27, 2006, http://upsidedownworld.org/main/venezuela-archives-35/335-revolutionary-radio-in-venezuela.

16   For more information, see Marian van der Zon, "Broadcasting on Our Own Terms," in *Autonomous Media: Activating Resistance & Dissent*, ed. Andrea Langlois and Frederic Dubois (Montreal: Cumulus Press, 2005), 31–46, http://www.cumuluspress.com/autonomousmedia.html.

17   For more information, see Stephen Dunifer, "Latitudes of Rebellion: Free Radio in an International Context," in *Islands of Resistance: Pirate Radio in Canada*, ed. Andrea Langlois, Ron Sakolsky, and Marian van der Zon (Vancouver: New Star Books, 2010), 23–33.

18   For more information, see Jerry Landay, "We're Part of the Restoration Process of Our People: An Interview with Mbanna Kantako (Human Rights Radio)," in *Seizing the Airwaves: A Free Radio Handbook*, ed. Ron Sakolsky and Stephen Dunifer (San Francisco: AK Press, 1998), 94–100; and Mbanna Konnadi Jr. and Ebony Kantako, "'Ghetto Radio' Rap Song," in *Seizing the Airwaves: A Free Radio Handbook*, ed. Ron Sakolsky and Stephen Dunifer (San Francisco: AK Press, 1998), 100–106.

19   For numerous examples, look to Langlois, Sakolsky, and van der Zon, *Islands of Resistance*. General information about setting up unlicensed radio stations is also available in this volume.

20   This chapter focuses on the potential to use pirate radio for empowerment. Many radio practitioners have no active interest in this goal. See, for example,

Radio Caroline as a vanity station; seemingly, it had greater interest in creating celebrity DJs than it did empowerment on a community level.

21 For more information on this example, see Andrea Langlois and Gretchen King, "Amplifying Resistance: Pirate Radio as Protest Tactic," in *Islands of Resistance: Pirate Radio in Canada*, ed. Andrea Langlois, Ron Sakolsky, and Marian van der Zon (Vancouver: New Star Books, 2010), or van der Zon, "Broadcasting on Our Own Terms."

22 Langlois and King, "Amplifying Resistance."

23 The term "Traditional Knowledge" includes Indigenous knowledge and local knowledge, wisdom, and teachings passed down culturally within the community.

24 TAR's background can be found in Chapter 9 of Marian van der Zon's "The Care and Feeding of Temporary Autonomous Radio," in *Islands of Resistance: Pirate Radio in Canada*, ed. Andrea Langlois, Ron Sakolsky, and Marian van der Zon (Vancouver: New Star Books, 2010). See also the original text, Hakim Bey, *The Temporary Autonomous Zone: Ontological Anarchy, Poetic Terrorism* (New York: Autonomedia, 1991).

25 Details about these music festivals can be found in van der Zon, "The Care and Feeding of Temporary Autonomous Radio."

26 See van der Zon, "The Care and Feeding of Temporary Autonomous Radio"; Marian van der Zon, "Gendered Pirates: Women's Roles in Temporary Autonomous Radio," in *Canadian Women in Radio*, ed. Geneviève A. Bonin and Lise Millette. Forthcoming.

27 *Desire & Machines: Auralizing Community*, Datastream-Literary Theory Research Group: Machine Communities Collaboration. Contributors: Daniel Burgoyne, Robin Davies, Alison Pitcher, and Marian van der Zon, http://www.frozenfox.com/machcom/index.html.

28 For more information on this process, see Langlois, Sakolsky, and van der Zon "Setting Sail," 17. Or see Gabriola Radio's (CKGI) website, http://www.ckgi.ca/.

29 Cj Your Dj, from CSSH, Shh, Rez Pirate Radio, 100.1FM, e-mail interview, October 28, 2010. A pseudonym has been used to ensure her anonymity.

30 Ibid.

31 Ibid.

32 Ibid.

33 She maintains a YouTube account with playlists, links to previously recorded interviews, and new videos (http://www.youtube.com/user/CjInventor). Since 2012, she has hosted a radio show on CHLY called *Shh, Rez Pirate Radio*.

34 For more information, see Neskie Manuel, "Secwepemc Radio: Reclamation of Our Common Property," in *Islands of Resistance: Pirate Radio in Canada*, ed. Andrea Langlois, Ron Sakolsky, and Marian van der Zon (Vancouver: New Star Books, 2010), 71–73; Charles Mostoller, "Awakening the 'Voice of the Forest': Radio Barriere Lake," in *Islands of Resistance: Pirate Radio in Canada*, ed. Andrea Langlois, Ron Sakolsky, and Marian van der Zon (Vancouver: New Star Books, 2010), 75–88; and Langlois, Sakolsky, and van der Zon, "Setting Sail." Also see Charles Fairchild, "The Canadian Alternative: A Brief History of Unlicensed and Low Power Radio," in *Seizing the Airwaves: A Free Radio Handbook*, ed. Ron Sakolsky and Stephen Dunifer (San Francisco: AK Press, 1998), 50.

35 Manuel, "Secwepemc Radio."

36 The author was active in the band Puzzleroot (2009–2012), http://www. puzzleroot.com, and in the multimedia performance project Meridian (2012– present), http://meridian.is/.

37 "The content of this book may be reproduced without the authors' permission in part or in its entirety provided it is distributed and made available to the reader for free, without service charges or any other fee. The authors further stipulate that the editors, individual writers, and visual artists all be credited for their work." See the copyright page in Langlois, Sakolsky, and van der Zon, *Islands of Resistance*.

38 See http://islandsofresistance.ca/.

39 After the book was published, individuals like pirate radio DJ Rick Dennis began to contact us with additional pirate radio stories.

40 For more information on women's roles in media, see van der Zon, "The Care and Feeding of Temporary Autonomous Radio"; van der Zon, "Gendered Pirates"; Rebekah Farrugia, "Spin-sters: Women, New Media Technologies and Electronic/Dance Music" (PhD dissertation, University of Iowa, 2004), 8–24, http://ir.uiowa.edu/cgi/viewcontent.cgi?article=1297&context=etd; Elizabeth L. Keathley, "Gendering the DJ" (paper presented to Music Educators' National Conference, Nashville, TN, April 10–14, 2002); Michelle Martin, "Capitalizing on the Feminine Voice," *Canadian Journal of Communication* 14, no. 3 (1989): 42–62; S. McClary, *Feminist Endings: Music, Gender, and Sexuality* (Minneapolis, MN: University of Minnesota Press, 1991); and Anja Rosenbrock, "I think I've never had a good idea inside the practice room," http://s171907168.onlinehome.us/andrasound/inandout/linked_items/rosenbrock.pdf.

41 "Fiji Women Community Radio Initiative Takes Suitcase Radio to the Field," *Communication and Information Sector's Daily News Service*, New Delhi, January 10, 2005, http://portal.unesco.org/ci/en/ev.php-URL_ID=17911&URL_DO=DO_TOPIC&URL_SECTION=201.html.

42 See http://www.prometheusradio.org/. In addition to Prometheus Radio's involvement with suitcase radios, its focus has also included making low-power FM (LPFM) stations viable in the United States, including lobbying the U.S. Congress to provide additional opportunities for LPFM.

43 Shauna Sylvester, "The Taliban Are Silencing the Voices of Afghanistan's Women," *Globe and Mail,* June 9, 2007, A19.

44 Margaretta D'arcy, *Galway's Pirate Women, a Global Trawl* (Galway, Ireland: Women's Pirate Press, 1996).

45 See "Timbuktu Mobile Radio Battles Locust Hordes," Webworld News Item, http://www.wantokent.com/Timbuktu.htm.

46 See "Timbuktu Mobile Radio Battles Locust Hordes." UNESCO donated four radio stations to Timbuktu, Mali. See also "Suitcase Radio for 'Radio Browsing' Programmes in Mali Donated by UNESCO," http://www.unesco.org/webworld/cmc.

SEVEN

ACTION RESEARCH AS ACADEMIC REFORM: THE CHALLENGES AND OPPORTUNITIES OF SHARED KNOWLEDGE

Patricia W. Elliott

Representing a rebalancing of power relations, action research upsets the status quo in institutions of power, including our universities. The reward is a more humane, just world for marginalized people and university-based researchers alike.

Why Action Research?

S imply put, action research engages community members in developing and carrying out research by and for themselves. Because of its participatory nature, the approach is often cited as an effective method to generate reliable, authentic, local knowledge that might otherwise remain hidden (Fals Borda, 1987, p. 333). Obviously this aspect has appeal to researchers and policy makers alike. "Involving local people as participants in research and planning has shown to both enhance effectiveness and save time and money in the long term," Cornwall and Jewkes note (1995). Citing such observations, many a research proposal declares that locally generated knowledge is valuable to scholarship and likely could not be cultivated by any other means. Having established this, the proposal may conclude: "Therefore I have chosen to employ participatory action research methodology to answer the research question." Yet Fals Borda, Cornwall, and Jewkes would very likely respond that such a statement denies the true nature of action research.

As researchers and community members alike, we must continually remind ourselves that action research is not a trowel for digging up information. Rather, it is a political stance derived from conditions of inequality and oppression. Foundational thinkers such as Orlando Fals Borda (2001) conceived their work as being intrinsically linked to the social transformation objectives of Third World liberationists such as Mahatma Gandhi, Paulo Freire, Julius Nyerere, and Camilo Torres (p. 29). This stance is nested within a broader world view that we are social beings in dialogue with one another, seeking health, happiness, and freedom together. Such a goal remains out of reach as long as "significant segments of society all over the globe are institutionally excluded from participating in the creation of their own world of thinking, feeling and acting subjects" (Park, 1993, p. 1). From this perspective, action research is seldom described by its proponents as a set methodology that comes with a prescribed set of methods to gain specific results on specific topics in specific situations. Indeed, feminist action researcher Jennifer Bickham Mendez (2006) argues that action research is so inherently situational and reflexive that "a 'how to' manual would be inappropriate" (p. 10). Davidson-Hunt and O'Flaherty (2007) add

> *This approach to research cannot simply be designed in advance by an outside researcher as though scrupulous attention to methodological detail will provide the opportunity to "get it right this time." It is but a step toward more fully engaging people as creative agents, coauthors in the research process. (p. 304)*

Understanding that action research is "not a list of procedures and protocols to be followed" (Davidson-Hunt & O'Flaherty, 2007, p. 304), its practitioners are more likely to describe their approach as a "way of being" that places researchers in the service of community members, and that seeks to address the imbalances that hinder our world from becoming a more equal and happy place for all, combining knowledge and action for social progress (Fals Borda, 1987, p. 332). In so doing, participants in action research must recognize that we ourselves are part of the power imbalance, whether we consider ourselves academics or activists, or both. Mendez (2006) notes, "the extreme disparities that structure our relationships mean that...equality is often difficult to approach in practice" (p. 18). Debates, challenges, struggles, and alliances become essential to a continually unfolding process of knowledge production. If nothing else, this perspective contains within it enough challenges, contradictions, and complications to ensure our community collaborations are never boring. There are plenty of opportunities for unexpected turns and intentions gone awry. The reward is research that has a life beyond our own narrow contributions, as community actors gradually gain traction within the process and take ownership over the next stage of action. Thus, while some projects may flame out spectacularly, we may take comfort that few projects face the alternative: a slow, whimpering decline on dusty shelves.

Facilitating Action Research

Despite its patina of a radical departure from the mainstream, the concept of action-oriented participatory research processes, in fact, has long-established roots in the academy, harking back to Aristotle's notion of *phrônêsis*—defined as "the design of problem-solving actions through collaborative knowledge construction with the legitimate stakeholders in the problem" (Greenwood, 2008, pp. 326–327). Later eclipsed by Descartes's mind-body dualism—with its "gods-eye" claim of an omniscient knowledge that could only be sullied by particularist, pedestrian human experience (Grosfoguel, 2008, pp. 4–5)—the intellectual tradition of socially engaged research nonetheless was carried through the ages via scholars such as Kant, Newton, Galileo, Bacon, Comte, and Marx, who all rowed against the notion that human affairs were of subordinate importance to "pure" scientific thought (Hammersley, 2004, p. 168; Fals Borda, 2001, p. 29). The current incarnation was coined "action research" in 1946 by German American researcher Kurt Lewin to describe a process in which theory is tested by its relevance to practical social action for change (Hammersley, 2004, p. 166; Kindon, Pain, & Kesby, 2007, pp. 9–10).

Later infusions of anticolonial, feminist, critical pedagogy, and pan-Indigenous discourses emphasized the participatory nature of action research, popularizing the term "participatory action research," or PAR. Today's application of PAR typically encompasses "a broad and messy array of disciplinary approaches, schools of thought and methodological practices" that have a common thread of realigning power relationships in knowledge production (Mendez, 2008, p. 139). No end of handbooks and guides offer excellent advice on how to embark on this process, authored by both scholars and community activists. From these sources, a number of common themes and recommended practices are evident. What follows is a basic but by no means exhaustive summary of key principles and approaches.

Problem Identification

Action research begins as a response to a problem identified by the community. It is one thing to say community members are involved in every step of the process. It is another thing to say community members decided on the first step, with the researchers following along behind (Hagey, 1997, p. 2).

Engagement

Trust building. Being part of the community. Simply enlisting community members to do surveys, or obtaining letters of support from community leaders is not engagement (Burhansstipanov, Christopher, & Schumacher, 2005, p. 72). It is this aspect that is identified most closely with the coinage "participatory action research."

Dialogic Research Planning

The research question and the approaches are discussed and debated in an open manner, and local participants are trained in the relevant methods to carry out the approach they settle on (Greenwood, 2008, p. 331). This can present a particular challenge for action researchers, because human need does not come neatly packaged in a discipline or methodology.

Participation as Process

Levels of participation are variable and processural. Participation cannot be mandated but is an "emergent process largely controlled by local conditions," although it can be enhanced and strengthened along the way as the community comes together to tackle pressing problems (Greenwood, Foote Whyte, & Harkavy, 1993, p. 176).

Solidarity

Action researchers do not sit on the fence. How can they? To gain the access and the level of trust required to truly partake in community action, one must clearly be on the side of the people (Vargas, 2008, p. 172).

Generation of People's Knowledge

Action research often engages in recovering a community's common knowledge, contained in traditional skills, stories, memories, and testimonials. It also produces new people's knowledge, by identifying problems and energizing people around the task of devising collective solutions (Park, 1993, p. 19).

Relationship Reflexivity
Reflexivity requires us to ask from the outset: What is the nature of the relationship between researchers and community actors? Reflexivity also requires us to recognize inner community dynamics: Who is being represented, who is being left out? As involvement shifts throughout the process, these questions should remain active and open (Sultana, 2007, pp. 376–383).

Empowerment
Action research includes the goal of engendering confidence and skills to carry local knowledge forward into action. The research cycle leads to action, which may, in turn, lead to further research, ideally research that finds itself more fully in the hands of the community with each step in the journey (Tang, 2008, p. 241).

Ownership
The data belongs equally to the community, and ultimately should be understandable, helpful, and used by the community, rather than mysterious, harmful, and used by outsiders. It should not unduly expose community members to police action, surveillance, or unwanted interventions. For reference, these principles are crystallized in the concept of Ownership, Control, Access, and Participation (OCAP), developed by the Steering Committee of the First Nations Regional Longitudinal Health Survey to ensure participating communities have access to, and physical control over, data (Schnarch, 2004, p. 80).

Accountability
Who precisely does the researcher work for? Do we answer to our research institutes, academic supervisors, and external funders? Or do we answer to the community? Hagey (1997) suggests, "The facilitator respects the autonomy of the people, avoiding speaking on their behalf, and he or she reports to the community when asked to play a mediator or interpreter role, always accountable to the people" (p. 5).

Action for Change
Simply writing up the problems of an oppressed community is not enough: "In fact, university libraries are filled with accounts of how aggrieved

communities, nations, and workers struggled and resisted, but in no way did these stories contribute to a shift in power relations" (Pulido, 2008, p. 352). At the core of action research is the idea of fundamentally challenging and changing not only oppressive conditions but also the structures of oppression.

Although these principles may seem straightforward, the challenges are many and the stakes are high. In the words of Park (1993):

> *We urgently need to recover people's wisdom and turn it into a potent force for emancipating the rest of humanity ... Saving the world from technological and spiritual destruction depends on transforming it into a human sphere of life where community and critical consciousness thrive. (p. 19)*

Action Research in Today's Academy: From Marginalization to Co-optation

Describing his work with Community Against Police Action (CAPA) in South Central Los Angeles, João H. Costa Vargas provides an excellent picture of the challenges of community-based research. Because the CAPA office was under FBI surveillance and had a history of infiltration by undercover police and agents provocateurs, it was essential from the outset for Vargas to establish himself not just as an anthropology student doing fieldwork but also as a fellow activist committed to ending police oppression in poor communities. He recalls,

> *I would not have become a CAPA collaborator if their members had not found my political commitment compatible with their program of social emancipation. Objectivity, if understood as detachment, was simply impossible, for a mere observer would not be welcome into the building on Western Avenue more than a few times. (Vargas, 2008, p. 172)*

Far from a fly-on-the-wall anthropologist, Vargas immersed himself in the work of the CAPA office, answering phones and doing other routine tasks throughout the day and recording his observations and reflections in the evening. He argues that this level of involvement and commitment to the cause was essential to the research process:

> *[U]nless your allegiance was beyond doubt, you would never gain the trust of CAPA activists or be able to circulate unencumbered in the building. So*

forget about being a graduate student in anthropology trying to do partici-
pant observation. You were an activist first and, circumstances permitting,
an observer second. (Vargas, 2008, p. 175)

This scenario makes eminent sense to anyone who has engaged in community research with a view to affecting social change. But where does it leave us in relation to the dominant paradigms that rule our lives? Whether in the university, the media, or policy circles, there is a tendency to dismiss the work of scholars like Vargas as nonscience. As Hagey (1997) notes, "PAR challenges the idea of seeing researchers as being neutral and unbiased, without vested interests, etc., because it purposely champions the community engaging in its own research" (p. 3). As well, participatory action research relies on relationship building and solidarity rather than the professional distance of traditional academic work. For example, José Antonio Lucero (2006) states that the most important fieldwork advice he received was "be a compañero" (p. 21). Social scientific work, he continues, must first be social, because it is "an intervention in people's lives and worlds that needs to be justified first and foremost to those people who make it possible," as opposed to extractive scientific inquiry (2006, p. 21). Park (1993) adds, "PAR represents interactive, holistic knowledge. As such, there is no 'proper' distance between the researcher and the researched, who are engaged in a collaborative process" (p. 16).

Presenting action research as science may involve developing and defining novel research methods. For example, Vargas (2008) described his work at CAPA as observant participation, rather than participant observation (p. 175). Another novel approach, arising from Canada, is the concept of place-based learning communities, developed by Indigenous communities in northern Manitoba and researchers at the University of Manitoba's Natural Research Institute. Davidson-Hunt and O'Flaherty (2007) define the model as "dialogic networks formed to generate cross-cultural understanding on local problems or events" (p. 295). This approach is based on the argument that there is more to research than the documentation of knowledge; engagement in dialogue about respective understandings of phenomena is a research process in itself, capable of creating new ways to frame questions and approaches, and based on mutually agreed upon goals (Davidson-Hunt and O'Flaherty, 2007, pp. 294–295).

Reinventing and refining methods is just one small step in a larger journey, however. Observing that every research paradigm has its own system of verification, Rahman (1991) calls on action researchers to develop clear statements on matters of objectivity, verifiability, and validity that distinctly relate to action research as the guiding philosophical and scientific framework, as opposed to accepting research assumptions designed for other research paradigms (p. 15). Along this line, Park (1993) suggests that the question of validity is settled in the application of PAR. If the collaboration leads a community to overcome obstacles, or to broaden empathy and connectedness—typical research objectives—then its validity as research is clear (p. 16).

Rather than turning one's back on science, then, it is more important to articulate clearly the science of action research. Such an articulation serves to legitimize people's knowledge systems, allowing grassroots actors to develop their own systems of verification and methods of inquiry (Rahman, 1991, p. 15). This answers Fals Borda's (1987) call for revolutionary science that "becomes a real possibility, not only a felt necessity" (p. 330). Natural science methods, for the most part, deal fairly effectively with observation of the physical world; PAR, for the most part, deals quite effectively with action in the social world. There is no reason one should hold trump over the other, or operate in seclusion. Well-rounded PAR projects make use of natural science methods, just as the natural sciences may use PAR to harness local knowledge in agriculture, climate-change tracking, medical botany, and myriad other examples. The growing acceptance of PAR approaches across disciplines is an obvious sign of greater scientific acceptance. Ironically, however, this acceptance raises a new challenge—the spectre of co-optation and exploitation.

As early as 1991, Rahman and Fals Borda raised the alarm that the "symptoms of PAR cooptation are evident" (p. 28). At the time, several universities had begun offering PAR instruction under the general heading of applied science, and PAR had been harnessed to a number of mainstream development projects as community verification systems. "Of course, not everything these institutions call participatory is authentic according to our ontological definitions, and much confusion has been sown in this regard," they observed, identifying the problem as "faulty assimilation" of the approach (Rahman and Fals Borda, 1991, p. 28). Similarly, in 1997, Hagey remarked on the growing presence of private research firms that purport to employ PAR yet work within oppressive power structures rather than against them:

In such cases, the principal investigator can passively be an agent for powers interested in managing the community. A close reading of their reports sometimes reveals an infantalization of community leaders or belittling of the community's problem-solving abilities and political institutions. (pp. 4–5)

As any citizen who has been drawn into an ostensibly "participatory" public consultation can attest, it has become standard practice for facilitators to serve up a limited set of options for consideration within a highly managed process that stifles debate and diverts community-offered alternative solutions as being "off the agenda." The process of infantilization spoken to by Hagey is often clear in final reports. For example, a privately contracted consultant's report on community consultations for the Regina Public School Board stated facilitators used a participatory process of "guided conversation" to gather feedback on a school closure plan (H. J. Linnen Associates, 2008, p. 5). Although parents arrived at the meetings armed with research on the global impacts of inner city school abandonment, and had worked across schools to develop a critique of the plan and offer alternative solutions, the contractor's report characterized school closures as "personal and emotional" issues, adding that "the closure situation created strong emotions in the affected schools" that "set a tone that resisted change," primarily related to the "closure of one's own school" (H. J. Linnen Associates, 2008, pp. 21, 24). Pointing to a carefully worded anonymous web survey as a better "census" of public opinion, and interpreting the survey results as mainly positive, the board-hired consultant recommended that the trustees continue with their closure plan while recognizing the challenge of "taking leadership decisions in these difficult environments" (H. J. Linnen Associates 2008, p. 24). Thereafter, the board publicly defended its decisions as taking place only after lengthy community consultation. This example illustrates a growing problem of research processes that peel away action research-style methods from the end goal of community control and emancipation. In the words of Hagey (1997): "Beware of research that uses the facilitator and the community members as puppets" (p. 5).

However, it is not only bureaucracies that take part in the co-optation of action research. Mendez (2008) notes that today's transnational social movements place heavy emphasis on the strategic deployment of information, while the rise of nongovernmental organizations (NGOs) creates greater demand for research and relevant data. In response, action researchers are increasingly called on to "translate" community narratives into the language of policy makers, lending scientific credibility to the arguments made by communities (Mendez, 2008, pp. 144–145). While this may be a helpful development, Vargas (2008) provides a contrary caution:

> It can be argued that translating scattered information into a linear narrative, besides unnecessarily changing the nature of the anarchic and

improvisational methods of community organizing, also makes such meth-
ods more easily domesticated and appropriated by individuals and institu-
tions who may not have the same political liberatory goals. (p. 178)

Kindon, Pain, and Kesby (2007) note that criticism of participatory approaches has intensified in concert with its commodification within top-down policy spheres (p. 2). For researchers, the implication of these critiques is clear. If we take part in research that employs so-called participatory methods to gather information and improve public relations, while failing to theorize and address inequality as the primary research goal, we are in danger of being as exploited as the community participants we work with. Emancipation must expand to the research process itself, a difficult prospect in an environment of chequebook consultants. We must continually remind ourselves that we work first and foremost for oppressed and marginalized communities, and not for those who would profess to help them.

From Paternalism to Partnership: Not an Easy Road

Lipsitz (2008) points out that anything worth doing can be done badly. "Combining scholarship and activism offers no automatic guarantee of either better scholarship or better activism," he warns (p. 91). Indeed, researchers who work closely with communities face an unusual array of complications, in both our collaborative undertakings and our personal/professional lives. We may fail to form good relationships, we may be inadequate to the task, and we may find ourselves enabling oppressive practices within communities. As well, the institutional structures we work for hinder equal relationships. Boog (2003) observes that the relationship between action researchers and participants "represents an experimental microcosm of the problematic social situation of the researched subjects, which was the initial reason for setting up an action research project" (p. 434).

It is no secret that the university-based researcher is an unusually privileged and empowered participant in an action research project. To begin with, we are used to presenting ideas in a forceful, confident manner. It is a part of our training—and not a part that prepares us well for community collaboration. Second, project financing is often funnelled through our personal and institutional research funds, putting us in the position of cheque writer, budgetary egg sitter, and final report author. This provides influence—whether intended or not—over the shaping of the project and how it is conveyed to others. Burhansstipanov, Christopher, and Schumacher offer a simple solution: hand over the chequebook. They suggest that "to make the transition from 'paternalism' to 'partnership,' research institutions and their employees must be willing to give up some control, power, and money" (2005, p. 72).

Unfortunately, individual researchers may have no influence over this situation, as the institutions they work for have their own internal processes of accountability and control. A strong argument might be made for counting a grant to a community association as a legitimate research expense, however it is not an argument one can reliably win in the absence of wider academic and institutional reforms. Indeed, there are few easy answers to the over-reaching architectures of class, race, gender, and privilege that seek to hold us where we are in relation to the research process. Herein lies the call for academic reform as an essential element of action research.

The Activist Scholar

Although action research is gaining wider acceptance, having been folded into the more institutionalized rhetoric of "community-based research" and "community-engaged scholarship," actively undertaking this type of research remains a risky business for researchers. For action researchers, our professional progress is tied to the uncertain path of community action, where we have little control—and are indeed committed to exercising little control—over the end results. Added to this is the fact that the research product could be a YouTube video, a workshop, or a protest march, rather than a published paper. It goes without saying that this is a difficult prospect for scholars who do not occupy secure positions in the academy, where lip service is paid to action research but fundamental structures and professional expectations remain unchanged. Elizabeth Oglesby (2006) offers the viewpoint of an untenured assistant professor:

> I have not engaged in what I would call more substantive research collaboration, i.e., generating research questions in tandem with research subjects or with social organizations in Guatemala. I will go on record admitting that the reason is fear, fear that the process would take too long, or that the very delicate relationships that one has to forge to sustain such a project might fall apart before a publication could be produced. Indeed, although it seems counterintuitive to me, by publishing in Spanish and diverse venues, I wonder if I have gone quite far out on a limb already. (p. 20)

Jessica Gordon Nembhard (2008) expresses similar concerns: "It is very difficult to be tenure track and know that even though my scholarship and commitment depend on my social justice activities and teaching, the tenure decision will be based on everything but that—and may suffer as a result" (p. 290). We should not conclude, however, that these challenges are confined to junior members of the academy, and that therefore gaining tenure will eventually solve the problem. Even senior, widely published academics such as Greenwood (2008) share a sense of marginalization: "Activist research in academic institutions is rare. A powerful set of forces, both external and internal to universities, are arrayed against it" (p. 319).

The basic complaints are well known and oft repeated. Academics are expected to act as university labourers, spending their time in committee meetings and administration tasks rather than working in the wider community (Lipsitz, 2008, p. 91). Increasingly, there are policies to ensure professors work in their offices on a nine-to-five basis. Here they are expected to produce knowledge products for their own tight-knit and highly privileged community, by publishing in approved, peer-reviewed journals (Mendez, 2008, p. 152). If they leave campus, it should be to present papers at international academic conferences, not to help out at local community centres. Inspired teaching and service to humanity are not given tangible credit (Gordon Nembhard, 2008, p. 290). Racism plays a role in marginalizing our work, as noted by Smith (1999):

> The form that racism takes inside a university is related to the ways in which academic knowledge is structured as well as to the organizational structures which govern the university. The insulation of disciplines, the culture of the institution that supports the disciplines, and the systems of management and governance all work in ways which protect the privileges already in place. (p. 133)

Admittedly, our professional struggles are puny compared to the struggles of marginalized and oppressed communities. Yet it would not serve to merely shrug our problems off and soldier on. These problems affect our functionality in the community, and stymie the process of legitimizing community knowledge and action as science. Writing from a perspective outside the academy, Freeman, Gust, and Aloshen (2009) observe that when universities accept and support community-engaged scholarship, it signals acceptance of the value of community cultural wisdom (p. 96). Their community-authored paper also addresses the practical value of tenure reform to community members:

Establishing respectful, trusting relationships takes a considerable amount of time and effort. Once a community partner or a community group is able to build such principled relationships with individuals within a college or university, we want to count on them being there well into the future. (p. 89)

At the same time, the authors generously acknowledge the challenges their colleagues inside the university face: "Sharing power—leveling the playing field—is a revolutionary act. It requires courage, tenacity, selfless-ness, transparency, ethical and moral leadership, and a commitment to do emotional and intellectual work for the common good" (p. 89).

Action research theorists have offered a range of possible responses to meet this considerable challenge. One option is to operate simultaneously and effectively in two spheres. This is the advice given by Canadian scholar and public health advocate Dennis Raphael in his "Ten Tips for Being a Public Scholar." Raphael's (2008) tip sheet includes choosing disciplines that allow the incorporation of politics into academic inquiry, as well as to "publish and publish even more" and "get tenured"—tasks he contends are "actually relatively easy for most academics to do" (pp. 411–412). This coincides somewhat with sociologist Francesca M. Cancian's (1993) advice: "Sociologists who do activist research and want a successful academic career ... have to bridge two conflicting social worlds" (p. 92). It must be noted, however, that she is far more critical of the publishing imperative than is Raphael. In either case, though, Cancian and Raphael deliver a prospect that is instantly familiar to working women: do it all, and do it better than anyone else. From experience, we may well suspect this is a process designed for our defeat as human beings.

One possible answer is to retreat to a standard division of labour. This appears to be the approach settled on by U.S.-based academic Don Mitchell, who relates the experience of being challenged by a group of students for being "all talk and no walk." Rather than feeling guilty for his lack of direct engagement in community protest, Mitchell (2008), who calls himself a "deskbound radical," argues there is a clear and justifiable division of labour between academics who do "intellectual work" and activists who press for change on the picket line (pp. 1, 453–454). For many action researchers, however, this approach is likely to be unsatisfying, in the same way that returning to traditional gender divisions of labour might be.

James and Gordon argue in favour of choosing community over academy, if a choice must be made. "Despite its political limitations, the fractured self of the radical subject desires what the academy cannot provide: relevancy and accountability to collectives resisting domination," they write (2008, p. 371). Therefore, an activist scholar would be better off seeking validation and belonging outside the academy, rather than risking becoming a "side-show attraction" on the inside (James and Gordon, 2008, p. 371). A historical precedent for this approach was set in 1970, when Fals Borda (2001) and his contemporaries "broke the shackles and left the academies" to establish alternative grassroots research institutions and practices, including the Rosca Foundation for Research and Social Action (pp. 27–28). Thus, we arrive at an important debate: Can PAR function within the traditional academy, and should it? What, if anything, is to be gained by taking on the additional burden of academic reform?

Action Research as Academic Reform

Overloaded by competing expectations, activist scholars are pulled in too many directions, with too much to do. Community-based activists face similar problems. They are often too harried in their daily lives to consider historical and theoretical questions, and may become impatient with academics who do so. Consequently, Lipsitz (2008) observes that they borrow from existing ideologies rather than creating or reforming ideologies. Further, the need for solidarity in a crisis makes them insular and isolated to criticism and resistant to new strategies (p. 92).

Even a casual observer might conclude the problems of scholars and activists are made for one another. As scholars, we can provide needed social and financial connections to make the lives of community members less harried. We can offer guidance in reflexive practice by raising important questions along the way, including questions insiders are reluctant to voice for fear of upsetting group dynamics. Our presence can open up established power cliques to new strategies and ideas from the grassroots. Through our grasp of action research theory, we can encourage communities to recognize the value of their own grassroots knowledge, rather than relying on external ideologies and practices that may not conform to local needs and aspirations.

In turn, community action has a contribution to make to scholarship. It challenges the templates we use, forcing us to acquire new knowledge about the world from new sources. Ultimately, community action advances human knowledge because it is in itself a unique form of knowledge in action. But it is knowledge that is not easy to grasp, being fluid and interactive. Rolling up our sleeves and joining in community activities provides insights and experiences that are difficult, if not impossible, to discover by traditional means. It is also a lot of fun. The goal of understanding and acting on the ensuing influx of new, dynamic, community-generated knowledge cannot help but benefit the academy as much as it benefits the grassroots.

Yet, within our institutions, we are confronted by significant barriers to the generation and dissemination of cogenerated, action-oriented knowledge. Herein may rest one of community activism's greatest contributions to scholarly work. Action research demands us to innovate rather than to accept the status quo. For example, our traditional knowledge products—journal articles—are largely inaccessible and of questionable relevance to the daily struggles of community collaborators. Even if community activists could afford the subscription fees, the arcane debates and competitive digs that are the hallmark of academic writing are of little use to them. Meanwhile, communities produce a wealth of excellent publications and other media products that are widely disseminated and discussed in a shared language that needs no translation. There is no reason we should not be contributing to these publications as a matter of course in our academic work.

In addition, researchers such as Smith (1999) advocate the creation of Indigenous research units, although she warns that such efforts only arise from a long struggle to gain recognition and funding within universities (p. 133). Although difficult, such internal struggles are not in vain. For example, a sign of the impact action research has had on research protocols is evident in the Tri-Council Policy's most recent draft section on "Research Involving Aboriginal Peoples." A review of recommended "good practices" clearly draws from the well of participatory action research, providing guidelines for community engagement in a spirit of mutual benefit, collaborative research agreements, strengthening local research capacity, and options for community review of research (Interagency Advisory Panel on Research Ethics, 2009, pp. 105–110).

A practical reform option available to Canadian researchers is to request support for community-based sabbaticals in project funding applications to the Social Sciences and Humanities Research Council (SSHRC). The University of Saskatchewan's Community University Institute for Social Research is one such organization that has on occasion offered sabbatical opportunities to employees of community-based organizations to take time off from their work to study community problems, with the support of SSHRC funding (see http://www.usask.ca/cuisr under "Funding and Training"). As well, any of us who have hired community-based research assistants in our projects are aware that university hiring practices are structured for hiring within our own student and staff pool, making the employment of community members a square peg in a round hole. All that would be required is some agreed-upon language for community-based job postings, and general institutional acceptance that not every assistant hired is a graduate student. This simple reform would help ensure community members are not always expected to contribute to projects for free, when university researchers get paid for the same work.

In the arena of performance review and tenure practice, beginning in 2011, Campus-Community Partnerships for Health (CCPH) and eight Canadian universities, including both Saskatchewan universities, undertook a nationwide Community-Engaged Scholarship (CES) initiative that holds as its primary goal "changing institutional culture and incentives in order to recognize and reward CES" (CCPH, 2010, p. 2). As a direct participant in this project, through my connection to the University of Regina Community Research Unit, I look forward to discovering whether or not this initiative will be able to genuinely move the institutional discourse beyond window dressing.

Action research approaches also call on us to develop new strategies in the classroom, so that our students are actively engaged in the community rather than sequestered in study halls. This may involve developing novel curriculum approaches. For example, we could create community internships that go beyond a few hours of volunteer work, and invite community activists to participate in curriculum development and delivery. What do they feel students need to know and read? What dialogues are important to engender? We could also explore new methods of peer review, on the understanding that anonymous, distant academics may not be the most reliable peers to evaluate community work. It is standard procedure to include evaluation processes in PAR projects; why should we not elevate this already well-established and well-formulated practice to the level of peer review? Who better to determine the validity of a project than members of an affected community? Indeed, Mendez (2008) argues that the simple yet profound act of holding research accountable to the community spirals outward into a reordering of relationships on a larger scale:

> In this way, scholar activists who are undertaking collaborative projects could contribute to a shift in the direction of North-to-South accountability, making the 'global power' of the scholar activist accountable to the 'local power' of the community or organization. (p. 152)

Thus, from individual struggles we begin to move mountains. This means having the courage to defend our own necks after we stick them out, so that it will be easier for others who follow. "Unless we challenge our obsession with publishing in obscure, albeit highly regarded academic journals, graduate students and early-career academics will have little choice but to do the same," warns Pickerill (2008, p. 485). She adds that this involves "not just writing more clearly and in more accessible locations, but spending more time with my community, friends and family ... creating space for passion in all our life endeavours" (2008, p. 486). I would argue that this is the most important part of action research: it turns us back into social beings. In this manner, the approach's utopian impulse extends far beyond our community projects. As Stringer (1996) argues, participatory, action-oriented research is ultimately an exercise of power (p. 159). It should come as no surprise, then, that it may upset the status quo not only within marginalized communities but also within power centres, including our universities. The potential reward is a more humane and just world for all.

References

Boog, B. W. M. (2003). The emancipatory character of action research, its history and the present state of the art. *Journal of Community and Applied Social Psychology, 13*, 426–438.

Burhansstipanov, L., Christopher, S., & Schumacher, S. A. (2005, November). Lessons learned from community-based participatory research in Indian country. *Cancer Control, 12*, 70–76.

Campus-Community Partnerships for Health. (2010). *Developing and rewarding community-engaged scholarship: Towards the transformation of university policies and practices.* Call for University Participants. University of Guelph, Guelph, ON.

Cancian, F. M. (1993, March). Conflicts between research and academic success: Participatory research and alternative strategies. *The American Sociologist, 24*(1), 92–106.

Cornwall, A., & Jewkes, R. (1995). What is participatory research? *Social Science and Medicine, 41*(12), 1667–1676.

Davidson-Hunt, I. J., & O'Flaherty, R. M. (2007). Researchers, Indigenous peoples, and place-based learning communities. *Society & Natural Resources, 20*(4), 291–305.

Fals Borda, O. (1987). The application of participatory action-research in Latin America. *International Sociology, 2*(4), 329–347.

Fals Borda, O. (2001). Participatory (action) research in social theory: Origins and challenges. In P. Reason & H. Bradbury (Eds.), *Handbook of action research: Inquiry and practice* (pp. 27–37). Thousand Oaks, CA: Sage.

Fox, J. (2004). Lessons from action-research partnerships. 2004 LASA/Oxfam America Martin Diskin Memorial Lecture. University of Santa Cruz, Santa Cruz, CA.

Freeman, E., Gust, S., & Aloshen, D. (2009). *Why faculty promotion and tenure matters to community partners.* Retrieved from http://www.eric.ed.gov/ERICWebPortal/search/detailmini.jsp?_nfpb=true&_&ERICExtSearch_SearchValue_0=EJ866775&ERICExtSearch_SearchType_0=no&accno=EJ866775

Gordon Nembhard, J. (2008). Theorizing and practicing democratic community economics: Engaged scholarship, economic justice and the academy. In C. R. Hale (Ed.), *Engaging contradictions: Theory, politics and methods of activist scholarship* (pp. 265–298). Berkeley and Los Angeles, CA: University of California Press.

Greenwood, D. J. (2008). Theoretical research, applied research and action research: The de-institutionalization of activist research. In C. R. Hale (Ed.), *Engaging contradictions: Theory, politics and methods of activist scholarship* (pp. 319–340). Berkeley and Los Angeles, CA: University of California Press.

Greenwood, D., Foote Whyte, W., & Harkavy, I. (1993). Participatory action research as a process and as a goal. *Human Relations, 46*(2), 175–191.

Grosfoguel, R. (2008). Transmodernity, border thinking, and global coloniality: Decolonizing political economy and postcolonial studies. *Eurozine.* Retrieved from http://www.eurozine.com/pdf/2008-07-04-grosfoguel-en.pdf

Hagey, R. S. (1997). The use and abuse of participatory action research. *Chronic Diseases in Canada, 18*(1). Retrieved from http://www.phac-aspc.gc.ca/publicat/cdic-mcc/18-1/a_e.html

Hammersley, M. (2004, June). Action research: A contradiction in terms? *Oxford Review of Education, 30*(2), 165–181.

H. J. Linnen Associates. (2008, February 20). *Renewing Regina public schools: Report on phase 4 consultations.* Regina, SK: Author.

Interagency Advisory Panel on Research Ethics. *(2009, December). Draft 2nd edition of the Tri-Council Policy statement: Ethical conduct for research involving humans (TCPS) Revised.* Ottawa, ON: Author.

James, J., & Gordon, E. T. (2008). Activist scholars or radical subjects? In C. R. Hale (Ed.), *Engaging contradictions: Theory, politics and methods of activist scholarship* (pp. 367–373). Berkeley and Los Angeles, CA: University of California Press.

Kindon, S., Pain, R., & Kesby, M. (2007). *Participatory action research approaches and methods: Connecting people, participation and place.* New York, NY: Routledge.

Lipsitz, G. (2008). Breaking the chains and steering the ship: How activism can help change teaching and scholarship. In C. R. Hale (Ed.), *Engaging contradictions: Theory, politics and methods of activist scholarship* (pp. 86–111). Berkeley and Los Angeles, CA: University of California Press.

Lucero, J. A. (2006). The comparative politics of *compañerismo* and collaboration. *LASA Forum, 37*(4), 21–22.

Mendez, J. B. (2006). Research as social justice work: Reflections on doing politically engaged scholarship. *LASA Forum, 37*(4), 10–12.

Mendez, J. B. (2008). Globalizing scholar activism: Opportunities and dilemmas through a feminist lens. In C. R. Hale (Ed.), *Engaging contradictions: Theory, politics and methods of activist scholarship* (pp. 136–163). Berkeley and Los Angeles, CA: University of California Press.

Mitchell, D. (2008). Confessions of a desk-bound radical. *Antipode*, 40(8), 448–454.

Oglesby, E. (2006). Research collaboration from a geographer's perspective. *Latin American Studies Association Forum*, 37(4), 19–21.

Park, P. (1993). What is participatory research? A theoretical and methodological perspective. In P. Park, M. Brydon-Miller, B. Hall, & T. Jackson (Eds.), *Voice of change: Participatory research in the United States and Canada* (pp. 1–20). Westport, CT: Bergen and Garvey.

Pickerill, J. (2008). The surprising sense of hope. *Antipode*, 40(1), 482–487.

Pulido, L. (2008). Frequently (un)asked questions about being a scholar activist. In C. R. Hale (Ed.), *Engaging contradictions: Theory, politics and methods of activist scholarship* (pp. 341–366). Berkeley and Los Angeles, CA: University of California Press.

Rahman, M. A. (1991). The theoretical standpoint of PAR. In O. Fals Borda & M. A. Rahman (Eds.), *Action and knowledge: Breaking the monopoly with participatory action research* (pp. 13–23). New York, NY: APEX.

Rahman, M. A., & Fals Borda, O. (1991). A self-review of PAR. In O. Fals Borda & M. A. Rahman (Eds.), *Action and knowledge: Breaking the monopoly with participatory action research* (pp. 24–35). New York, NY: APEX.

Raphael, D. (2008). Beyond positivism: Public scholarship in support of health. *Antipode*, 40(1), 404–413.

Schnarch, B. (2004). Ownership, control, access and possession (OCAP) or self-determination applied to research. *Journal of Aboriginal Health*, 1(1), 80–95.

Smith, L. T. (1999). *Decolonizing methodologies: Research and Indigenous peoples.* London, UK: Zed.

Stringer, E. T. (1996). *Action research: A handbook for practitioners.* Thousand Oaks, CA: Sage.

Sultana, F. (2007). Reflexivity, positionality and participatory ethics: Negotiating fieldwork dilemmas in international research. *ACME: An International E-Journal for Critical Geographies*, 6(3), 374–385.

Tang, S. S-L. (2008). Community-centred research as knowledge/capacity building in immigrant and refugee communities. In C. R. Hale (Ed.), *Engaging contradictions: Theory, politics and methods of activist scholarship* (pp. 237–264). Berkeley and Los Angeles, CA: University of California Press.

University of Saskatchewan, Community University Institute for Social Research. (n.d.). *Research funding and training.* Retrieved from http://www.usask.ca/cuisr/training/training.html

Vargas, J. H. C. (2008). Activist scholarship: Limits and possibilities in times of Black genocide. In C. R. Hale (Ed.), *Engaging contradictions: Theory, politics and methods of activist scholarship* (pp. 164–182). Berkeley and Los Angeles, CA: University of California Press.

PART 3

KNOWLEDGE SOVEREIGNTY: INDIGENOUS RESISTANCES AND RESILIENCIES

EIGHT

INDIGENOUS KNOWLEDGE: A K'ICHE-MAYAN PERSPECTIVE

Leonzo Barreno

The K'iche-Maya, the largest Mayan group in Guatemala, still preserves its own collective world view and their way of interpreting reality.

I ndigenous peoples have always had centres of learning, ranging from ceremonials in the bush to full-fledged universities. Common to them all has been the knowledge that "education" is a total process, in which (notwithstanding a division between men's roles and women's roles, men's sacred places and women's sacred places) the whole community is involved. The most fundamental knowledge the old impart to the young is that the world of matter and the world of culture/spirit are dialectically related. The truths are practical, without being cynically utilitarian: deeply moral (even, as with the Hopi prophecy, apocalyptic) but usually avoiding moralism and fanaticism.[1]

After a brief discussion of a clash between knowledge systems, western versus Indigenous; a brief description of Guatemala; and how the Mayan knowledge system has survived five hundred years of colonialism, this chapter discusses *one* characteristic of Indigenous knowledge particular to one group of people, the K'iche-Maya of the Guatemalan highlands. The topic explained in the following pages deals with the Mayan calendar of 260 days: its meaning, its practical use in ceremonies, and what role the calendar and time keeping mean in the knowledge system and social and cultural aspirations of the K'iche-Maya.[2] To discuss this topic, two sources of knowing are used: actual experience, or empirical observation, will be complemented with literature review about the Mayan calendar, time keeping, and Mayan social aspirations.

Different Societies and Clash of Knowledge Systems

Danermark, Ekström, Jacobsen, and Karlsson state that we cannot talk about "different 'conceptual frameworks' but rather of different 'viewpoints'."[3] In a world where history is written by the victor, it is not a question of "different ways of seeing things, but that we see different things."[4] In that regard, different people view and experience things differently even if they share the same time and space. As a result of social and cultural differences, power struggles result in producing victors who achieve domination by either hegemonic mechanisms or through coercion that may include state-sponsored violence. Victors of power struggles impose their language, concepts, and viewpoints as valid and, consequently, will have the means (education system and intellectuals) to define and produce explanations of social reality as they see fit into their theories and methodologies. As an example, the process of conquest and ongoing colonization of the Americas results in either the attempt to destroy Indigenous knowledge, which ends when a group is annihilated, or, on the other hand, in resistance when an Indigenous group continues to produce ideas and viewpoints emanated from their ancient beliefs.

As a consequence of the military conquest and colonization of the Americas, in particular the Mayan people of Guatemala, Indigenous peoples were classified into one single category: Indians. Such categorization denies the fact that there are hundreds of Indigenous groups in the continent and that each group possesses its own way of knowing and interpreting reality. While in some countries Indigenous peoples became a minority, such as in the case of Canada, in other countries, such as Guatemala, they are the majority. In this Central American country, there are twenty-one Mayan groups, comprising the majority of Guatemala's population.[5] The K'iche-Maya, the largest Mayan group, still preserves its own collective world view and their way of interpreting reality. It is necessary to clarify that each Indigenous group in Guatemala, and the continent, though sharing common experiences, and sharing similar symbols, each possesses its own viewpoints and its own interpretation of reality and social life. As a result, there is no

Indigenous knowledge, in the singular sense, but Indigenous knowledges in the plural sense, because the way a *Nehiyaw* (or Cree) of the Canadian Plains interprets time-space-energy (reality) is different to how a Kichua of Ecuador or a K'iche-Maya of Guatemala interprets it.

Colonialism, as already stated, denies the undeniable, which is the multiplicity of Indigenous peoples and knowledges. Colonization is a continuous process that blocks the promotion of Indigenous peoples' world views, affecting children the most. According to Cree intellectual Willie Ermine, a modern tool of colonizing Indigenous peoples is Western education that is turning Indigenous children into "indoctrinated children." The cultural monopoly, taught in the school system, is teaching Indigenous children how human beings should be according to Western standards.[6] Ermine acknowledges the good intentions of people who through their individual efforts attempt to "build bridges between cultures" but whose efforts are destroyed by "powerful currents."[7] Ermine mentions the concept of "ethical space" as the space that could be used, through meaningful dialogue, to understand each other's knowledge. Moreover, the Plains Cree do posses knowledge and have their own mediums to nurture and pass that knowledge to their children and to offer an alternative for intellectual dialogue. The situation is no different for the Mayan people of Guatemala.

Brief Historical Background

Guatemala, the northernmost Central American country, is 108,880 square kilometres in size. According to Fischer and McKenna Brown, the classic Maya city states (250–900 AD) developed in the northern lowlands, which by 900 AD, due to increasing population, overproduction, and environmental degradation, were abandoned.[8] At the time of the Spanish arrival, emerging Mayan states had developed in the Guatemalan highlands. The conquest of the main Mayan states took place between 1524 and 1531. Since conquest, and for most of colonization and the modern era, one of the main targets of suppression has been the Mayan belief systems.

As will be discussed in the following pages, the Maya of today still use pre-colonial symbols and material objects to represent their deities and to count time that their ancestors used and fought to keep. According to Severo Martínez, by 1693, or 169 years after conquest, the Maya still kept their "Indigenous paganism" that was the target of the conquistadors' descendants' hate and the object of "ruthless attacks."[9]

Despite living under slave-like conditions, the Maya, by then referred to only as Indians, fought to preserve stone representations of "ugly men and women, snakes, monkeys, eagles, and infinite other figures...that just sprung to surface out from the ground."[10] Colonizer, historian, and governor of Guatemala Francisco Fuentes y Guzman knew that the veneration of these stones represented a problem for the Spanish plans to fully dominate the Maya. Consequently, he ordered the removal of these stone idols out of his land (expropriated from Mayans) by throwing them into the abyss. To his surprise, the idols would appear again in the same place the day after he ordered them to be thrown out. Annoyed by the presence of the stone figures, he ordered the destruction of one of the main idols, using pickaxes that caused the Indians to be in a "state of shock when they saw how the idol was destroyed."[11] For Governor Fuentes, the Indians were worshipping the devil and he chastised the Catholic priest for not speeding up the process of Christianization.

Catholic priest Pedro Cortez y Larras described the Mayans' preservation of the stone figures: "[the] old idols, [show that] their Christianity is nothing but apparent and hypocritical."[12] Meanwhile, at the end of the seventeenth and beginning of the eighteenth centuries, Fray Francisco Ximenez found that the *Pop Wuj*, the sacred book of the Maya, was the main reason for these beliefs to be alive among the Indians. He alleged, "I found that this [Mayan] doctrine is what they learn from their mothers since birth and all of them know the doctrine by memory."[13] The Maya did not want anything Spanish nor anything that reminded them of conquest. The "doctrine" and the book *Pop Wuj* survived throughout Guatemala's colonial and modern history.

Guatemala was founded on the premise that anything Spanish was superior and anything Mayan was uncivilized. Furthermore, the education system created laws and programs to eradicate Mayan languages and the culture and assimilate the surviving population. People, their cultures, and their languages were portrayed as "detrimental to national progress."[14] Colonial mechanisms to eradicate the culture and the language included the 1646 policy of *Castellanización* (the use of Castilian Spanish only), imposing patronymic surnames, Spanish dress codes, and the mandatory use of Spanish, and only Spanish, in courts.[15] However, Mayan languages, belief systems, the use of ancient names, and symbols survived. Moreover, to the dismay of colonial and modern authorities, Mayan languages and other expressions of knowledge re-emerged despite centuries of oppression. Each Mayan group preserved its pre-colonization forms of knowing and how to know and interpret reality. One of the main vehicles used to obtain Mayan knowledge, in ceremonies and intense study about reality, is the K'iche-Mayan conception of time-space-energy expressed in the Mayan calendar *Cholq'ij*.

The Mayan Calendars and Their Numerical System

The calendar currently in fashion, due to the apocalyptic meaning it has received, is called the "Long Count" (or *Choltun*) or a cycle of 5,200 solar years that ended on December 20, 2012. A new Long Count began on December 21, 2012.[16] In the Gregorian calendar, the beginning of the current Long Count corresponds to August 11, 3114 BCE.[17] The Maya, however, had twenty other calendars. The main ones are the solar calendar (or *Ab'*) and the lunar calendar (Cholq'ij). The Ab' consists of 365 days divided into eighteen months of twenty days each, plus five days of reflection.[18] The Ab' is based on the rotation of the earth around the sun and the four distances of the earth in relation to the sun: two equinoxes and two solstices.[19] In Mayan mythology, the Ab' represents the sun and its animist representations are two male deities: Hun Ajpu (one hunter, when the sun is closer to the earth) and his father Hun Hunahpu (when the sun is farther from the earth). The other calendar, and the focus of this chapter, is the lunar calendar, also known a *Tzolkin* in Yucatec Maya or Cholq'ij in K'iche Maya. Together, calendars and deities represent life on the earth. The female deity, Ixmucane, Hun Ajpu's sister, represents the moon, while Ixquic, their mother, represents planet Earth.

All of the calendars used the vigesimal system of numeration. The table below shows the main symbols used to represent Mayan numbers, their respective decimal value, and their meaning.

Mayan Numbers	Value in Western Decimal System	K'iche-Mayan (English Pronunciation)	Meaning[20]
•	1	jun (huun)	finger tip
———	5	job (hob)	horizontal position of arm
⬭	0	winak (weenak)	eye, and the whole person

A graphic demonstration of the Mayan numbers (five to one), from bottom to top, is as follows:

•

• •

• • •

• • • •

———

According to Cabrera, this pyramidal system is essential to the Mayan understanding of the cosmos and life: the maximum use of the dots is four because they represent the four cardinal points and the four positions of the sun in relation to the earth. The maximum use of the bar is fifteen, or three bars, one above the other, because they represent the three levels of the Mayan cosmology: the underworld, life on the planet, and the cosmos.[21] The pyramidal system, using different variations of the solar calendar and the vigesimal system, can still be observed in the ancient Mayan buildings and in the weaving designs used by the Mayan women of Guatemala. The numbers, therefore, were used since the beginning of the Mayan civilization and continue to be used today.

The vigesimal system is counted from top to bottom and each level is multiplied by twenty. Counting, combining different variations using the three symbols, is infinite. Time is infinite. For example, using five dots in vertical Mayan order is equal to 168,421:

•   160,000
•   8,000
•   400
•   20
•   1

Interpreting Reality Using the Mayan Sacred Calendar

Reality is not simply what exists, and how to know what exists, but also time, space, and energy are important in the understanding of reality. According to Don Pascual, a Mam-Mayan timekeeper, as taught to Barrios, reality is viewed as the sum of time and space (or *Najt* in Mayan) and the pace or speed (the energy) in which time moves within that space.[22] Reality cannot be broken into parts or disassociate the human subject from it. It is for that reason, Don Pascual stated, the Cholq'ij

> is an instrument that allows each person to know his or her place in reality and in the world, and to know her predisposition, strengths and weaknesses to function within that reality. In that way, she will pursue her destiny using the right [or wrong] path in harmony [or disharmony] with her own purpose in life.[23]

To know her place in the (Mayan) world and guide her purpose in life, a person can use the Cholq'ij, the sacred or lunar calendar of the K'iche-Maya.

The Cholq'ij consists of 260 days (energies) divided into twenty cycles (or months) of thirteen days each: the days one to six represent frail energies, whereas the days eight to thirteen represent strong energies, while the number seven represents the balance of energies. According to Audelino Sac, "the Cholq'ij [represents] the moon's nine rotations around the earth and the time it takes to plant and harvest corn."[24] Meanwhile, Camacho Santay explains that it also represents the gestation of a human being in her mother's womb.[25] Therefore, the Cholq'ij represents the human person as a whole: *Jun Winak* (literally meaning one person) and also the sum of all their twenty parts (bone joints). In the K'iche-Mayan numerical system, when twenty is multiplied by the thirteen joints of the human body (ankles, knees, hips, wrists, elbows, shoulders, and neck), the result is the number 260.[26]

A new Cholq'ij (New Year) begins when it indicates *waxabi'b Bat'z* (eight monkey or eight cosmic threads) and ends when it indicates *wukub Tz'i'* (seven coyote or wild dog). Massive celebrations of a new Cholq'ij are now held all over Guatemala.

Consulting the Cholq'ij, a person obtains knowledge about her day of birth, the approximate date of her conception, and the respective Mayan symbols, or *Nawales* (protectors, the other selves), "governing" those dates. In total, a person "owns," and is owned by, four Nawales. A person, therefore, is not only an individual but also an individual who is part of reality (i.e., time-space-energy). According to Sac, a person becomes part of the collective and part of the Mayan philosophy: "I am you and you are I; whatever affects you affects me."[27] Each day, nonetheless, is a different symbol containing negative and positive energies, both of which are explained to each individual in order for that individual to maintain a balance in her life. The twenty symbols of the Cholq'ij are listed in the following table.

	Symbol[28]	Spanish Translation[29]	English Translation	Nawal (protector of)[30]
1	B'atz'	mono, hilo [cosmológico]	monkey [cosmological] thread	humanity, time, weaving
2	E	camino	road	four directions, food
3	Aj	caña	corn cane	arts
4	I'x	jaguar	jaguar	mayan altars, spirituality
5	Tz'ikin	pájaro	bird	material possessions
6	Ajmaq	búho	owl	deceased
7	No'j	idea, inteligencia	idea, intelligence	family, community
8	Tijax	daga de obsidiana	obsidian dagger	spiritual medicines
9	Kawoq	rayo, mujer	thunder, woman	women, midwives
10	Ajpu	cazador	hunter	music, agriculture, sports
11	Imox	lagarto, locura	alligator, craze	rain, water, craziness
12	Iq'	viento, luna	wind, moon	life
13	Aq'ab'al	amanecer	dawn	nature
14	K'at	red	net, web	jails, punishment
15	Kan	serpiente emplumada	feathered serpent	creation, justice
16	Kame	muerte	death	underworld, sickness
17	Kej	venado	deer	animals
18	Q'anil	semilla	seed	semen, germination
19	Toj	ofrenda	offering	fire and water
20	Tz'i'	perro, coyote	wild dog, coyote	authority, justice

Explanation of the Symbols and Their Use

Each symbol is the protector of abstract concepts, as well as the protector of human, cosmological, material, or natural elements. *Bat'z* (monkey or cosmological thread in English), the highest energy of all, for instance, is the Nawal of humanity and of time, represented by infinite, never-stopping rings weaving an imaginary cosmological thread.[31] It is within that weaving of time (*Bat'z*), space, and energy that the spiritual connection takes place. The second Nawal, *E*, represents and protects the four directions of the universe; the four cardinal points and the four positions of the earth in relation to the sun. Each and every symbol, one by one, with its negative and positive energies, is mentioned during a Mayan ceremony.

A Mayan ceremony requires a combination of mental concentration, counting, praying, and physical endurance, as a single ceremony can last from four to five hours. In Guatemala there are hundreds of sites that people have preserved to perform these ceremonies. Some are near human settlements and others are on tops of hills, mountains, or volcanoes, and near lakes or rivers. In the development of the ceremony, the *Ajq'ij ab* (or timekeeper) mentions hundreds of places where there are Mayan altars. Then, each of the twenty Nawales and its energies is revered and mentioned, beginning with the Nawal of the day before and ending with the symbol of the current day. Each of the twenty Nawales receives an offering after it is mentioned thirteen times. The spiritual connection during a ceremony is, therefore, a combination of counting time, of associating each Nawal, cosmological or earthly, to the human being.

Acquiring Knowledge: The Role of the Ajq'ij ab (Timekeeper)

Among the K'iche-Maya, and most Mayan groups, particularly among those living in the rural areas, there are midwives, natural medicine practitioners (derogatively called *curanderos*), traditional authorities, counsellors, conflict solvers, and the Ajq'ij ab or timekeeper (in Spanish, timekeepers are called *sacerdotes Mayas* or Mayan priests). To become an Ajq'ij ab, an individual has to follow the protocols and guidelines designed by an Elder Ajq'ij ab. A person can be trained from childhood, in agreement with their parents, or can decide to become one as an adult. There is no age and no gender restriction to begin initiation to become an Ajq'ij ab. I became a timekeeper in my adult life; however, I witnessed a young female of approximately thirteen years old performing the same duties as an adult: counting, narrating mythological as well as historical passages of the *Pop Wuj*, praying, and assisting people to understand their Nawal.

In addition to the use of the Cholq'ij, the Ajq'ij ab uses the *Pop Wuj*. In the book, most of the Cholq'ij symbols appear in mythological or historical accounts. The Ajq'ij ab mentions them and explains their role in Mayan mythology and history. For example, *Bat'z* (monkey or cosmological thread) appears in the form of two mythological figures, Hun Bat'z and Hun Chowen, twin brothers who, through tricks, were defeated by another set of younger twins, their brother Hun Ajpu and sister Ixbalanke. The former are converted into monkeys after their defeat and made to climb to a cosmological tree.[32] Hun Ajpu and Ixbalanke, after fulfilling their role on earth, which was to fight the lords of the underworld and to assist two female mythological deities (Ixmucane and Ixquic) to give life to human beings using corn, became the sun and the moon, respectively. *Aj* (corn cane) is described when the first four couples of Maya people are created and the material for their bones and flesh, after three failed attempts using other materials, was made out of corn.

The symbols, preceded by one of the Mayan numbers one to thirteen, were used to name people in pre-colonial times. In that regard, two of the last K'iche rulers, at the arrival of the Spanish conquistadors, were *Oxlajuj Kej* and *Belejeb Tz'i* (Thirteen Deer and Nine Coyote, respectively). They were also used to keep time. The Kakchiquel Maya used this system extensively and in that way they used dates and events to record the Spanish conquest in their historical text *Annals of the Kakchiquels*.

Conclusion: Mayan Social and Political Aspirations and the Cholq'ij

Although Mayan knowledge (materialized in mathematics, calendars, architecture, medicines, political systems, spiritual beliefs, languages, etc.) is not part of the education system of Guatemala, it does not mean it does not exist nor has it lost its relevance. Moreover, while Mayan children are indoctrinated into learning Spanish language, Spanish heroes, Western accomplishments, Western science, and Western religions, they do not learn anything Maya. Learning the language and cultural values takes place at home. Acquiring other types of knowledge (medicine, agriculture, midwifery, the Mayan calendar, etc.) is done either on an individual or collective basis.

The reasons why Mayan intellectuals, professionals, students, and activists are choosing to learn their ancient knowledge are debatable. The fact, nonetheless, is that the uses of Mayan languages and the expansion of Mayan ceremonies are becoming part of the modern Mayan struggles. According to Fischer and McKenna Brown, for Mayan intellectuals, students, and activists to achieve political and social participation in Guatemala, their approach in their pan-Mayan struggle goes "beyond scientific objectivity or literary self-reflection."[33] These Mayan intellectuals, students, and activists, in one way or another, have used the education system (that was supposed to assimilate them) to bridge the gap between their present and their past. Not even the 1981–1983 genocide against the northwest Maya stopped the modern Maya from fighting for several causes, specially the right of self-determination. Carol Smith, writes, "[O]ne would hardly have expected Maya self-determination to be the rallying cry to rise out of the ashes of Guatemala's holocaust."[34] However, the Mayan people are not a homogenous group, nor is there one way to achieve social, cultural, or political gains. While some attempt to achieve linguistic recognition, others attempt to achieve political representation. And while they diverge in their ways of achieving those goals, they are determined to become subjects of their own destiny through peaceful means.

However, as was taught to the author in the early 1980s, to achieve self-determination, even under the overwhelming and suffocating oppressive conditions of that decade, one must first know who one is and what his or her role in life is. The main vehicle to achieve that knowledge is to go back to the basis of the culture: language. Another vehicle, available to the author, is the Cholq'ij. The Cholq'ij is a vehicle to know what exists in both abstract and material things. More importantly, the Cholq'ij is a testimony to the continuation of time-space-energy, even after December 21, 2012.

Notes

1   Roger Moody, *The Indigenous Voice: Visions and Realities*, 2nd ed. (Utrecht, The Netherlands: International Books, 1993), 646.

2   The writer would like to clarify that this chapter is not about 2012. Therefore, it will not deal with the question of why the world did not end on that date, for such interpretation of the Mayan calendar was never discussed with the writer when he grew up in Guatemala, nor during his visits to such country, nor when he went through intensive training to become a timekeeper. If anything, this chapter is about Mayan knowledge that resisted religious, "scientific," social, and cultural censure, as well as brutal military conquest. The existence and use of the sacred calendar confirms the continuation of Mayan time, space, and energy as opposed to the apocalyptic, but profitable, interpretation given to

the Mayan Long Count calendar.

3   Berth Danermark et al., *Explaining Society: Critical Realism in the Social Sciences* (London, UK: Routledge, 2002), 29.

4   Ibid.

5   Edward F. Fischer and R. McKenna Brown, eds., *Maya Cultural Activism in Guatemala* (Austin, TX: University of Texas Press, 1999), 9–10.

6   Willie Ermine, as quoted by Dawn Ford, "The Space between Two Knowledge Systems," *Express News*, October 14, 2008, http://www.expressnews.ualberta. ca 10/14/2008.

7   Ibid.

8   Fischer and McKenna Brown, *Maya Cultural Activism*, 6.

9   Severo Martínez Peláez, *La Patria del Criollo* (Puebla, México: Universidad Autónoma de Puebla, 1982), 208.

10 Ibid., translation by author.

11 Ibid., 210.

12 Ibid., 213.

13 Ibid.

14 Fischer and McKenna Brown, *Maya Cultural Activism*, 208.

15 Ibid., 209.

16 Carlos Barrios, CH'UMILAL WUJ, *El libro del destino: Astrología Maya* (Guatemala, Guatemala: Cholsamaj, 2004), 27.

17 Fischer and McKenna Brown, *Maya Cultural Activism*, 7.

18 Nicolas Camacho Santay, *Libro Sagrado Maya* (Quetzaltenango, Guatemala: n.p., 2004), 17, translation of Nawals by author.

19 Audelino Sac, "Espiritualidad Maya, la Ciencia y el Pop Wuj" (Mayan Spirituality, Science and the *Pop Wuj*), in *Memorias del [Segundo Congreso sobre el Pop Wuj]* (Quetzaltenango, Guatemala: TIMACH y Xelapublicidad, 1999), 71.

20 Barrios, CH'UMILAL WUJ, *El libro del destino: Astrología Maya*, 46.

21 Edgar Cabrera, *El Calendario Maya: Su origen y su filosofía* (San José, Costa Rica: Liga Maya Guatemala, 1995), 132, 133.

22 Barrios, CH'UMILAL WUJ, *El libro del destino: Astrología Maya*, 106.

23 Ibid., 107.

24 Sac, "Espiritualidad Maya," 73.

25 Camacho Santay, *Libro Sagrado Maya*, 17.

26 Ibid., 75.

27 Sac, "Espiritualidad Maya," 70.

28 Barrios, CH'UMILAL WUJ, *El libro del destino: Astrología Maya*.

29 Spanish and English translations by the author.

30 Camacho Santay, *Libro Sagrado Maya*, 17.

31 As explained to the author by Don Carlos, K'iche-mayan timekeeper of Quetzaltenango, Guatemala, in October 2006.

32 Cabrera, *El Calendario Maya*, 287.

33 Fischer and McKenna Brown, *Maya Cultural Activism*, 2.

34 Carol Smith as quoted by Fischer and McKenna Brown, *Maya Cultural Activism*, 5.

NINE

GNARITAS NULLIUS (NO ONE'S KNOWLEDGE): THE ESSENCE OF TRADITIONAL KNOWLEDGE AND ITS COLONIZATION THROUGH WESTERN LEGAL REGIMES

Gregory Younging

Despite centuries of oppression, Indigenous knowledge is rich, varied, and continues to evolve.

Prior to contact with Western peoples between three hundred to six hundred years ago, Indigenous Nations had developed and evolved knowledge systems that flourished for millennia over the vast majority of the earth's land mass. These knowledge systems are integrated with the ecosystems in Indigenous territories, and are rich and varied, ranging from soil and plant taxonomy, cultural and genetic information, animal husbandry, medicine and pharmacology, ecology, zoology, music, arts, architecture, social welfare, governance, conflict management, and many others.[1] This chapter will begin by briefly outlining a small sampling of the manifestations of Indigenous knowledge systems that existed prior to European contact and colonization, most of which continue to exist and evolve.

Significant Contributions to Humanity: Devalued and Diminished

In the northern part of the continent of South America, Indigenous nations had charted the constellations, developed astrological charts, and constructed elaborate pyramids that parallel the pyramids in Egypt. In the mountains near the mid-west coast of the continent were complex city structures containing shaped stone buildings, stairs, walkways, and irrigation systems that still stand today. The ruins show precision-crafted buildings with neat regular lines, bevelled edges, and mortarless seams that characterize the best of Inca architecture.[2] In the interior of North America, Indigenous nations constructed gigantic mounds, some in the shape of animal and human figures that can only be identified from an aerial view. Entombed bodies and metal tools have been found inside these mounds, indicating "a complex and advanced civilization at work."[3] Along the northwest coast of the continent, intricate wood longhouses were constructed, comprising village structures that continue to intrigue architects. The three hundred or so tribal groups who lived in North America when Christopher Columbus arrived built their homes and arranged their settlements according to similar patterns and principles passed from generation to generation.[4]

Far beyond architecture, Indigenous design in North America had produced products including a variety of canoe designs, the kayak, snowshoes, sunglasses, and a multitude of farming and hunting implements. Gardening using hydroponics and advanced farming techniques were developed and practised on different continents by Indigenous peoples producing a range of crops including corn, squash, beans, tomatoes, wheat, potatoes, and varieties of fruits. Throughout the Amazon, basin Indigenous farmers had overcome problems with termites and other insects by utilizing extracts from trees that act as natural repellents—which Western scientists now struggle to understand and reproduce. Throughout North and South America, Indigenous farmers had a profound understanding of genetics, enabling them to experiment with new strains of potatoes. In the Andean region, Indigenous farmers knew that by taking pollen from one variety of corn and fertilizing the silk of another variety, they could create a corn with combined characteristics of the two parent crops.[5]

Major advances in the realm of health and herbal medicines had been developed throughout the continents of the Indigenous world. Shamans and traditional healers practised spiritual, herbal, and psychological techniques, including the placebo effect. Indigenous herbal specialists around the world gathered plants and studied and developed natural medicines that continue to surpass by far the advances in herbal medicine by non-Indigenous peoples. Indigenous knowledge systems have also made many significant contributions to the arts and humanities of the world. The technique of acid etching of designs of the Hohokam people in what is now southwestern Arizona (dating back to 500 BCE) predates the technique in Europe by three hundred years.[6] Stories of ancient times before human beings, stories of the creation of Indigenous peoples, and other stories of spiritual, mythological, and legendary figures are rooted in the oral tradition of Indigenous nations that has been passed down through generations and continues to fascinate many of the peoples of the world. Elaborate Indigenous artistic techniques and designs in sculpture, painting, music, drama, and dance continue to thrive in traditional and evolved forms, and have intrigued art historians and the art world for centuries.

In the area of governance, complex political systems exist among Indigenous nations and include chieftainships, monarchies, and evidence of universal rights and democracy prior to any such concepts in Europe. The Haudenausaunee People of the Longhouse practise a democratic form of government and formed the League of the Six Nations Confederacy that would later influence the development of American and European democracy. Oral history among the People of the Longhouse places the origin of the league at about 900 BCE,[7] although the Six Nations Confederacy was not officially formed until the early fifteenth century. Other United Nations structures along the northwest coast, eastern seaboard, and southern and northeast plains of North America developed between 2,500 and 1,500 years ago and far predate any such structures in Europe. Treaties and other economic, military, and political alliances between Indigenous Nations would continue through conflicts in the colonization process up to the present.

Indigenous knowledge systems represent the accumulated experience, wisdom, and know-how unique to nations, societies, and/or communities of people living in specific environments of America, Africa, Asia, and Oceania. These knowledge systems represent the accumulated knowledge of what was over 70 per cent of the earth's land mass prior to the era of colonization in the past few centuries—some ten thousand distinct peoples and cultures. In the past, Eurocentric knowledge has condescendingly associated Indigenous knowledge with the primitive, the wild, and the natural.[8] This is the prevailing negative Eurocentric perception of Traditional Knowledge (TK) that forms the basis for the status quo. Despite the advances made by knowledge systems throughout the Indigenous world, the Western world's general response throughout the colonial and most of the post-colonial periods was to dismiss the value of TK. Since only European people could progress, all Indigenous knowledge was viewed as static and historical.[9]

Not all TK originates from Indigenous peoples. Other forms of knowledge such as ancient Chinese medicine, Caribbean steel drum making and music, ancient Belgian weaving and lace-making techniques, and ancient Swiss yodelling have been considered to be forms of Traditional Knowledge. It is the case, however, that well over 95 percent of TK is derived from Indigenous peoples. The term "Traditional Knowledge" differs from the term "Indigenous knowledge" in that it does not include contemporary Indigenous knowledge and knowledge developed from a combination of traditional and contemporary knowledge. The two terms are, however, sometimes used interchangeably. Certain voices in the discourse prefer the term Indigenous knowledge because TK can be interpreted as implying that Indigenous knowledge is static and does not evolve and adapt.[10] However, Traditional Knowledge is the term used in most national discourses and virtually all the international forums. Indigenous knowledge is not only "technical" but also empirical in nature. Its recipients' integrative insights, wisdom, ideas, perceptions, and innovative capabilities pertain to ecological, biological, geographical, and other physical phenomena. It has the capacity for total systems understanding and management.[11]

The World Intellectual Property Organization Inter-Governmental Committee on Intellectual Property, Traditional Knowledge, Genetic Resources and Folklore (WIPO IGC) was established by the World Intellectual Property Organization (WIPO) General Assembly in October 2000 as a United Nations international forum for debate and dialogue concerning the interplay between intellectual property and TK. In carrying out its ongoing mandate to establish international standards for the protection and regulation of the use of TK, WIPO developed the following definition of Traditional Knowledge for the purposes of a 1998–1999 fact-finding mission that led to the establishment of the IGC (that has come to be regarded somewhat as a standard definition):

> *Traditional knowledge refer[s] to tradition-based literary, artistic or scientific works; performances; inventions; scientific discoveries; designs; marks, names and symbols; undisclosed information; and all other tradition-based innovations and creations resulting from intellectual activity in the industrial, scientific, literary or artistic fields. "Tradition-based" refers to knowledge systems, creations, innovations and cultural expressions which have generally been transmitted from generation to generation; are*

generally regarded as pertaining to a particular people or its territory; and,
are constantly evolving in response to a changing environment. Categories
of traditional knowledge could include: agricultural knowledge; scientific
knowledge; technical knowledge; ecological knowledge; medicinal knowl-
edge, including related medicines and remedies; biodiversity-related knowl-
edge; traditional cultural expressions ("expressions of folklore") in the form
of music, dance, song, handicrafts, designs, stories and artwork; elements
of language, such as names, geographical indications and symbols; and,
movable cultural properties. Excluded from this description would be items
not resulting from intellectual activity in the industrial, scientific, literary
or artistic fields, such as human remains, languages in general, and other
similar elements of "heritage" in the broad sense.[12]

Empirical-Like Knowledge as an Indigenous Methodology

The vast majority of Western-based research has been conducted through
the scientific process that has, in turn, produced most Western-based
knowledge. Vine Deloria Jr. has characterized the effect of the scientific
process as follows: "Eventually, we are told, the results of this research
with many other reports, are digested by intellects of the highest order and
the paradigm of scientific explanation moves steadily forward, reducing
the number of secrets Mother Nature has left."[13] In contrast to Western-
based scientific research methodology, there are emerging principles of
Indigenous-based research that draw on Indigenous traditional methods
of learning through lived experience including ecological and social interaction. Aspects of such methodologies can also be viewed in parallel with
Western-based theories of: 1) historical methodology, regarding primary
sources and oral tradition; and 2) discourse analysis, as expounded by
Vivien Burr[14] and Kenneth Gergen.[15]

   The historical method comprises the techniques and guidelines by which
historians use primary sources and other evidence to research and then write
history. The question of the nature, and indeed the possibility, of sound historical method is raised in the philosophy of history as a question of epistemology.[16] Aspects of the historical method and Indigenous epistemology
also converge in the use of oral tradition, whereby the oral transmission of
information from person to person is considered a legitimate method of
knowledge acquisition. Whereas oral testimony derived from a person who
was present at (or otherwise involved with) a past event can legitimately

inform present and future generations of history, oral transmission of cultural knowledge flowing from the past legitimately informs Indigenous heritage in proceeding generations. In both cases, a form of exclusive expertise is extended to the person with empirical knowledge of the event, or the Elder with empirical and transgenerational cultural knowledge. In many cases, the historical method's oral tradition and the Indigenous oral tradition are often the most reliable methods of knowledge acquisition, and, indeed, sometimes the best or only options.

With regard to discourse analysis, Burr and Gergen contended that "[o]ur ways of understanding the world are created and maintained by social processes."[17] Discourse is a form of social action that plays a part in producing the social world—including knowledge. Knowledge is created through social interaction in which we construct common truths and compete about what is true or false.[18] Although some understandings of TK can fit discourse analysis, more useful aspects are based fundamentally on Indigenous traditional methodologies that are now emerging as being useful to Indigenous research in contemporary contexts. Indigenous pedagogy paradigms are heavily based on the natural world and apprenticed relationships with Elders and other authoritative experts within Indigenous cultural confines. Within traditional Indigenous cultures, authority and respect are attributed to *Elders*—people who have acquired wisdom through life experiences, education (a process of gaining skills, knowledge, and understanding), and reflection.[19]

Perhaps the single most important precept of the Indigenous world view is the notion that the world is alive, conscious, and flowing with knowledge and energy. In his paper, "An Organic Arising: An Interpretation of Tikanga Based upon Maori Creation Traditions," Charles Royal states the following:

> *The natural world is not so much the repository of wisdom but rather is wisdom itself, flowing with purpose and design. We can say that the natural world is a mind to which all minds find their origin, their teacher and proper model. Indigenous knowledge is the fruit of this cosmic stream, arising organically when the world itself breathes through and inspires human cultural manifestation ... Leading from this view of the world being alive, conscious and wisdom filled is the obvious conclusion that all that we need to know, all that there is know and all that we should know already exists in the world, daily birthed in the great cycle of life. That is, human cultural production is a natural organic expression arising from the contours, shapes and colours of the environments in which we dwell.[20]*

In order to carry this Indigenous principle into the contemporary context, it must be acknowledged that many Indigenous peoples no longer dwell solely in what was "the world" to their ancestors (for example, the natural world). Many Indigenous peoples are now located in a world that consists of a complex physical and cultural layering of principles derived from nature and modernity. However, as emerging Indigenous research methodologies express, this does not mean that traditional models are not applicable and adaptable. Therefore, in contemporary research, Indigenous models can be adapted in the following ways: 1) interaction with the contemporary environment and the subsequent gained experience can be an important and relevant way of acquiring knowledge; and 2) authoritative figures who have accumulated a wealth of experience over time on particular aspects of the contemporary world can be afforded an Elder-like status for the purposes of research.

This Indigenous model of learning through experiencing is articulated further in Linda Tuhiwai Smith's *Decolonizing Methodologies: Research and Indigenous Peoples* as "intervening" and "connecting." Smith contends that, "[i]ntervening takes action research to mean literally the process of being proactive and becoming involved as an interested worker for change." Intervening and getting involved in a process occurring in the world is therefore a legitimate method of acquiring knowledge through the benefit of an insider perspective to the process, while also engaging and affecting the process. With regard to connecting, Smith states, "[c]onnectedness positions individuals in sets of relationships with other people and with the environment."[21]

Sources of Indigenous Knowledge

Some key sources of Indigenous knowledge include:

1. learning from observation of cyclical patterns in ecosystems and other natural law;
2. learning from animals;
3. spiritual knowledge acquired through ceremonies;
4. learning through teachings in Indigenous stories and philosophies;
5. trial and error;
6. Indigenous empirical-like knowledge;
7. oral tradition;

8. learning from Elders' interpretations and intuition;
9. ancient ancestral knowledge;
10. learning through Indigenous theories and methodologies;
11. learning through unique aspects of the contemporary Indigenous condition.

However, these high-capacity, time-tested Indigenous knowledge systems have been devalued and diminished by having Eurocentric perceptions and institutions imposed upon them. In the process, many of the systems have been debased through misrepresentation, misappropriation, unauthorized use, and the separating of the content from its accompanying regulatory regime.

Customary Laws: Developed Legal Regimes Devalued and Diminished

Indigenous peoples have numerous internal customary laws associated with the use of Traditional Knowledge. These customary laws have also been called "cultural protocols" and are part of the laws that Indigenous Nations have been governed by for millennia and are primarily contained in the oral tradition. Although, in lieu of the increased outside interest in TK and problems with interaction between TK and intellectual property rights (IPR) systems, there is a current movement among many Indigenous Nations to document their laws around the usage of their knowledge in written and/or digital format. In addition, many Indigenous Nations are developing methodologies for adapting and evolving customary laws so they will be effective in present-day situations.

Customary laws around the use of Traditional Knowledge vary greatly between Indigenous Nations.

- Certain plant harvesting, songs, dances, stories, and dramatic performances can only be performed/recited and are owned by certain individuals, families, or clan members in certain settings and/or certain seasons and/or for certain Indigenous internal cultural reasons.
- Crests, motifs, designs, and symbols, as well as herbal and medicinal techniques, are owned by certain individuals, families, or clan members.

- Artistic aspects of Traditional Knowledge, such as songs, dances, stories, dramatic performances, and herbal and medicinal techniques can only be shared in certain settings or spiritual ceremonies with individuals who have earned, inherited, and/or gone through a cultural and/or educational process.
- Art forms and techniques, and herbal and medicinal techniques cannot be practised, and/or certain motifs cannot be used until the emerging trainee has apprenticed under a master of the technique.
- Certain ceremonial art and herbal and medicinal techniques can only be shared for specific internal Indigenous cultural and/ or spiritual reasons and within specific Indigenous cultural contexts.

These are but a few general examples of customary laws that Indigenous Nations around the world have developed over thousands years to regulate the use of Traditional Knowledge. Indigenous customary laws are intimately intertwined and connected with TK and form what can be viewed as whole and complete, integrated, complex Indigenous knowledge systems throughout the world. For example, speaking about clan ownership in Nlaka'pamux customary law, Shirley Sterling states: "This concept of ownership by clans, nations and family groups and individuals of stories and other knowledge must be respected. The protocols for the use of collective knowledge from each cultural area and each First Nation would have to be identified and followed."[22]

Indigenous customary law, like other sources of law, is dynamic by its very nature. Like its subject matter—culture, practices, and traditions—it is not frozen in time. It has evolved with the social development of Indigenous peoples. Indigenous customary law also has an inextricable communal nature. The social structures that recreate, exercise, and transmit this law through generations, and the protocols that govern these processes, are deeply rooted in the traditional territories of Indigenous peoples, and, understandably, are inalienable from the land and environment itself.[23] Indigenous customary law is inseparable from Indigenous knowledge. In some Indigenous Nations, the abstract subtlety of Indigenous customary law is indivisible from cultural expressions such as stories, designs, and songs. That is, a story may have an underlying principle of environmental law or natural resource planning.[24] A song may explain the custodial relationship that a certain community has with a particular animal species. A design may be a symbol that expresses sovereignty over a territory, as well as the social hierarchy of a Nation's clan system. A watchman's pole may be considered an assertion of Aboriginal title, tell a story of a historical figure, and have a sacred significance.[25]

Neither the common law nor international treaties place Indigenous customary law on equal footing with other sources of law. As a result, Traditional Knowledge is particularly vulnerable to continued misuse and appropriation without substantive legal protection. Indigenous jurisprudence and law should protect Indigenous knowledge. In relation to Eurocentric law, Indigenous jurisprudence of each heritage should be seen as an issue of conflict of laws and comparative jurisprudence. With regard to its authority over Indigenous knowledge, Indigenous law and protocols should prevail over Eurocentric patent, trademark, or copyright laws.[26] However, due to a series of historical realities that will be considered below, the status quo is that Indigenous knowledge has become subjugated under European legal regimes, and intellectual property rights and other Eurocentric legal regimes trump or fail to recognize Indigenous law. This has created a situation where TK is taken out of its Indigenous context and placed in Western contexts without the accompanying Indigenous law, thus leaving TK vulnerable and often devoid of, or lacking in, its integrity.

European Systems: Intellectual Property Rights

One of the greatest ironies of the status quo in the interface between European and Indigenous knowledge management systems is that Indigenous systems predate European systems by centuries. This point can be highlighted by the historical reality that when Christopher Columbus landed in the Americas, hundreds of integrated knowledge systems, complete with regulatory regimes, had been functioning on the continent for generations, while no such regulatory regimes were in existence in Europe. What would now be termed "piracy," "unauthorized disclosure," and "copyright infringement" was common practice in sixteenth-century Europe. In the period of time leading up to the mid-sixteenth century, European authors' works were produced and sold without permission,[27] and inventors began to boycott the trade fair circuit based around Frankfurt because they would commonly have their ideas misappropriated. This section will briefly outline the development of some of the important milestones in Europe that led to the concept of "intellectual property" and the development of what became the intellectual property rights (IPR) system.

Copyright

The word "copyright" came into being as a reference to the sole right of the Stationers' Company to copy texts, first enacted in the second half of the sixteenth century in England. The Stationers' Company was a London-based booksellers' cartel that enjoyed a legislative monopoly over the trade in books in exchange for assistance in the suppression of "seditious" and "blasphemous" texts. An idea akin to the modern notion of copyright was developed in fifteenth-century Venice, predating the Industrial Revolution when creations were imbued with unprecedented social and economic value. The first such legislative award was made in 1486 to historian Marc Antonio Sabellico. The grant of copyright protection by Venetian authorities was meant to compensate inventors and stimulate invention. In 1545, the Venetian Council of Ten demanded that booksellers secure written proof that their publications had received authorial consent.[28]

Copyright as we know it began in 1710 with the enactment in England of the Statute of Anne. Prior to this, publishing was regulated by means of the Licensing Act, which required that all books be registered with the Stationers' Company. Thus, copyright was not introduced to deal with concerns of authors but to regulate the trade in books and to assuage the concerns of the booksellers and printers. The mention of the rights of authors in the preamble had more to do with window dressing than substantive protection. The preamble stated:

> *Whereas Printers, Booksellers and other persons have lately frequently taken the Liberty of printing, Reprinting and Publishing or causing to be Printed, Reprinted and Published Books and other writings without the consent of Authors or Proprietors of such Books and Writings to their very great Detriment, and too often to the ruin of them and their families.*[29]

With the Statute of Anne came a time limit on the rights of authors: twenty-one years for the books already on the Stationers' register, and up to twenty-eight years for new books. It also introduced the concept of the public domain, a commons that encompasses documents and material of all kinds no longer protected by copyright. Regardless of ownership, once the term of copyright expires, intellectual property becomes the property of everyone. The physical embodiment of it may continue to belong to individuals or institutions, but the intellectual property falls into the public domain. However, if a new work is created that incorporates a work that is in the public domain, the new work is protected.

The enactment of this statute meant that two authorities governing the rights of authors existed in England: common law (the law created by decisions of judges), and statute law (the law created by legislation). The decisive case came in 1769 with the judgment in *Millar v. Taylor*. Millar was a London-based bookseller who brought the suit for copyright infringement against Taylor, a rival bookman who had published "The Seasons," a poem Millar "owned." Millar grounded his case in common law, arguing that he had purchased the rights to the poem in perpetuity. Taylor based his defence on the Statute of Anne, claiming that Millar's copyright had run its course and the poem was in the public domain.

The judge decided in favour of common law and Millar stated: "It is just, that an author should reap the pecuniary profit of his own ingenuity and labour. It is just, that another should not use his name without his consent. It is just that he should judge when to publish, or whether he will publish. It is fit he should not only chose the time, but the manner of publication, how many, what volume, what print. It is fit, he should choose to whose care he will trust the accuracy and correctness of the impression."[30] The Millar decision in favour of authorial rights stood for only five years. It was overturned in 1774 in the case of *Donaldson v. Beckett* (Donaldson being a pirate publisher, and Becket being an author) that established the notion of the balance of interests between creators and users in copyright.

Droit moral and droit d'auteur
Moral rights came into being in France in the eighteenth century. The moral rights theory holds that a creator is a sovereign individual and therefore his/her work is sovereign, and as such, must be respected. In Article 27, the United Nations Declaration of Human Rights states, "Everyone has the right to the production of moral and material interests resulting from scientific, literary or artistic production of which he is the author." This is balanced by article 2(1), which states that "[e]veryone has the right to freely participate in the cultural life of the community to enjoy the arts and to share in its benefits."[31] The Berne Convention for the Protection of Literary and Artistic Works of 1886 was the first international agreement on copyright in Europe. The convention enacted a moral rights clause at its Rome Congress in 1928. Article 6 of the convention states: "Independently of the author's economic rights, and even after the transfer of said rights, the author shall have the right to claim authorship of the work and to object to any distortion, mutilation or other modification of, or other derogatory action in relation to, the said work which would be prejudicial to his honour or reputation."[32] The

concept of *droit moral* (moral rights) was introduced, which in turn led to the concept *droit d'auteur* (author's rights). *Droit moral* theory holds that the author/creator is sovereign, and therefore his/her work is sovereign and must be respected as such. *Droit d'auteur* holds that the rights of the author/creator are natural and inalienable rights and that the author/creator must be identified with, and credited for, the work.

Originality

The key criterion for copyright protection is that the work be "original." Originality does not mean that a work must be unique, one of a kind, and unlike anything else but rather that it be an original expression of the author, and not a copy of another work. The explanation of one American jurist, Judge Learned Hand, in 1936, is often quoted as a definition: "Borrowed work must not be for the plagiarist who is not himself *pro tano* an 'author'; but if by some magic a man who has never known it were to compose a new Keats 'Ode on a Grecian Urn,' he would be an 'author,' and, if he copyrighted it, others might not copy that poem, though they might of course copy Keats's."[33]

Ownership

Copyright in a work belongs in the first instance to the creator. Subsequently, it may be licensed or assigned, for example, to producers, publishers, and distributors who manufacture and market the work. If a work is produced during the course of employment as part of the employee's duties, however, the law stipulates that the rights are the employer's. Similarly, if a photograph, portrait, engraving, or print is commissioned, the person ordering the work and paying for it is deemed to own the copyright, unless there is an agreement to the contrary. There are thus two kinds of copyright owners operating in the cultural sector: corporations or businesses, and individual creators. In some countries, in order to have copyright protection, a work must be registered. In Canada, when someone creates a work, it is automatically protected under the Copyright Act, so long as the creator is Canadian or is resident here, or in a country that is a signatory to the international conventions, such as the Berne Convention, to which Canada belongs.

The so-called Anglo-American copyright systems (in Canada and the United States, and influencing and being adopted in other countries) have a primarily utilitarian logic. In return for enriching the public, creators are allowed to reap some of the fruits of their creative labours. But the monopoly thereby granted by the state is temporary, and the law expresses an interest in protecting the public's right to copyright material in the long term through the concept of the public domain. Hence, copyright's concern with "balance." In public policy terms, this can be understood as the tension between individual rights and public freedoms—that is, between the property rights of individuals and the right of society to its cultural heritage and to the freedom of information.

The continental system is based on the concept of the *droit d'auteur* as the "natural and inalienable" right of individual creators. The interests of creators are paramount, not those of the public, and moral rights are central. Moreover, these are deemed to be human rights, attached to the individual creator. They indicate that besides being a product, service, or a performance, a creation is connected to the person of its creator. Behind the painting, the text, or the film, lies the reputation of its author.[34]

Patents and Trademarks

The regulation of patents protecting industrial inventions, the oldest form of intellectual property, goes back to the Venetian Decree of 1474.[35] The concept of patents did not get widespread recognition in Europe with the passage of England's 1624 Statute of Monopolies. The Statute of Monopolies spoke of granting patents for "any manner of new manufactures." The Paris Convention for the Protection of Industrial Property was passed in 1883. The European Patent Convention was passed in 1973. Patents are granted to inventors to protect their inventions from being copied or used by others for a fixed time period, usually between seventeen and twenty years. Most industrialized countries now have a patent office to administer the application and regulation of patents. The main criteria for the granting of patents are that the invention must be "new, useful and unobvious ideas with practical application." This can include "new machines, products, processes, or improvements on existing technology."[36]

As European societies became increasingly industrialized, it became apparent that patents and copyright were not sufficient to protect all forms of intellectual property. In the eighteenth century, European countries in the process of industrialization developed the concept of "trademark," which was later legislated in the form of national trademark acts. Patent and trademark, along with copyright, now make up the current IPR system. Trademarks are used to support a company's claim that its products are unique as compared to similar products from other companies. The main criteria for granting trademarks are that the product is "authentic" and "useful." Most industrialized governments now have agencies to grant and administer trademarks. Once a trademark is applied for in its country of "origin," the trademark applicant can apply to have it registered in other countries to which it may wish to export its products. Some groupings of countries have multilateral trademark agreements, such as the Madrid Agreement Concerning the International Registration of Trademarks, which enables an applicant to be granted trademark in the thirty signatory countries with a single application.

Ratification by Canada of the latest versions of the Paris Convention (1967) and Berne Convention (1971) requires Canada to bring its intellectual property laws in line with the conventions. In the Irwin Essentials in Canadian Law Series, titled *Intellectual Property Law: Copyright, Patents, Trade-Marks*, David Vaver notes that "early in its history, Canada came to protect foreign authors and enterprises alongside its native born—at least its native born descended from settlers."[37] Vaver further states, "Both the *Paris and Berne* conventions were highly Eurocentric treaties that ignored the culture of indigenous peoples."[38] Native culture was thought to be free for the taking, the product of many and so the preserve of none—except when it was transformed by the mediation of Europeans, whereupon it magically gained cultural legitimacy. Although TK can have fundamental characteristics that differ from European-based intellectual property, Traditional Knowledge *is* intellectual property owned collectively by Indigenous Nations or groupings therein. However, this collective ownership is not acknowledged by the IPR system.

Case Studies in IPR/TK Interface

This section will detail examples of Traditional Knowledge that have been misappropriated and otherwise protected or unprotected under copyright, patents, and trademarks. The case studies will be analyzed in terms of the insights they provide about the functionality of the intellectual property rights system and its ability to incorporate TK and the interests of Indigenous peoples—where TK originates. The section will highlight concerns that existing regimes of protection are not able to protect certain forms of TK; and, therefore, will support the argument that new systems of protection need to be developed and implemented (that could both include, and work in conjunction with, Indigenous customary law). The three main mechanisms of the IPR system—copyright, patent, and trademark—will be examined through specific cases to show how they have impacted TK. Through the examination of the case studies, some brief analysis of how each mechanism interacted with TK will also be provided.

Interaction between TK and IPR Systems

As stated earlier, in the process of transporting European institutions into various parts of the world occupied by Indigenous peoples, the intellectual property rights system has now been imposed upon the Traditional Knowledge system. Many issues have arisen in the past ten years regarding problems resulting from the existing IPR system's apparent inability to protect TK. The main problems with TK protection in the IPR system are

- that expressions of TK often cannot qualify for protection because they are too old and are, therefore, supposedly in the public domain;
- that the "author" of the material is often not identifiable and there is thus no "rights holder" in the usual sense of the term;
- that TK is owned "collectively" by Indigenous groups for cultural claims and not by individuals or corporations for economic claims.

The Public Domain Problem

Under the intellectual property rights system, knowledge and creative ideas that are not "protected" are in the public domain (that is, they are accessible by the public). Generally, Indigenous peoples have not used IPR to protect their knowledge, and so Traditional Knowledge is often treated as if it is in the public domain without regard for customary laws. Another key problem for TK is that the IPR system's concept of the public domain is based on the premise that *the author/creator deserves recognition and compensation for his/her work because it is the product of his/her genius, but that all of society must eventually be able to benefit from that genius.* Therefore, according to this aspect of IPR theory, all knowledge and creative ideas must eventually enter the public domain. Under IPR theory, this is the reasoning behind the time period limitations associated with copyright, patents, and trademarks.

The precept that all intellectual property, including Traditional Knowledge, is intended to eventually enter the public domain is a problem for Indigenous peoples because customary law dictates that certain aspects of TK are not intended for external access and use in any form. Examples of this include sacred ceremonial masks; songs and dances; various forms of shamanic art; sacred stories; prayers; songs; ceremonies; art objects with strong spiritual significance such as scrolls, petroglyphs, and decorated staffs; rattles; blankets; medicine bundles and clothing adornments; and various sacred symbols, designs, crests, medicines, and motifs. However, the present reality is that Traditional Knowledge is, or will be, in the public domain (that is, the intellectual property rights system overrides customary law).

Case Studies

After providing some background as to the key reasons behind the IPR systems' deficiencies in protecting Traditional Knowledge, the remainder of this section turns to some specific examples. Indeed, there are hundreds of such case studies, many of which are referred to in literature and discourse. However, for the purposes of illustration, the number of case studies will be limited to two or three under the categories of copyright, patent, and trademark. The cases will attempt to show that an intellectual/legal analysis of reasons for IPR deficiencies can be made simpler by looking at some concrete examples. An effort has also been made to provide a balance between positive and negative examples in terms of IPR/TK interaction in the selection of the cases.

Copyright Cases

This section will first contrast two cases where Indigenous stories have been published in children's books. The first case is one in which a non-Indigenous author overtly appropriated and copyrighted stories. The second case involved an Indigenous publisher who attempted to adopt aspects of customary law into the publishing process. A third example of a case of music copyright is also included.

THE CAMERON CASE. In 1985, the Euro-Canadian author Anne Cameron began publishing a series of children's books through Harbour Publications based on West Coast Indigenous traditional stories. These books include *The Raven, Raven and Snipe, Keeper of the River, How the Loon Lost Her Voice, Orca's Song, Raven Returns the Water, Spider Woman, Lazy Boy, and Raven Goes Berrypicking*. Cameron had heard the traditional stories by Indigenous storytellers and/or had been present at occasions when the stories were recited. The original printing of the books granted Anne Cameron sole authorship, copyright, and royalty beneficiary, and gave no credit to the Indigenous origins of the stories. As the discourse around Indigenous cultural appropriation emerged in the 1990s, Cameron's books came under severe Indigenous criticism, not only on the grounds of cultural appropriation, but also because the Indigenous TK-holders asserted that some of the stories and aspects of the stories were incorrect. This led to a major confrontation with Indigenous women authors at the Third International Women's Book Fair in Montreal in 1988.[39] At the end of the confrontation, Cameron agreed not to publish any more Indigenous stories in the series. However, the books continued to be reprinted and new books in the series continued to be published. Some minor concessions have been made in subsequent reprints of books in the series, as well as in new additions to the series. Reprints of the books that were produced after 1993–1994 contained the disclaimer: "When I was growing up on Vancouver Island I met a woman who was a storyteller. She shared many stories with me and later gave me permission to share them with others...the woman's name was Klopimum." However, Cameron continued to maintain sole author credit, copyright, and royalty payments. In a further concession, the 1998 new addition to the series, *T'aal: The One Who Takes Bad Children*, is co-authored by Anne Cameron and the Indigenous Elder/storyteller Sue Pielle, who also shares copyright and royalties.

THE KOU-SKELOWH CASE. The Kou-Skelowh Series, published by Theytus Books, could be viewed as proper and ethical process within Indigenous cultural confines. The series contains traditional Okanagan stories that have been translated into English, illustrated, and made into children's books. The original Kou-Skelowh Series was published by Theytus Books in 1984. The redesigned, second versions of the series were published by Theytus in 1991. One of the most valuable aspects of the series is how its development attempted to incorporate Indigenous cultural protocols into the publishing process. Firstly, in the early 1980s, on behalf of Theytus, Okanagan author Jeannette Armstrong approached the Okanagan Elders Council and asked if some traditional legends could be used in the project. When the Elders gave permission for three legends to be used, Armstrong then condensed the legends and translated them into English. The English versions were then taken back to the Elders Council for examination and edited until they were approved.

The Elders Council was then asked if Theytus Books could have permission to publish the stories for the book trade. After lengthy discussions, Theytus was granted permission on the grounds that several conditions were met, including that no one individual would claim ownership of the legends or benefit from the sales. The Elders Council was also then asked to name the series: *Kou-Skelowh*, meaning "we are the people." The series does not name an author; instead, each book contains the caption, "An Okanagan Legend." The series is also copyrighted to the Okanagan Tribal Council, as the Okanagan Elders Council is not an incorporated entity. The methodology implemented in the Kou-Skelowh Series could stand as a model in which concerns about Indigenous cultural protocols were considered. The methodology that was used in the Kou-Skelowh Series could also stand as an example of the uniqueness of Indigenous editorial practice.

THE MBUBE CASE. In its original Indigenous version, the "Mbube Song" is traditionally sung with a Zulu refrain that sounds, to English-speaking people, like "wimoweh." "Mbube" was a big hit throughout Southern Africa, selling nearly one hundred thousand copies in the 1940s of the recorded version by South African singer Solomon Linda, who was regarded as the master singer of the song. Linda recorded the tune in 1939, with his group the Evening Birds, and it was so popular that a style of Zulu choral music became known as Mbube Music. Decca Records in the United States accessed a copy of the recording in the 1950s and passed it on to the singer Pete Seeger, who was apparently enchanted by Mbube, especially the "wimoweh" refrain. Seeger then recorded it with the American folk group, the Weavers. American musicologists claim the song really gained notoriety with the Weavers' live version at Carnegie Hall in 1957. Linda was not credited as the writer; it was credited to Paul Campbell, a member of the folk group. The Kingston Trio released their version in 1959, with the writer credit listed as "traditional; adapted and arranged by Campbell-Linda."

A subsequent version by the Tokens was performed in an audition with the top RCA production team of Hugo (Peretti) and Luigi (Creatore) in 1960. Hugo and Luigi decided the song needed new lyrics. With George Weiss, they keyed in on what they saw as the song's "jungle origins" and wrote "The Lion Sleeps Tonight," including the "wimoweh" refrain that was Seeger's mistranslation of Linda's original. The Tokens recorded the quintessential pop version in May 1961 at RCA Studios. The song became a huge international hit and was given another round of popularity and financial benefit when it was featured as the theme song in the Disney movie, *The Lion King*. Linda or his heirs have not received any substantial royalties from a song that is perhaps one of the most well-known worldwide hits.[40] Prior to his recent passing, Seeger made concessions with the Linda family over this issue.

ANALYSIS. While the Kou-Skelowh case shows that publishers and editors can make moral decisions to respect TK, the Cameron case shows that the copyright system does not protect traditional stories from appropriation should the "author" choose to continue to maintain copyright. The Indigenous TK-holders of the original stories could find no recourse within copyright law.

As such, they could only make their grievances known, and together with the Indigenous women authors, make a moral appeal to the copyright holder. This appeal was only moderately effective in that it only led to some minor concessions. Although the Kou-Skelowh case is a more optimistic model for TK within copyright, it fundamentally only represents an innovative use of the system based on the good will of the publisher to respect TK protocols. In the Mbube case, Soloman Linda also had no recourse within copyright law. According to music copyright, a person(s) who does fresh work on an existing work may, however, claim to be the author of the resulting product.[41]

Patent Cases

Misappropriation of TK through patents is the area in which the greatest number of misappropriations exists, as thousands of patents on TK have been licensed to corporations and individuals worldwide. At the seventh meeting of the WIPO IGC in November 2005, a representative from the Indian national delegation quoted a recent study in which "a random selection of 300 patents in India revealed that over 200 contained TK.[42] The extent of the problem has become a major concern for WIPO, being the body that grants international patents. The organization has conducted several major research studies on the topic in recent years, some of which refer to such cases as "erroneous patents" and propose mechanisms to revoke such patent licences. Many of these controversial patent licences pit small Indigenous communities against large national and multinational corporations. Noting that there is a wealth of test cases that could be selected, this section will examine two cases: one involving an Inuit corporation's unsuccessful attempt to patent Inuit TK in Canada, and the case of the patenting of a plant from Africa by corporations in the United States.

THE IGLOOLIK CASE. An example of the failure of the Patent Act to respond to Inuit designs is the Igloolik Floe Edge Boat Case.[43] A floe edge boat is a traditional Inuit boat used to retrieve seals shot at the floe edge (the edge of the ice floe), to set fishing nets in summer, to protect possessions on the sled when travelling by snowmobile or wet spring ice, and to store hunting or fishing equipment. In the late 1980s, the Canadian government sponsored the Eastern Arctic Scientific Research Centre to initiate a project to develop a floe edge boat that combined the traditional design with modern materials and technologies. In 1988, the Igloolik Business Association (IBA) sought to obtain a patent for the boats. The IBA thought that manufactured boats using the floe edge design would have great potential in the outdoor recreation market. To assist the IBA with its patent application, the Canadian Patents and Developments Limited (CPDL) agency initiated a preproject patent search that found patents were already held by a non-Inuit company for boats with similar structures. The CPDL letter to the IBA concluded that it was difficult for the CPDL to inventively distinguish the design from previous patents and, therefore, the IBA patent would not be granted. The option of challenging the pre-existing patent was considered by the IBA; however, it was decided that it would not likely be successful due to the high financial cost and risk involved in litigation.

THE TAUMATIN CASE. Taumatin is a natural sweetener made from the berries of the katemfe shrub that are traditionally used by Indigenous peoples in Central Africa. The protein is about two thousand times sweeter than sucrose without any of the health risks. In 1993, researchers from the Lucky Biotech Corporation and the University of California acquired a U.S. patent on all transgenetic fruits, seeds, and vegetables containing the gene responsible for producing taumatin.[44] Although taumatin has still not reached the United States and other markets, with the high cost and low production scale of growing taumatin on plantations in Africa, and a $900-million-per-year, low-calorie sweetener market in the United States, it is highly likely that African katemfe plantations will not be used; as a result, the countries where katemfe is grown will not be able to benefit from exporting the berries.[45]

ANALYSIS. The Igloolik and tautmatin cases show that TK can be patented by non-Indigenous corporations, leaving the Indigenous originators with no financial benefits and no recourse other than litigation. Typically in patent challenge litigation, corporations have their own lawyers and financial resources to provide effective legal support, whereas local (Indigenous) communities rarely have such resources or advocates. Even if a case goes to court, the company may well succeed in convincing the court that its product, use, or process is sufficiently different from the original to constitute an invention.[46]

Trademark Cases

As most Indigenous communities are far behind in terms of establishing businesses, most trademarking of TK involves a non-Indigenous corporation trademarking an Indigenous symbol, design, or name. This practice has been curtailed by laws in the Philippines, the United States, and other countries. However, it remains rampant in most countries around the globe (for instance, the 2010 Vancouver Olympics logo). Again, many cases could have been examined in this chapter, but only two have been chosen: one case involving the Snumeymux Band trademarking petroglyphs through the Canadian Patent Office, and one involving an international corporation's patent licence being the subject of an intense international Indigenous lobbying effort.

THE SNUMEYMUX CASE. The Snumeymux people have several ancient petroglyphs located off their reserve lands near False Narrows on Gabriola Island, British Columbia. In the early 1990s, non-Indigenous residents of Gabriola Island began using some of the petroglyph images in coffee shops and various other business logos. In the mid-1990s, the Island's music festival named itself after what had become the local name of the most well-known petroglyph image: the dancing man. The Dancing Man Music Festival then adopted the image of the dancing man as the festival logo and used it on brochures, posters, advertisements, and T-shirts. The Snumeymux Band first made unsuccessful appeals to the festival, businesses, and the Gabriola Island community to stop using the petroglyph symbols. In 1998, the Snumeymux Band hired Murray Brown as its legal counsel to seek protection of the petroglyphs. At a 1998 meeting with Brown, Snumeymux Elders, and community members, the Dancing Man Festival and Gabriola Island business and community representatives were still defiant that they had a right to use the images from the petroglyphs.[47]

On the advice of Brown, the Snumeymux Band filed for a Section 91(n) Public Authority Trademark for eight petroglyphs and was awarded the trademark in October of 1998.[48] The trademark protects the petroglyphs from "all uses" by non-Snumeymux people and, therefore, the Dancing Man Festival and Gabriola Island business and community representatives were forced to stop using images derived from the petroglyphs.

THE AVEDA CASE. In 2000, the Aveda Corporation, headquartered in Minneapolis and New York City, introduced a cosmetic product line called "Indigenous," which included an aroma candle, essential oil, and hair and body shampoo. The products in the line were infused with cedar, sage, and sweetgrass, and the symbol of the line featured on all labelling and promotional material was the Medicine Wheel. The trademark application, No. 75/76,418 under the word "Indigenous," was filed with the United States Patent and Trademark Office on September 9, 1999, and was granted on November 15, 1999. The "Indigenous" trademark application was submitted to the Canadian Intellectual Property Office on September 15, 1999, and granted on July 16, 2003.

Indigenous lobbying against the "Indigenous" line began to grow through-out 2000–2002 in the United States, Australia, and New Zealand. The lobby-ing efforts attempted to disseminate the message that the line was offensive to Indigenous peoples, mainly because the word "Indigenous" was trade-marked by a non-Indigenous corporation, and the Medicine Wheel symbol was being used in a culturally inappropriate manner. The cross-cultural issues were somewhat clouded by the fact that the cedar, sage, and sweetgrass were obtained from Native Americans and other Native Americans endorsed the products. For instance, Robby Romero, president of Native Children's Survival, made the following statement that was printed on one of the bro-chures: "Indigenous™ express[es] a reverence to Mother Earth, devotion to the environment, and an alliance with Wisdom Keepers of the World."

Eventually, Indigenous lobbyists from the United States and Australia began working together and managed to arrange a meeting with Dominique Conseil, Aveda's president, in September 2003. In the meeting, Conseil was persuaded to drop the line and the trademark, and Aveda issued the follow-ing statement in a press release dated November 4, 2003:

> *Aveda Corporation today announced the discontinuation of its Indigenous product line as well as its intention to abandon the "Indigenous" trade-mark. The Indigenous collection...will cease production immediately....The decision was reached following a meeting among representatives of several indigenous nations of the Americas and Australia and representatives of Aveda....We are discontinuing the Indigenous product line to demonstrate our ongoing support and respect for indigenous peoples in their efforts to protect their traditional knowledge and resources...Aveda will discontinue marketing any products under the "Indigenous" trademark and, to empha-size its respect, will begin the formalities necessary to abandon any rights it may have in this trademark...By its action, Aveda also hopes to stand in solidarity with indigenous peoples in their quest for recognition of intellec-tual property rights in their traditional wisdom.[49]*

ANALYSIS. While the outcomes of the Snumeymux and Aveda cases appear to shed an optimistic light on trademark protection of TK, a closer exam-ination of the cases still reveals problems with TK and IPR interaction. The Snumeymux trademark did "work" to protect the petroglyphs but not as the trademark system is intended. According to trademark theory, the system is intended to be "offensive," allowing the rights holder to freely use the mark for the promotion and advancement of the product into the marketplace. In the Snumeymux case, the petroglyphs were trademarked for "defensive" purposes—that is, so they would not be used. Like the Kou-Skelowh case, the Snumeymux case represents an innovative use of the IPR system that negotiated within the system's limitations and found a way to make it work to protect TK.

The Aveda case may be a great Indigenous lobbying victory, but it is not such a great victory for TK protection within the IPR system. In this case, the extenuating circumstances of a strong and organized lobby, a company eager to protect its naturalist, purest, earthy image, and an open-minded company president, led to the cancelling of the line and the trademark. However, like the author Anne Cameron's minor concessions, the cancelling was the result of a willing concession on the part of the rights holder based on a moral appeal. There is nothing within the IPR system that would have compelled Aveda to abandon the mark if the company, for example, chose to make an economic decision based on investment in developing and manufacturing the line, and ignore the moral issue presented before it.

Summary of Case Studies
The case studies have shown that serious conflicts exist between the IPR and TK systems that leads to the conclusion that it constitutes a major problem that Indigenous peoples must resolve with the modern states they are within and with the international community. In contrast to Eurocentric thought, almost all Indigenous thought asserts that property is a sacred, ecological order and manifestations of that order should not be treated as commodities.[50] It is clear that there are pressing problems in the regulation of TK. It is also clear that the IPR system and other Eurocentric concepts do not offer a solution to some of the problems. There have been cases of Indigenous people using the IPR system to protect their TK. However, the reality is that there are many more cases of non-Indigenous people using the IPR system to take ownership over TK by using copyright, trademark, and especially patents. In some such cases, this has created a ridiculous situation whereby Indigenous peoples cannot legally access their own knowledge.

A study undertaken on behalf of the Intellectual Property Policy Directorate (IPPD) of Industry Canada and the Canadian Working Group on the Convention on Biodiversity Article 8(j) concludes:

There is little in the cases found to suggest that the Intellectual Property system has adapted very much to the unique aspects of Indigenous knowledge or heritage. Rather, Indigenous peoples have been required to conform

to the legislation that was designed for other contexts and purposes, namely
western practices and circumstances. At the same time, there is little evi-
dence that these changes have been promoted within the system, i.e., from
failed efforts to use it that have been challenged (IPPD-2002).

Such conclusions, among many being drawn in other countries and international forums, and the case study examples discussed here, support the
argument that new systems of protection need to be developed. *Sui Generis*
models based on and/or incorporating customary laws have been proposed
and developed in many countries and are being discussed in the WIPO IGC.

Terra Nullius and the Colonization of Traditional Knowledge

Between thirty thousand and 520 years ago, Traditional Knowledge systems
developed and thrived, protected and regulated by their associated customary laws, upon approximately 90 per cent of the earth's landmass that was
occupied by thousands of Indigenous Nations. In this pre-colonization era,
Indigenous peoples were the vast majority of the world population and lived
in balance with natural laws in their respective territories. In the early colonial
period, Western perspectives interpreted Indigenous Nations through the
lens of Social Darwinism as subhuman and primitive. Consequently, despite
its immense universal value, TK was also seen by the Western perspective to
be of little or no value. Christopher Columbus came to Indigenous America
as an invader and a colonizer without regard for the original inhabitants he
"discovered."[51] The arrival of Columbus signified the beginning of a period
of colonization in which Indigenous peoples were subjected to Western legal
norms in replacement of their own. By 1493, the patterns were set for the
next 520 years in the Americas and other places where European coloniz-
ers relocated and dispossessed Indigenous peoples from their lands and
resources.[52] Throughout the early period of colonization, debates and discussions around Europe considered whether Indigenous peoples were human
beings or not, largely concluding the latter. Theories of Social Darwinism
added further justification that Indigenous, black, and other brown-skinned
peoples were lesser evolved than Western European peoples.

  Indigenous peoples' territories were interpreted by Western legal regimes
as being *terra nullius*, literally meaning "land belonging to no one." *Terra*
nullius justified the idea and legal concept that when the first Europeans
arrived, the land was owned by no one and therefore open to settlement.

In the sixteenth century, when Spanish, British, and French colonial forces began large-scale encroachment upon the thirty million Indigenous peoples in North America, *terra nullius*, Social Darwinism, and the Doctrine of Discovery were the dominant ideologies that prevailed through colonial institutions to many current, modern, Western institutions.

North American Colonization and Residential Schools

Early settlers in North America benefitted from Indigenous peoples sharing their Traditional Environmental Knowledge, especially in the Arctic and semi-Arctic regions of the continent—now Canada. This early history of the relationship between the British Crown/Canada and Indigenous Nations was based on international law, nation-to-nation negotiations, and treaties. However, soon afterward, Canada began to stray down a path leading away from international law toward an adversarial/hostile, dominating relationship with Indigenous peoples. This era continues through to today, including the residential school system and several other breaches of international law. With the Act for the Gradual Civilization of Indian Tribes of 1851, Upper and Lower Canada began passing laws designed to eliminate Indigenous peoples without their consent. In this era, the government viewed Indigenous peoples as an obstacle to acquiring complete control of the resources and territories of Canada. It began to speak of "the Indian Problem." With the implementation of an official policy of assimilation carried out through the Indian Act of 1876, the colonial project was in full force.

Throughout the period of 1879 to the late 1980s, the Canadian government, in conjunction with Catholic, Protestant, and Anglican churches, displaced whole generations of Indigenous children from their homes, families, Elders, and communities into the Indian residential school (IRS) system. The vision was anchored in the fundamental belief that to educate Aboriginal children effectively, they had to be separated from their families, thereby suggesting that the parenting process in Aboriginal communities had to be disrupted.[53] The children were taught to be ashamed of who they were, and they were physically, mentally, and sexually abused. Thousands lost their lives at these schools, many due to disease.[54] The IRS system was the hallmark institution of the assimilation policy. In 1920, Canadian Superintendent of Indian Affairs Duncan Campbell Scott made his (in)famous statement, "Our object is to continue until there is not a single Indian in Canada that has not been absorbed into the body politic."[55]

The overriding goal of the IRS system was to divest Indigenous peoples of their TK, and thereby their attachment to (and knowledge related to) their territories forevermore within a few generations. In the schools, children were punished for displaying all aspects of their original cultures. Resetting the child's cultural clock from the "savage" setting—the seasonal round of hunting and gathering—to the hourly and daily precision required by an industrial order was seen by the Department of Indian Affairs as an issue of primary consideration.[56] As Indigenous peoples were being divested of their TK throughout the IRS era, some of the following disciplines and third parties were actively engaging in the following practices: 1) anthropologists, archaeologists, and some missionary groups were in the process of documenting TK in data banks; 2) museums and collectors were confiscating Indigenous cultural artifacts containing and representing TK; 3) third-party corporations were appropriating Indigenous artistic designs, such as symbols and totem poles, and functional designs, such as canoes and snowshoes; and 4) Canada was developing its IPR regime while at the same time subjecting TK and Indigenous peoples to it. This was the era of intense colonization and was the first wide-scale colonization of TK. The impacts of residential schools are not buried in the past; they continue through the ongoing loss of TK and other multigenerational traumatic effects. Still many Canadians today are unaware of the impacts of residential schools, including the loss and colonization of TK.

Gnaritas Nullius (No One's Knowledge)

Just as Indigenous territories were declared *terra nullius* in the colonization process, so, too, has TK been treated as *gnaritas nullius* (no one's knowledge) by the IPR system, which has meant it has consequently flowed into the public domain along with Western knowledge. In effect, Indigenous knowledge has been colonized, along with many other Indigenous institutions and possessions. In this colonization process based on *gnaritas nullius*, manifestations of, and practices derived from, Indigenous knowledge—such as the canoe and kayak design, bungee jumping, snowshoes, lacrosse, surfing, and sustainable development—are embraced by Western peoples as their own (without acknowledgement of the source), just as lands were taken in the colonization process based on *terra nullius*. This has occurred despite widespread Indigenous claims of ownership and breach of customary law. The problem is that advocates for the public domain seem to see knowledge as the same concept across cultures, and impose the liberal ideals of freedom and equality to Indigenous knowledge systems. Not all knowledge has the same role and significance within diverse epistemologies, nor do diverse world views all necessarily incorporate a principle that knowledge can be universally accessed. Neither can all knowledge fit into Western paradigms and legal regimes.

A central dimension of Indigenous knowledge systems is that knowledge is shared according to developed rules and expectations for behaviour within frameworks that have been developed and practised over millennia. Arguments for a public domain of Indigenous knowledge again reduce the capacity for Indigenous people's control and decision making over their knowledge and cannot be reasonably made outside the problematic frameworks of the colonization of TK and *gnaritas nullius*. Intellectual property law is largely European in derivation and promotes particular cultural interpretations of knowledge, ownership, authorship, private property, and monopoly privilege. Indigenous peoples do not necessarily interpret or conceptualize their knowledge systems and knowledge practices in the same way or only through these concepts.[57] Thus, Indigenous peoples and their allies continue to argue for recognition of Indigenous laws' jurisdiction over Indigenous knowledge and the development of *sui generis* regimes that incorporate and complement Indigenous laws at local, national, and international United Nations levels such as the WIPO IGC.

Notes

1   Catherine Hoppers, ed., *Indigenous Knowledge and the Integration of Knowledge Systems: Towards a Philosophy of Articulation* (Claremont, South Africa: New Africa Books, 2002), 11.

2   Jack Weatherford, *Indian Givers: How Native Americans Transformed the World* (New York: Crown Publishers, 1988), 59.

3   Daniel Francis, *The Imaginary Indian: The Image of the Indian in Canadian Culture* (Vancouver: Arsenal Pulp Press, 1992), 193.

4   Peter Nabokov and Robert O. B. Easton, *Native American Architecture* (Oxford: Oxford University Press, 1989), 12.

5   Weatherford, *Indian Givers*, 85.

6   Lee Francis, *Native Time: A Historical Time Line of Native America* (New York: St. Martin's Griffin, 1996), 14.

7   Ibid.

8   Sakej Henderson, "Traditional Indigenous Knowledge" (unpublished manuscript, 2004), 1.

9   Ibid., 6.
10   Sakej Henderson, "Postcolonial Indigenous Legal Consciousness," *Indigenous Law Journal* 1 (Spring 2002): 1–56.
11   Ibid., 2.
12   World Intellectual Property Organization (WIPO), International Committee on Intellectual Property and Genetic Resources, Traditional Knowledge, and Folklore, *Traditional Knowledge: Operational Terms and Definitions.* Third Session (Geneva, Switzerland: WIPO, June 13–21, 2002).
13   Vine Deloria Jr., *Red Earth, White Lies: Native Americans and the Myth of Scientific Fact* (New York: Scribner, 1995), 42.
14   Vivien Burr, *An Introduction to Social Constructionism* (New York: Routledge, 1995).
15   Kenneth J. Gergen, "The Social Constructionist Movement in Modern Psychology," *American Psychologist* 40, no. 3 (March 1985): 266–275, http://dx.doi.org/10.1037/0003-066X.40.3.266.
16   Wikipedia, "Epistemology," http://en.wikipedia.org/wiki/Epistemology.
17   Louise J. Phillips and Marianne W. Jorgensen, *Discourse Analysis as Theory and Method* (London: Sage Publications, 2002), 5.
18   Ibid., 5.
19   Jo-ann Archibald, *Indigenous Storywork: Educating the Heart, Mind, Body and Spirit* (Vancouver: University of British Columbia Press, 2008), 63.
20   Charles Royal, "An Organic Arising: An Interpretation of Tikanga Based upon Maori Creation Traditions" (unpublished manuscript, 2007).
21   Linda Tuhiwai Smith, *Decolonizing Methodologies: Research and Indigenous Peoples* (London: Zed Books, 1999), 147.
22   Shirley Sterling, "The Grandmother Stories: Oral Tradition and the Transmission of Culture" (PhD dissertation, University of British Columbia, 1997), 39.
23   Merle Alexander, "Customary Laws: Appling Sharing within Communities to International Instruments" (unpublished manuscript, 2003), 9.
24   See John Borrows, *Canada's Indigenous Constitution* (Toronto: University of Toronto Press, 2010); Hoppers, *Indigenous Knowledge and the Integration of Knowledge Systems*, 17–20, for an interpretation of an Anishinabek resource law regarding Nanabush v. Deer, Wolf et al.
25   Alexander, "Customary Laws," 11.
26   Henderson, "Traditional Indigenous Knowledge," 9.
27   Susan Crean, Caldwell Taylor, and Gregory Younging, *Handbook on Creator's Rights* (Toronto: Creator's Rights Alliance, 2003).
28   Ibid., 8.
29   Ibid.,10.
30   Ibid., 16.
31   Universal Declaration of Human Rights, December 10, 1948, UN General Assembly Res. 217.
32   Berne Convention for the Protection of Literary and Artistic Works, September 9, 1886, as revised at Paris on July 24, 1971, and amended in 1979, S. Treaty Doc. No. 99–27 (1986).

33 Ibid.
34 Ibid.
35 David Vaver, *Intellectual Property Law: Copyright, Patents, Trade-Marks* (Concord, ON: Irwin Law, 1997), 1.
36 Ibid., 120.
37 Ibid.
38 Ibid., 2.
39 Laura Smyth Groening, *Listening to Old Woman Speak: Natives and alterNatives in Canadian Literature* (Montreal: McGill University Press, 2004).
40 Bill Brent and Fred Glenman, "Translated Hits," http://www.bobshanon.com/stories/hesofine.html.
41 Vaver, *Intellectual Property Law*.
42 WIPO Intergovernmental Committee on Intellectual Property and Genetic Resources, Traditional Knowledge and Folklore: Seventh Session (WIPO/GRTKF/IC/7), intervention of Indian delegation, http://www.wipo.int/meetings/en/details.jsp?meeting_id=6183.
43 Violet Ford, "The Protection of Inuit Cultural Property" (paper presented at the meeting of the Creator's Rights Alliance National Conference on Traditional Knowledge, Montreal, QC, June 4, 2004), 20.
44 Gregory Younging, "Competing Jurisdictions over Traditional Knowledge in the North Americas," (presentation to the WIPO Panel on Indigenous and Local Communities' Concerns and Experiences in Promoting, Sustaining and Safeguarding Their Traditional Knowledge, Traditional Cultural Expressions and Genetic Resources, Intergovernmental Committee on Intellectual Property and Genetic Resources, Traditional Knowledge and Folklore, Tenth Session, Geneva, Switzerland, November 30, 2006).
45 Darrell Posey and Graham Dutfleid, *Beyond Intellectual Property: Toward Traditional Resource Rights for Indigenous Peoples and Local Communities* (Ottawa, ON: International Development Research Centre, 1996), 82.
46 Ibid., 94.
47 Michael Brown, *Who Owns Native Culture?* (Cambridge, MA: First Harvard University Press, 2003).
48 Ibid.
49 "Aveda Announces Discontinuation of Indigenous Product Collection," media release, November 11, 2003, http://ip.aaas.org/tekindex.nsf/9703c8d7edc467d685256ae10074187f/e632f81fb2b671b085256ddc00545a9e?OpenDocument.
50 Marie Battiste and James Youngblood Henderson, *Protecting Indigenous Knowledge and Heritage: A Global Challenge* (Saskatoon, SK: Purich Publishing, 2001), 145.
51 Sharron Venne, *Our Elders Understand Our Rights: Evolving International Law Regarding Indigenous Rights* (Penticton, BC: Theytus Books, 1998), 2.
52 Ibid., 4.
53 John Milloy, *A National Crime: The Canadian Government and the Residential School System* (Winnipeg, MB: University of Manitoba Press, 1999), 23.

54 Connie Walker, "New Documents May Shed Light on Residential School Deaths," CBC, January 7, 2014, http://www.cbc.ca/news/aboriginal/new-documents-may-shed-light-on-residential-school-deaths-1.2487015.

55 Duncan Campbell Scott, cited in John Leslie, *The Historical Development of the Indian Act*, second edition (Ottawa: Department of Indian Affairs and Northern Development, Treaties and Historical Research Branch, 1978), 114.

56 Ibid., 36.

57 Jane Anderson, "Indigenous/Traditional Knowledge & Intellectual Property," Center for the Study of the Public Domain, Duke University School of Law, 2010, http://www.law.duke.edu/cspd/itkpaper.

RENEGOTIATED RELATIONSHIPS AND NEW UNDERSTANDINGS: INDIGENOUS PROTOCOLS

Jane Anderson and Gregory Younging

Intellectual property law has been slow to develop new frameworks that can incorporate Indigenous needs and expectations around knowledge use, access, and control. The development of alternative protocols needs to be a collaborative effort.

Introduction

National and international experiences have acknowledged that Indigenous cultural expressions are commonly misrepresented and misused, and that the development of protocols is often an effective means of dealing with such misappropriation. Protocols provide guidelines for behaviour; they can function as a means for changing people's understanding of an issue and, thus, how they act in relation to it. In the context of the sharing, usage, and storage of Indigenous knowledge, protocols are being utilized as a strategic way of increasing reflective behaviour around Indigenous rights in cultural knowledge. One clear advantage of protocols is that they can be flexible and adaptable to specific contexts and local interests. This makes them ideal tools for guidance on appropriate and/or ethical behaviour and practice. In the absence of formal legal intellectual property mechanisms for recognizing and protecting rights in Indigenous cultural knowledge, and in ever increasing contexts where relationships with Indigenous peoples are sought, or where Indigenous knowledge is used, protocols are providing a productive tool for negotiating new kinds of equitable relationships.

Protocols

The possibility of using protocols emerged out of the problems that Indigenous, traditional, and local communities have with intellectual property (IP) law. In short, intellectual property, and copyright in particular, demand that Indigenous knowledge and Indigenous people are identified and categorized in ways that do not necessarily reflect Indigenous laws, epistemology, ontology, systems of governance, or personhood. For example, copyright law requires both an individual author and a work to provide copyright protection. A work is a tangible expression of an idea in the form of a book or a photograph, etc. Indigenous knowledge systems do not necessarily mark the transition from intangible knowledge to tangible property in the same way. The cultural specificity of intellectual property law (IPL), especially its Western emergence and development, creates frameworks that do not map easily onto Indigenous knowledge systems. This has produced a range of problems—including the misuse and appropriation of diverse Indigenous knowledge for non-Indigenous use.

While IPL has been slow to develop new frameworks that can incorporate Indigenous needs and expectations around knowledge use, access, and control, questions about what practical alternatives exist for protecting Indigenous knowledge use, which are not dependent upon a specific legislative remedy, have emerged. It is in this context, and in responding to a lack of protection within current national and international legislation and intellectual property norms, that the possibility of protocols have been raised, developed, and utilized. Protocols seem to have become a legislative alternative for various interested parties—especially and initially in the arts. However, their development spans various domains and institutions that have intersections in Indigenous knowledge access and use; two examples include the arts (generally speaking) and within libraries/archives.

But what are protocols? What do they do? How do they work? What do they seek to achieve? And to what extent are they successful?

Protocols remain perceived as relatively neutral cultural forms—but they are part and parcel of the legal dynamics that they have been set against. They are not made up counter to legal experience but are informed by and respond to formal legal failings or inadequacies. In this sense, protocols are a practical adjunct to law-making processes and demonstrate a shift to a postmodern ordering of the relations between society and legal networks. The shift to protocols is itself illustrative of current trends in intellectual property toward private law making, for example, through agreements and consents.

Quite clearly protocols are guidelines for conduct. They provide information about ways for dealing with a particular problem or issue, and they offer informed instructions about direction and action. But how do they do this (particularly given their nonbinding nature)? Why would we follow protocols—do we have to believe in them in part to follow them, or do they need to become inscribed in a social and cultural context, where not following them becomes an improper act? There is an inherent power to protocols—as the adoption of protocols occurs in order to achieve certain ends, for example, respecting rights or alerting attention to alternative ways of social and cultural engagement.

Protocols could be understood as context-driven policy. They are produced through a complex matrix of relations exercised through ongoing and changing cultural engagement that is always already invested with politics. Protocols are not neutral forms. They are prescriptive in that they prescribe particular types of behaviour. Like guidelines, codes of conduct, and policy, they have the capacity to convey a mode of behaviour that individuals are presumed to follow. Protocols work precisely through the self-governing capacity of individuals. Protocols prescribe modes of conduct through emphasizing or normalizing particular forms of cultural engagement. The presumption is that we read a protocol, we take on the advice, and we act accordingly. Whilst this effect is not given, over time protocols do have the capacity to influence change in ways that differ to stringent bureaucratic or legislative programs. However, a key point of interest for protocols is that they offer choice as their differential: an individual, or even an institution, either chooses to follow them or not. Over time, the adoption and usage of protocols can establish cultural standards that lead to more binding forms of enforcement, such as policy, legislation, and law.

Protocols are not value-neutral but enhance or consolidate systems of value that may already be socially circulated within a particular context. In this sense, they provide the possibility for accounting for changing cultural values and norms, and that these may vary from context to context, community to community.

The proliferation of protocols in the area of intellectual property and Indigenous knowledge is very important but not necessarily surprising. Other areas of IPL, challenged by various social, bureaucratic, or governmental values and demands, have also found themselves co-existing with a body of protocols that draws from law and further imbues social relationships with legal mechanisms. An easy example is to point to the variety of protocols relating to digital and communicative technologies. For example, the entire internet is governed by set protocols and a series of developing and emerging protocols.

Perhaps the increase of protocols dealing with Indigenous knowledge protection suggests a particular movement and direction relating to Indigenous rights and the protection of Indigenous knowledge. It is representative of activity that is occurring throughout IPL, where protocols are part and parcel of repositioning certain agendas. The practical utility of protocols is that they are playing a crucial role in changing attitudes and perspectives about how certain industries deal with Indigenous knowledge. The hidden power of protocols is that they effect change by encouraging actors to make a choice about how they behave in relation to a particular issue—this is as a compliment to more stringent, court-based methods.

It is useful to consider protocols as a very specific instrument for pushing the limits of law in terms of providing specific, context-driven approaches that incorporate useful elements of IPL, as well as bridging the sizable gap between what the law says and how it actually works in contexts that require new forms of knowledge management.

Australian Examples of Protocols

There are certain elements of protocols that have been or are currently in circulation, and several others that are currently being developed. Many of these protocols have been developed in Australia and draw significantly from the work of the Indigenous lawyer Terri Janke.

Aboriginal and Torres Strait Islander Library and Archive Protocols
The Aboriginal and Torres Strait Islander Library and Archive Protocols were developed in 1994 and 1995.[1] They sought to provide a guide to libraries, archives, and information services about interaction with Aboriginal and

Torres Strait Islander people and communities, as well as how to handle material with Aboriginal and Torres Strait Islander content. Specifically, the protocols encouraged

- the recognition of moral rights of Aboriginal and Torres Strait Islander peoples "as the owners of their knowledge";
- the need to address issues arising from Indigenous content and perspectives in documentary materials, media, and traditional cultural property; and
- the need to address issues of access to libraries, archives, and information resources amongst other things.[2]

The protocols sought to chart a path for best practices that acknowledged and respected Indigenous rights in an area haunted by colonial pasts and practices—where Indigenous people featured as subjects of the archive rather than active participants in interpreting past and present cultural production.

In a context where, as far as the law of copyright goes, Indigenous people own very little of the material found in such institutions, the protocols began a process of recognition and standard setting. They began to address certain historical power imbalances that the law was really unable to deal with. The protocols prescribed a change of behaviour—that Aboriginal and Torres Strait Islander people did have rights in relation to the material, and while these would not be recognized legally, the institutions themselves could be proactive in recognizing them. Institutions could choose to be respectful and acknowledge differing, while not necessarily legal, rights. Whilst the exact nature of Indigenous intellectual property remained ambiguous, the step of encouraging reflection about rights and interests previously excluded because they were not legally recognizable, and hence unenforceable, was the explicit purpose of the protocols. The protocols have been effective in that they have raised the level of expectation about the actions of libraries, archives, and information services in relation to Indigenous material.

NAVA Protocols

With similar intentions about raising the profile of Indigenous rights in the arts, the National Association for the Visual Arts developed the NAVA protocols for working with the Australian Indigenous Visual Arts and Crafts Sector in 2001. With a hint of purpose in the title—"Valuing Art, Respecting Culture"—the protocols positioned themselves within a field of similarly intentioned protocols from other sectors like museums, galleries, and libraries.[3]

Drawing authority from the United Nations Draft Declaration on the Rights of Indigenous Peoples, the NAVA protocols endorsed a series of principles regarding Indigenous rights to retain control of their cultural heritage and to regard these rights as intellectual property rights. In doing so, the protocols posit that elements not traditionally associated as intellectual property should be recognized as such. The NAVA protocols explain that

> Protocols provide a means of complying with the customs and cultural value systems of a particular situation, group or culture, in order to acknowledge and respect the situation or people involved, and to ensure that negotiations and transactions are able to be undertaken in a spirit of co-operation and goodwill. The importance of respecting the protocol requirements of every cultural group involved in collaboration and transactions should be acknowledged.[4]

Here we get a good idea about the nature of protocols; what they seek to achieve and realize is an increase in understanding certain cultural nuances that have not historically been easily accessible. The protocols seek to bring certain principles and guidelines for correct conduct into a more public, visible space. In compiling these general principles, the protocols prescribe how the art sector should engage with Indigenous artists as a different category of artists.

It is worth noting that the audiences for these protocols are not usually Indigenous people but rather those working in fields where Indigenous interests are involved. That is to say that the protocols have not been about translating traditional intellectual property rights into Indigenous contexts but more translating a range of Indigenous rights, utilizing the language of intellectual property, into frameworks perceived to be lacking in understanding and/or at risk of bad behaviour.

Australia Council

Following on the heels of the NAVA protocols, the Australia Council launched a series of protocols that were designed to specifically deal with translating intellectual property rights. This is clear in the way in which the protocols are separated into intellectual property classificatory rubrics: art, song, dance, performance, and digital technology. Constituting divisions in copyright, the protocols explain copyright and when certain uses of works might arise that involve copyright issues.

These protocols are general guides. They are full of information about principles governing good conduct in relation to respecting Indigenous heritage. The five separate documents dovetail each other in information and direction. As a whole, they are seen as a kind of kit—instructive in the different divisions of copyright law as this relates to Indigenous arts.[5]

It is fair to say that protocols have become the popular option in pushing for recognizing Indigenous rights. There is a wide range of other protocols being developed in Australia—for example, through the Ara Iritja Archive, Federation of Aboriginal and Torres Strait Islander Languages (FATSIL), and State Library of Queensland protocols. These protocols are being produced to respond to quite site-specific and contextual needs. They are also, importantly, being seen as tools for communities that are conversant with community needs in this area, and are driven from the specific needs of the locale, rather than as a general interpretive grid. These new protocols are both explanatory intellectual property protocols and community protocols.

Further Things to Think About

One difficulty with protocols is their accessibility. In a sense, they have traditionally had a very specific audience, one that is predominately educated and literate. The utility of protocols has been to alter perspectives of Indigenous rights—but it has not necessarily been to alter perspectives in communities about law and rights—and find some practical middle road in between what is popularly described as "two bodies of law." In many ways, this maintains a perspective about the incommensurability of IPL for Indigenous knowledge. This perspective rests on specific narratives of what intellectual property is, does, and means. There is a gulf here, but it is not being bridged necessarily through protocols. For instance, communities still retain very limited understandings of intellectual property.

Canadian Context for Protocols

In the late 1980s and early 1990s, the Indigenous arts community in Canada was instrumental in bringing the issues of cultural appropriation and repatriation to the forefront of the national consciousness. The mobilization of Indigenous artists at the 1987 Telling Our Own Story Conference in Vancouver, BC; protests by Indigenous artists against *The Spirit Sings* exhibit at the Glenbow Museum in Calgary, AB, and the National Gallery of Canada in Ottawa, ON, in 1986–1987; and the lobbying effort of Indigenous members in the Writers Union of Canada in 1988 all contributed to an increased awareness among progressive elements in Canada. These efforts have led to increased recognition of the importance of respect and protection for Indigenous cultural expressions.

The Creator's Rights Alliance (CRA) was formed in 2002 to represent the intellectual property interests of artists in Canada at a national and international level, and, therefore, also has an interest in Traditional Knowledge (TK) issues and Indigenous artists. The CRA Indigenous Peoples Caucus has maintained an effort to hold ongoing discussions on related issues within the Indigenous artist community and government departments and agencies in Canada, and to lobby for Indigenous cultural expression rights at the World Intellectual Property Organization (WIPO) and other United Nations forums. The Intellectual Property Policy Directorate (IPPD) of Industry Canada also has a domestic policy development work program on TK issues.

Indigenous Artist Research Project

The Creator's Rights Alliance (CRA) approached representatives of the IPPD in 2004 for funding assistance to conduct three regional symposia dealing with Traditional Knowledge-related issues, as well as a national conference coinciding with the CRA annual meetings in Montreal in June 2005. The entire project was named the Indigenous Artist Research Project (IARP). Throughout the symposia conducted for the project, participants pointed out that TK raises serious challenges for the intellectual property law (IPL). Many argued that the current IPL does not respond to the concerns of TK holders. One overarching problem identified is that the IPL is designed to eventually release all intellectual property into the public domain after time periods of protection expire. Many participants insisted that Indigenous protocols dictate that certain aspects of TK should be regulated and protected. In each region, artists and others indicated the need for support from the federal government for organization around these issues at the local level in order to allow them to contribute better to these discussions. The IARP managed to bring together a wide range of individuals, federal government departments, and organizations interested in finding answers to the complex and sensitive issues related to TK, in a positive and productive manner. It is hoped that the information gathered will be a useful contribution to current work on Traditional Knowledge underway within the federal government and Indigenous communities, and that collaboration will continue to take place in the future.[6]

The National Gatherings on Indigenous Knowledge

Traditions: National Gatherings on Indigenous Knowledge (NGIK) was the third in a series of national gatherings organized by the Department of Canadian Heritage (DCH), with the goal of developing "practical strategies for working together in areas where the mandate, expertise and experience of the Department of Canadian Heritage would coincide with the aspirations of Aboriginal peoples."[7] DCH proposed that the process would "inform Canadian Heritage how it might better acknowledge, celebrate and support the rich contributions of Aboriginal peoples across the country" and "raise awareness of the need to take action now to ensure the continuing vitality of Aboriginal languages and cultures and to ensure that the artistic expressions of First Nations, Inuit and Métis peoples remain under their control."[8]

The preamble to the NGIK *Final Report* states that three target areas for further study and action emerged from a series of discussion gatherings held across Canada in 2005: languages and cultures; intellectual and cultural property; and artistic expression.[9] The gatherings provided a forum in which Canadian Heritage came together with Indigenous communities and representatives from other government sectors to discuss a framework for the recognition, respect, protection, and celebration of Indigenous knowledge in all the ways it is used and expressed. The NGIK allowed delegates to share information about best practices and support available from federal departments and agencies, and it encouraged open and relevant discussions of key issues and brainstorming on opportunities and strategies for change.

During the months of May and June 2005, national gatherings on Indigenous knowledge were held in eight locations across Canada: Rankin Inlet, Edmonton, Penticton, Wanuskewin, Yellowknife, Wendake, Eskasoni, and Six Nations. They brought together over four hundred representatives of Indigenous communities with DCH and other government representatives. Each gathering took place over three days and involved approximately fifty invited delegates. Gatherings consisted of small breakout circles and plenary discussions focused on the following themes: 1) Indigenous knowledge and languages and cultures; 2) Indigenous knowledge and intellectual and cultural property; and 3) Indigenous knowledge and artistic expression.

Within each of the three themes, delegates were asked to consider what issues should be considered priorities and what were the main vulnerabilities; the possibilities for action; and the roles and responsibilities for addressing the issues in diverse communities. The process of engagement used by the National Gatherings Secretariat is founded on key principles that have guided the Canadian Heritage in coming together with federal departments, provincial and territorial governments, Aboriginal governments and leaders, and communities alike. According to the NGIK report, the process contributed to the goal of devising "new ways to plan for the future with the support and collaboration of representatives from various levels of government, including our own Indigenous governments."[10]

Although each gathering and, indeed, each circle discussion, had its own unique conception of Elders' Councils, the underlying message was that guidance and advice from Elders is essential because traditional laws and protocols govern virtually all aspects of community life, including finding solutions and strategies to address critical issues. The NGIK process was an example of a national government inviting Indigenous communities to take part in a process and express their views. It remains to be seen if the NGIK will have any significant impact on DCH and Canadian government policy on Traditional Knowledge.

To be sure, Canada has the benefit of learning from the Australian examples and the opportunity of building on recent initiatives and the 2010 Olympics—including the controversial appropriated Inukshuk in the Olympics logo. Canada appears to be at a similar stage that Australia was at a decade ago, in that, after about two decades of Indigenous peoples raising Traditional Knowledge issues, the state has slowly begun to acknowledge the problem. Perhaps the Indigenous Artist Research Project, the National Gatherings on Indigenous Knowledge, and other grassroots initiatives among Indigenous artists and communities could lead to the beginning of a movement to act on Traditional Knowledge issues more substantively in Canada. However, as with the Australian examples, this work requires the support of government and arts agency funding.

International Context

The World Intellectual Property Organization Intergovernmental Committee on Intellectual Property and Genetic Resources, Traditional Knowledge and Folklore (WIPO IGC) was established by the WIPO General Assembly in

October 2000 as an international forum for debate and dialogue concerning the interplay between intellectual property and Traditional Knowledge, genetic resources, and traditional cultural expressions (folklore). The WIPO IGC has developed draft provisions for the protection of traditional cultural expressions. The objectives of the draft provisions are to "[p]revent the misappropriation of traditional cultural expressions/expressions of folklore" and "provide indigenous peoples and traditional and other cultural communities with the legal and practical means, including effective enforcement measures, to prevent the misappropriation of their cultural expressions."[11]

The United Nations Educational, Scientific and Cultural Organization's (UNESCO's) third convention, the Convention on the Protection and Promotion of the Diversity of Cultural Expressions, is intended to be the last in UNESCO's trilogy of conventions to protect the world's culture. Traditional Knowledge is not specifically mentioned in the articles in the convention, although it is in the part of the preamble text that reads: "Recognizing the importance of traditional knowledge as a source of intangible and material wealth, in particular the knowledge systems of indigenous peoples, and its positive contributions to sustainable development, as well as the need for its adequate protection and promotion."[12]

The Declaration on the Rights of Indigenous Peoples maintains that all national and international standards on Indigenous knowledge issues should conform to Article 31 of the declaration, which states:

1. Indigenous peoples have the right to maintain, control, protect and develop their cultural heritage, traditional knowledge and traditional cultural expressions, as well as the manifestations of their sciences, technologies and cultures, including human and genetic resources, seeds, medicines, knowledge of the properties of fauna and flora, oral traditions, literatures, designs, sports and traditional games and visual and performing arts. They also have the right to maintain, control, protect and develop their intellectual property over such cultural heritage, traditional knowledge, and traditional cultural expressions.

2. In conjunction with indigenous peoples, States shall take effective measures to recognize and protect the exercise of these rights.[13]

Conclusion

Protocols that address the arts and rights in Indigenous knowledge have been built upon over a ten-year period. The utility of protocols and, indeed, their pragmatics, derive from their positioning between law and the social, thus drawing legitimacy and authority from both domains. They can be informative, educational, and convey new meaning about an issue to that which previously existed. To date, many of these protocols function to inform a disparate public about differing Indigenous expectations of intellectual property law. However, this has also been done without necessarily translating key elements of intellectual property law back into communities. The flow has been monodirectional. The development of protocols needs to occur in collaboration—that is, the only way they can be effective is if communities are involved in drafting their own, and changing them over time, as is needed.

Given the influence and increased circulation of protocols, it seems inevitable that they will continue to proliferate—as new needs develop. For example, it is highly likely that protocols regarding biodiversity and access sharing will be developed before any legislative measures are developed that address Indigenous rights in biodiversity. It will be important to make these protocols useful for communities, as well as for industry groups. In making them only relevant to industry and other interested groups, Indigenous people and communities remain marginalized from information that will be useful to make decisions regarding use of genetic resources. This should be one of the lessons learned from a reflexive look at protocols and their utility.

The challenge for the next wave of protocols is to make them practically accessible. For the utility of protocols is that they can entertain cultural specificity and context in ways that law cannot. Whilst they are still dependent upon people choosing to follow their direction, they do maintain the capacity to exert influence in a variety of domains. Significantly, they are instructive—providing guidelines for possible modes of engagement. In this sense, they hold the capacity to respond to contextual needs in a given locale. Whilst protocols offer a practical possibility for protecting Indigenous knowledge, they can also be unintelligible, general, and useless. This means that in making decisions to use and develop protocols, there is an urgent need to reflect upon who they are being designed for, what perspectives they are presenting, and to what purpose.

Bibliography

Anderson, J. "Access and Control of Indigenous Knowledge in Libraries and Archives: Ownership and Future Use." Paper presented for Correcting Course: Rebalancing Copyright for Libraries in the National and International Arena, American Library Association and the MacArthur Foundation, Columbia University, New York, May 5–7, 2005.

Anderson, J. "Access, Authority and Ownership: Traditional Indigenous Biodiversity-Related Knowledge." In *Australian Indigenous Knowledge and Libraries*, edited by M. Nakata and M. Lanton, 72–82. Canberra, Australia: Australian Academic & Research Libraries, 2005.

Anderson, J. *Law, Knowledge, Culture: The Production of Indigenous Knowledge in Intellectual Property Law.* Cheltenham, UK: Edward Elgar Press, 2009.

Anderson, J., and K. Bowrey. "The Politics of Global Information Sharing." *Social and Legal Studies* 18, no. 4 (2009): 479–504.

Australia Council for the Arts. *Protocols for Working with Indigenous Artists: Protocol Guides for Music, Writing, Visual Arts, Media Arts and the Performing Arts.* Strawberry Hills, NSW, Australia: Australian Council for the Arts, 2007. http://www.australiacouncil.gov.au/about/protocols-for-working-with-indigenous-artists/.

Australian Broadcasting Commission, Indigenous Programs Unit. *Cultural Protocols for Indigenous Reporting in the Media.* 2003.

Australian Institute of Aboriginal and Torres Strait Islander Studies. *Guidelines for Ethical Research in Indigenous Studies.* 2nd ed. Canberra, Australia: AIATSIS, 2012. http://www.aiatsis.gov.au/_files/research/GERAIS.pdf.

Australian Library and Information Association (ALIA) and the Aboriginal and Torres Strait Islander Library and Information Resource Network (ATSILRN). *Aboriginal and Torres Strait Islander Protocols for Libraries, Archives and Information Services.* Canberra, Australia: ATSILRN, 2012. http://aiatsis.gov.au/atsilirn/docs/ProtocolBrochure2012.pdf.

Bostock, L. (1997) *The Greater Perspective: Protocols and Guidelines for the Production of Film and Television on Aboriginal and Torres Strait Islander Communities.* Sydney, Australia: Special Broadcasting Services, 1997.

Bowrey, K. "Alternative Intellectual Property? Indigenous Protocols, Copyleft and New Juridifications of Customary Practices." *Macquarie Law Journal* 6 (2006): 65–95.

Canadian Heritage. *Traditions: National Gatherings on Indigenous Knowledge: Final Report.* Ottawa: Canadian Heritage, 2008.

Denardis, L. *Protocol Politics: The Globalization of Internet Governance.* Cambridge, MA: The MIT Press, 2009.

Federation of Aboriginal and Torres Strait Islander Languages Corporation (FATSIL). *FATSIL Guide to Community Protocols for Indigenous Language Projects.* 2004. http://www.fpcc.ca/files/PDF/guide-to-community-protocols-for-indigenous-language-projects.pdf.

Galloway, A. *Protocol: How Control Exists after Decentralization.* Cambridge, MA: The MIT Press, 2004.

Janke, T. *Minding Cultures Report*. Geneva, Switzerland: The World Intellectual Property Organization (WIPO), 2002. http://www.wipo.org/globalissues/studies/cultural/minding-culture/index.html.

Janke, T. *New Media Cultures: Protocols for Producing Indigenous Australian New Media*. Sydney, Australia: The Australia Council, 2002.

Janke, T. *Our Culture: Our Future*. Report on Australian Indigenous cultural and intellectual property rights produced for the Australian Institute of Aboriginal and Torres Strait Islander Studies (AIATSIS) and the Aboriginal and Torres Strait Islander Commission (ATSIC). Surry Hills, Australia: Michael Frankel and Company Solicitors, 1998.

Janke, T. *Visual Cultures: Protocols for Producing Indigenous Australian Visual Arts and Crafts*. Sydney, Australia: The Australia Council, 2002.

Janke, T. *Writing Cultures: Protocols for Producing Indigenous Literature*. Sydney, Australia: The Australia Council, 2002.

Johnson, D. *Indigenous Protocol*. Sydney, Australia: Special Broadcasting Commission, 2004.

Jones, Annabel, and Bryony Barnett. *Guidelines for Ethical and Effective Communication for Researchers Working in Torres Strait*. Report to CRC Torres Strait. 2006. http://www.tsra.gov.au/__data/assets/pdf_file/0008/2051/torres_protocols.pdf.

Mellor, D., and T. Janke. *Valuing Art, Respecting Culture: Protocols for Working with the Australian Visual Arts and Crafts Sector*. Potts Point, NSW, Australia: National Association for the Visual Arts, 2001.

Nakata, M., and M. Langton. *Australian Indigenous Knowledge and Libraries*. Canberra, Australia: Australian Academic and Research Libraries, 2005.

Palmer, L. "Agreement Making, Outcomes, Constraints and Possibilities." In *Honour among Nations? Treaties and Agreements with Indigenous People*, edited by M. Langton, M. Tehan, L. Palmer, and K Shain, 251–254. Melbourne, Australia: Melbourne University Press, 2004.

Raven, M. "Protocols and ABS: Recognising Indigenous Rights to Knowledge in Australian Bureaucratic Organizations." *Indigenous Law Bulletin* 39 (2006). http://austlii.law.uts.edu.au/au/journals/ILB/2006/39.html#Heading47.

United Nations. Draft Declaration on the Rights of Indigenous Peoples. UN Doc. E/CN.4/Sub.2/1994/2/Add.1. http://www1.umn.edu/humanrts/instree/declra.htm.

United Nations Educational, Scientific, and Cultural Organization (UNESCO). Convention on the Protection and Promotion of the Diversity of Cultural Expressions. October 20, 2005. http://www.unesco.org/new/en/culture/themes/cultural-diversity/cultural-expressions/the-convention/convention-text/.

United Nations General Assembly. *United Nations Declaration on the Rights of Indigenous Peoples*. Resolution adopted by the General Assembly. October 2, 2007. A/RES/61/295. http://www.refworld.org/docid/471355a82.html.

World Intellectual Property Organization (WIPO). The Protection of Traditional Cultural Expressions: Draft Articles. Compiled from the Intergovernmental

Committee on Intellectual Property and Genetic Resources, Traditional Knowledge and Folklore (IGC) 22nd Session, July 9–13, 2012. Geneva, Switzerland.

Internet Resources for Protocols

- Aboriginal and Torres Strait Islander Library and Information Resources Network: http://www1.aiatsis.gov.au/atsilirn/protocols.atsilirn.asn.au/indexoc51.html?option=com_frontpage&Itemid=1
- Australian Arts Council—Indigenous Arts Protocols: http://www.australiacouncil.gov.au/research/aboriginal_and_torres_strait_islander_arts
- Australian Broadcasting Commission—Cultural Protocol: http://www.abc.net.au/indigenous/education/cultural_protocol.htm
- Biocultural Community Protocols: http://www.unep.org/communityprotocols/PDF/communityprotocols.pdf
- Development of a Protocol Framework for Meaningful Consultation with Canada's Aboriginal People on Forest Management: http://www.cec.org/grants/projects/details/index.cfm?varl an=ENGLISH&ID=108
- Hopi Cultural Protocols: http://www.nau.edu/~hcpo-p/hcpo/index.html
- Indigenous Knowledge: Place, People and Protocol: http://www.pch.gc.ca/pc-ch/org/sectr/cp-ch/aa/trd/ppr-eng.cfm
- Protocols for Native American Archival Materials: http://www2.nau.edu/libnap-p/protocols.html

Notes

1 In conjunction with the Aboriginal and Torres Strait Islander Library and Information Resource Network (ATSILIRN).
2 Aboriginal and Torres Strait Islander Library and Information Resource Network, "Protocols," 2012, http://aiatsis.gov.au/atsilirn/protocols.php.
3 D. Mellor and T. Janke, *Valuing Art, Respecting Culture: Protocols for Working with the Australian Indigenous Visual Arts and Crafts Sector* (Potts Point, NSW, Australia: National Association for the Visual Arts Ltd., 2001).
4 Ibid., 43.
5 Australia Council for the Arts, *Protocols for Working with Indigenous Artists: Protocol Guides for Music, Writing, Visual Arts, Media Arts and the Performing Arts* (Strawberry Hills, NSW, Australia: Australian Council for the Arts, 2007), http://www.australiacouncil.gov.au/about/protocols-for-working-with-indigenous-artists/.
6 *Indigenous Artist Research Project, Final Report*, 2004.
7 Canadian Heritage, *Traditions: National Gatherings on Indigenous Knowledge: Final Report* (Ottawa: Canadian Heritage, 2008), 2.
8 Ibid., 3.

9 Ibid., 7.

10 Ibid., 46.

11 World Intellectual Property Organization (WIPO), *The Protection of Traditional Cultural Expressions: Draft Articles* (compiled from the Intergovernmental Committee on Intellectual Property and Genetic Resources, Traditional Knowledge and Folklore (IGC) 22nd Session, July 9–13, 2012, Geneva, Switzerland, 3).

12 UNESCO Convention on the Protection and Promotion of the Diversity of Cultural Expressions, Paris, October 20, 2005, para. 9.

13 UN General Assembly, *United Nations Declaration on the Rights of Indigenous Peoples*, resolution adopted by the General Assembly, October 2, 2007, A/RES/61/295, Article 31.

PART 4

REFRAMING THE FUTURE: EMERGING IDEAS AND UNDERSTANDINGS

ELEVEN

THE ECONOMICS OF INFORMATION IN A POST-CARBON ECONOMY

Joshua Farley and Ida Kubiszewski

The challenges we face are immense, and information will play a critical role in building a post-carbon economy—but today's markets are not equipped to produce the information we need to survive.

conomics is frequently defined as the allocation of scarce resources among competing desirable ends. Most economists focus on markets as the ideal allocative mechanism. One critical resource required for any economic activity, from gathering edible plants to genetically engineering them, is information, or knowledge. As a result of the exponential increase in new technologies and knowledge, we now live in what is commonly called the information age. Another critical resource is energy, an essential input into any economic activity. Explosive advances in knowledge during the eighteenth century allowed human society to shift from the finite flow of current solar energy, available at a fixed rate over time, to the finite stock of fossil energy, which can be used virtually as fast as we like. We have become so dependent on fossil fuels that we could not feed ourselves without them—we currently use an estimated seven to ten calories of hydrocarbons to produce, process, transport, and prepare each calorie of food we consume (Pimentel & Pimentel, 2008). Access to such concentrated energy allowed humans to increase the rate of extraction of raw materials from nature and in waste emissions back into nature, with all the harm to ecosystems and human well-being inherent to both activities. The market economy emerged simultaneously with the fossil fuel economy. Though most economists attribute the explosive economic growth of the past two centuries to the magic of the market, it would have been impossible without the magic of fossil fuels.

Fossil fuel stocks are finite. Discoveries peaked during the 1960s then declined precipitously during subsequent years. In spite of amazing advances in technology, conventional oil production peaked around 2006 (International Energy Agency [IEA], 2010). We have likely used half the planet's finite supply already, and remaining oil is less accessible, of lower quality, and requires more energy to extract, offering a lower energy return on energy invested (Campbell & Laherrere, 1998). Even if fossil fuels were infinite, we have exceeded the planet's capacity to absorb their waste products, threatening catastrophic destabilization of the global climate. Whether due to source or sink constraints, if human society is to thrive, it must shake its dependence on fossil fuels and undo the damage it has caused.

Information will play a central role in this transition. Addressing climate change and peak oil will require major advances in low-carbon energy technologies. Creating sustainable food systems will require technologies that increase agricultural yields while reducing ecological impacts and dependence on fossil fuels. Addressing natural resource depletion and environmental degradation will also require new green technologies.

Given the central and growing importance of information in our economy, it is critical that we assess what types of economic institutions are most effective at allocating resources toward the production of appropriate information and that information among different users. Economists recognize that information has the unique characteristic that it improves through use. Information is therefore not a scarce resource in an economic sense, and we cannot assume that markets efficiently create and allocate new information. There has nonetheless been a tremendous global effort in recent decades to force information increasingly into the market economy, strengthening patent protection across international borders, lengthening patent and copyright duration, and extending intellectual property rights to ever more types of information (Boyle, 2003; Jaffe, 2000).

The goal of this chapter is to assess the effectiveness of market forces for producing the most potentially valuable information at the lowest costs, for maximizing its value among users, and to compare markets with alternative economic institutions. To achieve this, the chapter

- identifies appropriate criteria for assessing different economic institutions for the production and dissemination of information;
- analyzes the unique physical characteristics of information and the most pressing problems confronting human society that require new information and technologies in order to be solved;
- assesses the effectiveness of markets in producing the most desirable information, and in minimizing the costs of production;
- assesses the effectiveness of markets in allocating information among potential users; and
- explores alternative mechanisms for producing appropriate types of information at minimum cost that maximize its value after production.

Assessment Criteria: The Desirable Ends

Implicit in the definition of economics are the criteria for assessing economic institutions: How effectively does a given institution achieve some particular set of desirable ends? Economists have conventionally defined the desirable ends of economic activity as utility maximization, where utility is a measure of relative satisfaction, or "the greatest happiness," for the greatest number of people (Bentham, 1907; Mill, 1871). Conventional economists typically assume that consumption provides utility and what we pay for the goods we consume is an objective measure of the utility they provide. They also claim that we cannot meaningfully compare utility between people, and therefore our goal should be to maximize total monetary value in the economy.

Under certain rigid assumptions, markets achieve this goal. Markets use the price mechanism to decide how to allocate resources among different products and how to allocate those products among different users. The basic mechanism can be split into two parts: the allocative function of prices and the rationing function We can think of the allocative function as how raw materials are apportioned among different products. Many different firms are competing for raw material inputs into production, such as oil and steel, and whoever is willing to pay the most wins the resource. If I am able to convert the resource into a product of higher value than my competitor, I can afford to pay more than my competitor. This ensures that resources are allocated toward the highest-value products. The rationing function of price awards products to whichever consumer is willing to pay the most for them. This ensures that those products go to whoever values them the most in monetary terms. Markets therefore maximize monetary value on both the production and consumption sides. When economists state that markets are efficient, they mean that markets maximize monetary value. If maximizing monetary value is our goal, then markets would appear to be an excellent economic institution (Farley, 2008).

However, the "greatest number of people" should include future generations, in which case ensuring sustainability takes precedence over maximizing current monetary value. Future generations cannot participate in today's markets, and market values do not reflect their preferences. To ensure sustainability, we must not deplete renewable resources faster than they can reproduce, cannot deplete essential nonrenewable resources such as oil faster than we can develop renewable substitutes, and cannot emit waste into the environment faster than it can be absorbed (Daly, 1990). Our efforts to maximize monetary value for the current generation come at the cost of sustainability.

But even if we ensure sustainability, it is not at all clear that monetary value is what we want to maximize. Monetary value is determined by preferences weighted by purchasing power. Someone who is destitute and starving does not value food, someone who is destitute and ill does not value health care. The conventional economist's assumption that we cannot compare utility between individuals is unrealistic: a good meal obviously provides more utility to a starving person than to an overfed one by almost any metric besides that of monetary value.

This chapter will take the position that the desirable ends of economic activity must include the satisfaction of basic biological necessities for growing populations now and in the future. Concern for future generations means that we must ensure sustainability. The most serious threats to basic needs and sustainability include global climate change, peak oil, natural resource depletion, food security, biodiversity loss, and global pandemics, among others. Information must play an important role in solving any of these problems. Given the severity and urgency of these threats, we must ensure that our economic institutions are well suited for producing the required knowledge and disseminating it as effectively as possible.

The Nature of the Resource: Characteristics of
Information Relevant to Its Allocation

Economics typically focuses on scarce resources. If I burn a barrel of oil, that oil is no longer available for you to burn; if ecosystems sequester the CO_2 I spew into the atmosphere, they have less ability to sequester yours. Because my use leaves less for you to use, we must compete for access to the resources. Economists use the terms "rival" or "subtractive" to describe such resources: use by one person leaves less for others. If society fails to ration access to scarce rival resources, anyone who wants them can use them. The likely result is unsustainable overuse or underprovision, unjust distribution, and inefficient allocation toward activities that do not generate the greatest monetary value or toward people who do not value them the most.

However, information is a nonrival resource: one person's use of information has no impact on the amount of information left for others to use. More accurately, information is actually an additive resource that improves through use (Kubiszewski, Farley, & Costanza, 2010), and this additive nature of information is what led to the rapid development of technologies and civilizations. If we look back over time, the rate of technological progress was exceptionally slow for the first two hundred thousand years or so of human existence—small bands of hunter-gatherers roamed the countryside looking for food, and technological advances were separated by millennia. The invention of agriculture, however, allowed denser populations and the more rapid circulation of ideas, which improved through use. Written language emerged, allowing ideas to be stored and transmitted more easily. As the rate of flow of information increased, so did the rate of technological change. Mercantilism and industrialization led to more rapid communication of ideas between cities and across cultures, contributing to an even more rapid rate of increase in knowledge (Diamond, 1997). For example, when Genghis Khan conquered most of Asia, the Middle East, and Eastern Europe, he adopted new technologies and spread them across his empire. Equally important, he opened up and protected trade routes, allowing people and ideas to continue to spread. As ideas spread, new users found ways to improve them. The spread of information through Genghis's conquest may have ultimately paved the way for the European Renaissance and the Industrial Revolution to which it led. Genghis Khan could be considered the father of the modern age (Weatherford, 2004).

Many low-carbon alternatives to fossil fuels are effectively nonrival. For example, no matter how many photons we capture for solar energy in North

America, it will have no impact on the number available in the rest of the world. If we freely share technologies for capturing solar energy with other countries, those countries are likely to burn less fossil fuel, improving everyone's quality of life. The more scientists and industries experiment with these new technologies, the faster they are likely to improve.

As many people in the commons movement point out, information is like grass that grows longer and more nutritious the more it is grazed upon, so everyone should be free to graze on it as much as possible. In reality, however, an increasing amount of information is patented or copyrighted. People are not allowed to use it unless they pay. The World Trade Organization's Agreement on Trade-Related Aspects of Intellectual Property Rights was the greatest expansion of intellectual property rights in history (Tansey, 2002). In spite of this expansion in intellectual property rights, neither patents nor copyrights can make access to information completely excludable, so that even those who do not pay may benefit. The result is that the private sector is likely to invest less in research and development (R&D) than is socially optimal (Arrow, 1962). Accumulating evidence suggests that restricting access to information has slowed the rate of growth of knowledge (Heller & Eisenberg, 1998; Paul, 2005; Runge & Defrancesco, 2006).

Why Price Information? The Logic of the Market

Competent economists recognize that the price mechanism only maximizes monetary value for resources that are competitive in use, also known as rival or subtractive resources. The rationing of nonrival resources creates artificial scarcity and actually reduces the economic value of the resource.

Paradoxically, the value of existing nonrival resources is maximized at a price of zero. This is readily evident from an example. If someone develops an inexpensive, safe, and carbon-free substitute for fossil fuels, the more people that adopt this technology, the better off society is. Placing a high price on the technology (that is, the information required to produce it) would reduce adoption and increase the probability and severity of climate change. In more technical terms, net benefits to society increase whenever the marginal social benefits (i.e., the benefit from one additional "unit") of an activity exceed the marginal social costs. The marginal cost to society of disseminating information is nearly zero. Individuals continue consuming resources as long as the marginal benefits they receive are greater than the price, and if forced to pay for access to information or other nonrival resources, they will stop consuming them long before their marginal benefit falls to zero. In economists' terms, this creates a dead-weight loss of economic surplus—a loss of value. The price mechanism fails to maximize value for nonrival resources.

Prices also pose problems for the creation of new knowledge. If we accept the conventional economist's notion of value, then the marginal value (for instance, the value of an additional unit) of a rival resource is determined by the greatest amount any single individual is willing to pay for it. If this exceeds the cost of producing an additional unit, profit is possible, or at least a fair return on the labour and resources used in production. However, the marginal value of a nonrival resource is given by summing the marginal benefits across all users (Samuelson, 1954). The sum of marginal benefits to all users of the clean-energy technology described above may far exceed the R&D costs at a price of zero. However, as soon as the producer charges for use, the number of users and hence total value of the technology decreases. Again, the value to society is maximized at a price of zero, but at such a price there is no market incentive to produce new information.

Patents and copyrights are an effort to solve this paradox. Intellectual property rights, in essence, give a state-protected monopoly to information for a limited time. According to article 1, section 8, of the United States Constitution, their purpose is "To promote the Progress of Science and useful Arts, by securing for limited Times to Authors and Inventors the exclusive Right to their respective Writings and Discoveries." When the patent expires, the price of information reverts to zero, maximizing the value of the invention. The belief, albeit far from unanimous, was that positive incentives for innovation overwhelmed the negative impacts of monopoly.

Both patents and copyrights initially lasted fourteen years, and were national, not international. Fourteen years of monopoly profits were considered adequate incentive for the private sector to develop new ideas. When such patent laws were first put in place, technology moved slowly, and inventions might have had a useful life of many decades. Governments were often much smaller, with fewer resources to invest in publicly sponsored R&D. In such a context, intellectual property rights were perhaps a good idea, though even this is subject to debate (Arrow, 1962; Boyle, 2003; Jaffe, 2000).

However, under the aegis of the World Trade Organization (WTO), patents are now international, and last twenty years. Copyrights in the United States have been extended to seventy years beyond the death of the author or to ninety-five years for anonymous works or those produced for others (e.g., corporations). The cost and ease of transmitting information around the world has plunged to almost zero, making information increasingly non-rival and nonexcludable, more of a pure public good. The contribution of information to value-added has also increased. Society has responded by trying to strengthen intellectual property rights to maintain the incentives for innovation (Boyle, 2003) at considerable cost. At the same time, the rate of change of technology has increased exponentially, and new technologies frequently have a useful lifespan shorter than the patent or copyright that protects them. In essence, governments now spend considerable money protecting monopolies for the useful life of a product or idea, even as costs of dissemination approach zero.

In the presence of such dramatic changes, we must assess whether or not the market price mechanism is an effective institution for allocating resources toward the production of knowledge that is the most valuable to society, then allocating that knowledge among users in a way that maximizes its value once it has been produced.

The Production Side

There are two separate questions relevant to the production of information. First, what types of economic institutions will produce the information that provides the greatest net benefits to society? Second, for any type of information society does produce, what economic institutions will generate it at the lowest total cost?

Do Markets Produce the Most Desirable Information?
The first question asks whether or not market forces allocate scarce resources (scientists, laboratories, etc.) toward the production of knowledge that helps people satisfy basic biological needs and promote sustainability (i.e., maintain the conditions to satisfy basic biological needs for future generations). Markets systematically allocate resources toward whatever knowledge maximizes monetary value and generates the most profit. This presents three basic problems.

First, people unable to satisfy their basic biological needs are destitute by definition and, as explained above, have negligible market demand. It is far more profitable to provide luxuries for the rich than necessities for the poor, and this fact determines what type of information markets are likely to provide. The example of eflornithine provides a clear illustration. Scientists discovered in 1979 that eflornithine kills trypanosomes, the parasites responsible for African sleeping sickness. The only other treatment for sec-ond-stage sleeping sickness is arsenic-based, extremely painful to administer, not very effective, and sometimes lethal. Nonetheless, poor Africans could not afford to pay for the new drug, so very little was produced for that pur-pose. However, it turned out that eflornithine also removes unwanted facial hair in women, which is a very lucrative market (Gombe, 2003). In pursuit of profit, the allocative function of price apportions few resources toward devel-oping cures for lethal diseases that afflict the poor (Trouiller et al., 2002) but billions toward cosmetics. Although most people would presumably think saving lives is a more valuable use of resources than developing cosmetics, market demand is a function of preferences weighted by wealth and income. Markets allocate resources toward those who have money and unmet wants, not toward those who have unmet needs. Markets provide few incentives to create technologies that help the poor meet basic biological needs.

Second, markets will only allocate resources toward knowledge that pro-tects or provides goods and services that can be bought and sold on the mar-ket. A stable climate, the ozone layer, the ecological resilience provided by biodiversity, and a host of other ecosystem services are essential to human survival, yet cannot be privately owned (in economic jargon, such resources are nonexcludable). Property rights are a prerequisite for conventional mar-kets to function. Technologies that convert ecosystem structure into eco-nomic products, inevitably generating waste in the process, are therefore likely to be far more profitable than technologies that conserve or restore ecosystems to provide critical ecosystem services. Markets provide few incentives to create technologies that promote sustainability.

Markets in information also influence academic research, as obstacles exist in gaining access to patented information, including research tools. A survey by the American Association for the Advancement of Science (AAAS) found that 35 per cent of academics in the biosciences, for example, reported difficulty in acquiring patented information necessary for their research. Among all scientists reporting such difficulties, 50 per cent had to change the focus of their research, and 28 per cent had to abandon it all together (Hanson, Brewster, & Asher, 2005). In AAAS surveys in the United States, Germany, and Japan, over 40 per cent of scientists agreed that, "Obtaining access to technologies owned by others often involves contractual restric-tions on publications that cause significant constraint[s] on academic free-dom" (as cited in Lei, Juneja, & Wright, 2009, p. 38).

Most people presumably believe that saving individual lives or promoting the survival of our species are more desirable ends than getting rid of unwanted facial hair. Markets are unlikely to develop the information required to solve some of the most serious problems faced by society. This would be less of a problem if scientists and other resources required to produce information were available in infinite quantities, but that is not the case. Every scientist hired to develop cosmetics for the rich is no longer available to develop life-saving cures for contagious diseases or technologies that protect the environment.

A third problem is that the cost of creating new information can be very high, while the cost of providing that new knowledge to another user has become negligible—little more than the cost of transmission over the Internet. The average cost of information therefore declines as more people use it. Figure 1 depicts an example of a hypothetical new technology for generating methane from sewage that simultaneously sterilizes it and converts it to a safe organic fertilizer. The costs of retrofitting existing sewage plants to use this technology are met by subsequent sales of methane and fertilizer, so the only cost to adopters is payment for the information underlying the technology. The technology will have important ecological benefits that are not priced in the market and have no impact on private sector decisions. A private sector firm estimates that the technology will cost $80 million to develop. Average cost per user declines as more users adopt the technology, as depicted in Figure 1. The firm has also estimated the demand curve for the product, also depicted in Figure 1. The demand curve is an estimate of how many sewage utilities will purchase the technology at a given price. Demand curves are determined by the marginal benefits of adoption, so the area under the curve provides a measure of total benefits to society. The total market benefits minus the total costs equal the net benefits to society.

However, firms are interested in profits, which are determined by total revenue (sales price x quantity sold) minus total costs, in this case $80 million. The problem is that to sell more products, the firm must lower prices. At some point, the falling prices outweigh the increasing sales, and total revenue falls. In economists' jargon, products with these characteristics are natural monopolies, as will be explained below.

Though developing clean energy sources is arguably one of the most important challenges for society today, as a result of the problems described above, the energy sector is one of the least innovative industries. The sector invests about 6 per cent as much, relative to capital intensity, as the manufacturing sector as a whole, with a minimal share of these investments dedicated to the needs of the poor. There are very high costs to developing new technologies and scaling them up, and when one firm bears the costs, other firms capture many of the benefits (Avato & Coony, 2008). Private sector investment in energy technology (research, development, and deployment) has fallen steadily since the 1980s, and accounts for only 0.3 per cent of sales in the United States (Coy, 2010).

In summary, the private sector directs research efforts toward market goods that satisfy the desires of the rich rather than public goods and benefits for the poor. The fact that most resources are currently allocated by market forces, along with the rule of diminishing marginal utility, suggests that allocating resources toward public goods and the poor would yield greater welfare benefits at the margin than markets. Even if we accept the goal of maximizing the net monetary benefits of production, there are circumstances in which market forces cannot profit from creating information for marketable products, though society as a whole would benefit.

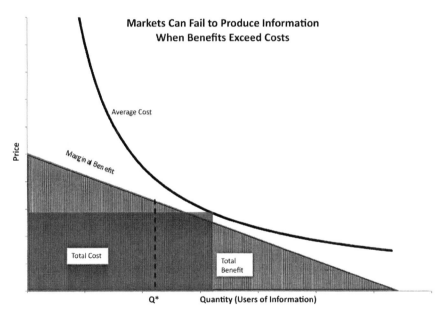

Figure 1: Information has high fixed costs and negligible marginal costs, so the average cost declines with the number of users. Total benefits, measured by the area under the demand curve, increase with number of users. However, to sell more patented information, firms have to lower the cost. As a result, there is no price at which the firm will recoup the costs of producing the information, even though for any number of users greater than Q*, market benefits exceed costs. In this hypothetical illustration, the firm can never earn enough revenue (price x quantity) to cover the total costs of production (average costs x quantity), and therefore will not develop the technology. Social benefits equal total costs at Q*, and exceed them for any greater level of adoption, reaching a maximum at a price of zero. Even with patent protection, the private sector fails to create the new technology.

Do Markets Produce Information at Lowest Cost?
Regardless of the information produced, economic efficiency demands that it be produced in the most cost-effective manner possible. The most important input into the production of information is information. Under the market paradigm, teams of scientists, typically working for corporations, compete to bring a patentable technology to market. These teams are unlikely to share information that may help competitors. This implies that considerable research is likely to be duplicated, and synergies may be lost. If several teams are taking very similar paths, when one arrives at a patentable technology first, the work of the other teams has simply been wasted. Since information improves through use, the more freely it circulates, the more likely it is to improve. For an equal level of investment, one must assume that collaborating teams of scientists freely sharing knowledge are likely to make more rapid progress than isolated competitive teams hoarding knowledge.

Considerable evidence suggests that the proliferation of patents has indeed slowed the advance of knowledge. In the medical sector, the proliferation of patents has made it much more difficult and costly to develop new drugs (Heller & Eisenberg, 1998). A survey of its members by the AAAS found that the 40 per cent of those who had acquired patented technologies for their research had difficulty doing so, and as mentioned above, many of these were forced to change or abandon their research (Hanson et al., 2005). In another recent survey of academics in the biosciences, a majority disagreed with the statement that, "Intellectual property rights on research tools provide incentives to invent more tools and/or conduct related research, and advance the research in your area," while a majority agreed that, "Overall, the intellectual property protection of research tools is having a negative impact on research in your area" (Lei et al., 2009, p. 38). Curiously, the major research impediment was not patents per se, but rather complying with university guidelines for seeking and respecting patents.

Intellectual property rights create numerous other costs unrelated to the research itself. First are the costs of applying for patents, which can be substantial and can favour large corporations over individuals. The legal costs of enforcing patents can also be quite high for both the patent owner and the court system. Estimates suggest that over 1 per cent of patents end up in litigation (Lanjouw & Lerner, 1998), with typical cases costing $2 million or more (Margiano, 2009; Tyler, 2004). In the case of patent trolling, firms create or purchase patents they do not intend to use simply to challenge the patents of other firms, and challenged firms frequently settle out of court simply to avoid litigation costs (Magliocca, 2006). Firms also patent technologies they do not plan to use simply to keep others from using them, thus slowing innovation (Turner, 1998). All of these extraneous costs reduce the quantity of money that could otherwise be made available for research.

The Consumption Side: Do Markets Efficiently Allocate Information among Consumers?

Once information has been produced, it must be allocated among consumers in a way that maximizes its value. Patents create private property rights in information, allowing it to be bought and sold. The problem with this is that prices ration access—only those willing to pay the price are allowed to use the information. However, additional use of information imposes no additional costs. In fact, it has long been recognized that information generation has positive externalities in the form of facilitating the creation of new information, which justifies subsidies for information generation (Foxon, 2003). Furthermore, use of green technologies and cures for contagious diseases generate additional positive externalities, which means that society could increase net social benefits by subsidizing use.

The inefficiency of price rationing information is clearly illustrated through example. Under the Convention on Biological Diversity, countries essentially have property rights to their biodiversity and the genetic information it contains (United Nations Environment Program, 1992). Traditionally, countries that find new strains of contagious diseases make them available to the World Health Organization, which allows anyone to develop vaccines or cures for those diseases. Typically this means that the genetic information would be passed on to private sector corporations, which would compete to develop a vaccine. As discussed above, competition is likely to be a less effective means for developing new medicines than co-operation. Indonesia recently discovered a new strain of avian flu. In terms of allocating a successful vaccine, Indonesia realized that a private corporation would likely price the vaccine at a cost too high for most of the world's poor, including Indonesia's citizens. Indonesia therefore threatened to sell the virus to a single corporation, presumably with the requirement that any resulting vaccine be made available to Indonesia's citizens (McNeil, Jr., 2007). Rationing access to the virus would reduce the likelihood of discovering a vaccine, while rationing access to the vaccine would increase the likelihood of a pandemic.

Charging for information leads to the grossest sort of inefficiency. Returning to the example of a technology for generating methane and fertilizer from sewage, imagine that the hypothetical firm discussed above makes a breakthrough and realizes it can develop the technology for only $60 million. This shifts the average cost curve down, as shown in Figure 2 below, and makes it profitable to create, patent, and sell the technology. With the patent protecting the firm from competition, the firm can choose a profit-maximizing price and quantity. The area in the lower left shows the total costs to the firm, and the area above, its maximum possible profits. The net market benefits to society are given by the private profits plus the triangle between the profits and the demand curve. However, the triangle depicts the additional *net* market benefits to society if the technology were to be given away free of charge. In economists' terms, the failure to realize these additional benefits is a deadweight loss to society caused by patent pricing. The technology, of course, also creates methane that replaces carbon emissions from fossil fuels, organic fertilizer that replaces highly polluting chemical fertilizers, and less pollution from sewage disposal, all nonmarket benefits of immense value.

If other firms saw the large profits being made from this technology, they might decide to develop a "me-too" product. However, this would presumably cost an additional $60 million in development costs simply to replicate an existing product. In other words, the more firms that develop competing

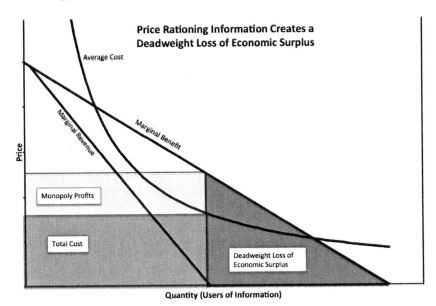

Figure 2: The private sector will develop a new technology when the monopoly profits are positive, but this generates a deadweight loss of economic surplus.

products, the greater the total costs to society, with negligible additional benefits, which is why products with high fixed costs and low marginal costs are known as natural monopolies.

Alternative Economic Institutions

Both theoretical and empirical evidence suggest that markets are unlikely to produce the most desirable types of information, fail to produce information at the lowest possible cost, and lead to suboptimal "consumption" of information. Compounding the inefficiency of these failures, both the government and private sectors waste substantial resources creating and protecting the patents essential to the market production of information. For some types of information, the benefits of market production might outweigh the costs. However, the most serious threats to today's society, ranging from global climate change to global pandemics, involve public goods. Markets inherently fail to prioritize public-good production. Rather than forcing solutions to such problems into the market model, we need a more scientific approach that adapts economic institutions to the nature of the problem. We need to foster economic institutions that reduce or eliminate these inefficiencies.

The challenge is to develop institutions that stimulate production of the technologies we need to solve our most serious societal challenges, then disseminate that information as quickly and broadly as possible. We will review a variety of existing mechanisms based on who covers research costs: the public sector, the not-for-profit sector, market forces, individual efforts, or some combination thereof.

Public-Sector Provision

As information has the characteristics of a public good, public-sector provision seems an obvious solution, especially for information required to protect and restore public goods. There is, of course, a long tradition of government-financed R&D. Organized public support for R&D in agriculture, with results freely disseminated as public goods, dates back over 150 years (Tansey, 2002), with the land grant universities in the United States as just one example. However, while the most serious problems society currently faces are increasingly public good in nature, the share of public funding for research has declined dramatically in recent decades. In the United States, federal funding for R&D has fallen from well over 60 per cent for most of the 1960s to well under 30 per cent in recent years, with the private sector making up most of the difference. Federal funding continues to account for the bulk of basic research, however, and the bulk of funding for universities (National Science Foundation, 2010).

While in theory the public sector should focus research efforts on public goods and pay less attention to potential monetary returns, it is not clear that governments are effectively allocating R&D resources toward solving society's most pressing problems. As in the private sector, government support of alternative energy R&D has fallen substantially since the 1980s. In the United States, the President's Council of Advisors on Science & Technology has recommended an increase in energy R&D funding from $6 billion to $16 billion, though an actual increase of that magnitude seems unlikely given the resistance from recently elected Republicans (Johnson, 2010). Global climate chaos could have dramatic impacts on quality of life and life expectancy, while advances in health care can at best add a few years to our lives. Nonetheless, well over half of nondefence R&D in the United States is spent on health, while investments in energy and the environment are negligible (Knezo, 2005), and in other Organisation for Economic Co-operation and Development (OECD) countries nonhealth R&D merits little more than an asterisk. Furthermore, the Bayh-Dole Act of 1980 allows private sector businesses and universities to patent publicly funded research, with the potential for seriously restricting its dissemination.

Prizes
Another possibility is prizes for innovative research, which dates at least to 1714, when the British government offered a prize for developing a method to estimate a ship's longitude. Such prizes are primarily designed to direct research toward solving specific problems. Competitors undertake much of the risk, so the prize essentially leverages private sector resources. If the winner of the prize must also place the resulting technology in the public domain, then prizes effectively turn the innovation into a public good and address the problem of dissemination (Stiglitz, 1999). However, the best-known prize is currently the XPRIZE, which allows inventors to retain full intellectual property rights to their inventions. In this case, the only advantage of the prize is to stimulate research on a specific topic.

The XPRIZE foundation has the motto, "revolution through competition," and describes itself as "an educational nonprofit organization whose mission is to create radical breakthroughs for the benefit of humanity thereby inspiring the formation of new industries, jobs and the revitalization of markets that are currently stuck" (http://www.xprize.org/). In spite of these lofty goals, it is highly questionable that the research it inspires actually addresses humanity's most pressing problems. The first prize essentially went to the development of space-based tourism. A current prize focuses on cheap and rapid sequencing of the human genome, in order to "improve help and ameliorate suffering," but such medical advances will likely be available only to the wealthy. Other prizes, such as that awarded to the 100 mpg car, may prove more beneficial, though cars are also likely to remain the privilege of the global wealthy.

Such prizes do attract considerable attention and publicity, which may be more important than the money they offer (Ledford, 2006). Prizes work "not only by identifying new levels of excellence and by encouraging specific innovations, but also by changing wider perceptions, improving the performance of communities of problem-solvers, building the skills of individuals, and mobilizing new talent or capital" (McKinsey & Co., 2009, p. 7). The America COMPETES Act, passed by Congress on December 22, 2010, authorizes all government agencies to conduct prize competitions.

In spite of some advantages of the prize approach, in particular when the resulting innovations become public goods, it still stimulates competition in research and fails to achieve the benefits of sharing information in the innovation process.

Commons-Based Peer Production

Another approach to innovation, arguably the oldest of all, is commons-based peer production, whose "central characteristic is that groups of individuals successfully collaborate on large scale projects following a diverse cluster of motivational drives and social signals" (Benkler, 2002, p. 2). By its very nature, such research is freely available to all. Commons-based peer production tends to be most successful when research equipment is quite cheap (e.g., computers), problems can be broken down into small modules of different sizes, and integration of the modules is relatively easy. The modular nature allows contributors to determine their own level of contribution and self-select for the tasks at which they excel (Benkler, 2002).

In spite of economists' assumptions about self-interested behaviour, we know empirically that individuals freely contribute enormous amounts of time to collaboratively solving problems and generating new technologies. Benkler (2004) argues that "instead of direct payment, commons-based production relies on indirect rewards: both extrinsic, enhancing reputation and developing human capital and social networks; and intrinsic, satisfying psychological needs, pleasure, and a sense of social belonging. Instead of

exclusive property and contract, peer production uses legal devices like the
GPL [General Public License], social norms, and technological constraints
on 'antisocial' behavior" (p. 1110). Within this peer production community,
monetary returns may actually have negative connotations, and can potentially decrease co-operation (Benkler, 2002). Although some computer pro-
grammers report being paid for their contributions (Todd, 2007), there is
actually evidence from behavioural economics and psychology that monetary incentives can make people more selfish (Vohs, Mead, & Goode, 2006,
2008) and "crowd out" the intrinsic motivations to co-operate, which drive
much of this research (Frey, 1997; Frey & Jegen, 2001). It thus appears that
most contributors participate to be part of a gift economy, for the status
conferred, or to make the world a better place. However, it does not really
matter what the particular motivation is for an individual to participate—
different individuals can participate for different reasons (Boyle, 2003).

This approach may be particularly effective for software development
but should work for any problem that can be modelled on a computer.
Throughout history, technological advances in stone knapping, agriculture, architecture, government, and others involved a similar approach, as
did language, culture, and music. The advantage of this approach is that it
does not require any changes in intellectual property rights. The problem is
that some of the most important societal problems we currently face, such
as alternative energy technologies, may require substantial and expensive
investments in basic science, additional investments to apply the research,
and a significant learning curve to achieve economies of scale.

Dissemination: Open Access and Open Source

Once information has been produced, there is still the problem of dissemination. The value of technologies that address society's most serious problems is clearly maximized when made freely available for all. When there are
positive externalities to use, which is the case for any green technologies or
cures for contagious disease, it may even be socially efficient to pay people
to use the technology.

There are currently two dominant approaches to making information
freely available: open access and open source. Open access refers to information that is freely available for all but which cannot be modified. Open
source refers to information that is freely available to all and can be modified
by anyone.

There are important differences between the two models. In the scientific realm, most open-access publications and the research behind them are generated by academics, and paid for with salaries or grants, which may also cover the costs of publication. Publications typically contribute to promotions and higher salaries, but nonmonetary compensation such as status and prestige provide considerable incentive. There is also a strong element of reciprocation, or "gift economies," as scientists know that they will also benefit from the contributions of others. Such payments allow researchers to devote full time to specific problems and the knowledge required to address them. However, many academics jealously guard the data underlying their research, at least until publication, which reduces the value of the data to society. Also, at the same time that open-access publications are becoming more common, so, too, are patents on research results.

Open-source information is generally produced via commons-based peer production. It can be used as is or modified, as long as it is properly cited. More importantly, it is typically protected by a General Public License (GPL) or copyleft. Though anyone can use and alter the work, all subsequent work is protected by the same licence and can never by patented or placed under conventional copyright.

One promising alternative for production and dissemination is a hybrid of the open-source and open-access approaches. One example is the Alzheimer's Disease Neuroimaging Initiative, in which a large consortium of researchers looking for biomarkers for Alzheimer's shares all its data and makes findings public immediately. No one owns the data and no one submits patent applications. Scientists on the project are paid for their research with salaries and grants, primarily from universities or the public sector, and also gain status and other nonmonetary benefits. Participants have referred to the results as "unbelievable" and "overwhelming" (Kolata, 2010, p. A1). There are other open-source initiatives in the health sciences focused on diseases of the poor, which provide little opportunity for profit in any case (Hale, Woo, & Lipton, 2005; Maurer, Rai, & Sali, 2004).

The advantage of this hybrid approach is that it allows scientists to work full-time on problems that serve the public good. We suspect that in general scientists would prefer to find cures for life-threatening diseases or improve technologies that mitigate environmental catastrophes rather than develop cosmetics for the rich.

One major obstacle with public funding, however, is pooling adequate resources. In the United States, for example, the Republicans are proposing dramatic cuts in government-supported R&D. While government-sponsored research might require an increase in taxes, it could also reduce other demands on both government and private resources. Health care provides one of the most obvious examples. Most people are not aware that even in the United States, over half of every dollar spent on health care is provided by the government (Woolhandler & Himmelstein, 2002). The skyrocketing cost of pharmaceuticals is rapidly increasing both private sector and government expenditures. If government-sponsored research on pharmaceuticals was freely shared by all, pharmaceutical costs would likely plunge, freeing up government resources to spend on research and private sector resources that could be used to pay additional taxes. The private sector can fund research through profits on patents, but those profits ultimately come from the taxpayer's pocket. Should it matter to the taxpayer whether they pay for R&D through monopoly profits or through higher taxes? Even if the government proves unwilling to dedicate as much money to R&D as the private sector, if knowledge were better directed and freely shared, presumably much less money would be required.

The big question is where such money should come from in a time of fiscal crisis? The answer is actually quite obvious—from the sectors causing the problems. On the source side, oil companies have earned record profits in recent years and, as pointed out earlier, invested very little in R&D. In economic theory, a firm deserves a fair return on labour and capital. Additional returns are from the value of the resource in the ground, which is created by nature, and are known as rent, or unearned income. Most countries enjoy sovereign rights to mineral resources and are entitled to the rent they generate. Furthermore, it is well established in theory and practice that capturing rent by charging royalties does not create any loss of economic surplus. It is also obvious that nonrenewable resources cannot be equally divided across generations. Justice and sustainability instead demand that enough of the rent generated by such resources be invested in renewable substitutes such that the resource is depleted no faster than those substitutes are developed (El Serafy, 1981). Society should also capture additional revenue on the sink side, either through carbon taxes or a cap and auction system on carbon emissions, which could be invested in other green technologies. The wealthy countries have done the most to cause the problems we face and are the most capable of contributing resources to a global, open-source, R&D program. However, any single country can begin the initiative and will still benefit by sharing results with all countries due to the public-good nature of knowledge and the benefits it provides (Beddoe et al., 2009).

Conclusion

Human society has made a dramatic transition from an environment in which ecosystem goods and services, including fossil energy, were abundant, and human-made artifacts scarce, to one where the opposite is true. Market economies proved very effective at converting energy and natural resources to human-made artifacts, but that is no longer our most pressing challenge. Economics addresses the allocation of scarce resources and must adapt to reflect these new scarcities. The challenges we face are immense and information will play a critical role in building a post-carbon economy. Although market-based allocation systems have the advantage of providing incentives for the private sector to create certain new information, they fail to correctly determine what information best promotes society's desired ends, fail to produce information at the lowest cost, and they make information artificially scarce after it has been produced.

The correct sequence for economic analysis is to decide on the desirable ends, assess the physical characteristics of the scarce resources necessary to attain them, and only then determine what economic institutions are most appropriate for allocation. If we apply this analytic sequence to the problem of developing a sustainable post-carbon economy, we see that the production of information should be based on co-operative approaches rather than competitive markets, and information once produced should be open-access, freely available to all. There are a number of economic institutions available for achieving this. Perhaps the most promising is open-source R&D, publicly funded at the global level. We should test this and various other options using a scientific approach of adaptive management in which we strive to improve upon effective institutions and discard ineffective ones. We can no longer afford to take an ideological approach in which we predetermine that markets are the most effective allocative institutions, regardless of the desirable ends and scarce resources in which we test various options.

A different allocation system is required for both the production and consumption of information. Since information is the basis of economic production, common ownership, or elimination of property rights, of information would significantly increase information transfer and produce a greater rate of innovation. It will also provide a means of allocating information toward the desirable ends of society and the common good by allowing a larger number of scientists and researchers access to the information.

References

Arrow, K. (1962). Economic welfare and the allocation of resources for invention. In R. Nelson (Ed.), *The rate and direction of inventive activity* (pp. 609–625). Princeton, NJ: Princeton University Press.

Avato, P., & Coony, J. (2008). Accelerating clean energy technology research, development, and deployment: Lessons from non-energy sectors. Washington, DC: The World Bank.

Beddoe, R., Costanza, R., Farley, J., Garza, E., Kent, J., Kubiszewski, I., ... Woodward, J. (2009). Overcoming systemic roadblocks to sustainability: The evolutionary redesign of worldviews, institutions and technologies. *Proceedings of the National Academy of Sciences*, 106, 2483–2489.

Belluck, P. (2010, June 13). For forgetful, cash helps the medicine go down. *New York Times*, p. A1.

Benkler, Y. (2002). Coase's penguin, or, Linux and the nature of the firm. *Yale Law Journal*, 112(369). Retrieved from http://digitalcommons.law.yale.edu/fss_papers/3126/

Benkler, Y. (2004). Commons-based strategies and the problems of patents. *Science*, 305, 1110–1111.

Bentham, J. (1907). An introduction to the principles of morals and legislation. Oxford, UK: Clarendon Press.

Boyle, J. (2003). The second enclosure movement and the construction of the public domain. *Law and Contemporary Problems*, 66(1 & 2), 33–74.

Campbell, C. J., & Laherrere, J. H. (1998). The end of cheap oil. *Scientific American*, 278, 78.

Coy, P. (2010). The other U.S. energy crisis: Lack of R&D: R&D neglect is holding back innovative energy technologies. *Bloomberg Business Week*. Retrieved from http://www.businessweek.com/stories/2010-06-16/the-other-u-dot-s-dot-energy-crisis-lack-of-r-and-d

Daly, H. E. (1990). Towards some operational principles for sustainable development. *Ecological Economics*, 2(1), 1–6.

Diamond, J. (1997). Guns, germs and steel. New York, NY: W. W. Norton and Company, Inc.

El Serafy, S. (1981). Absorptive capacity, the demand for revenue, and the supply of petroleum. *Journal of Energy Development*, 7, 73–88.

Farley, J. (2008). The role of prices in conserving critical natural capital. *Conservation Biology*, 22, 1399–1408.

Foxon, T. J. (2003). Inducing innovation for a low-carbon future: Drivers, barriers and policies. London, UK: The Carbon Trust.

Frey, B. S. (1997). On the relationship between intrinsic and extrinsic work motivation. *International Journal of Industrial Organization*, 15, 427–439.

Frey, B. S., & Jegen, R. (2001). Motivation crowding theory. *Journal of Economic Surveys*, 15, 589–611.

Gombe, S. (2003, November). Epidemic, what epidemic? *New Internationalist*, (362). Retrieved from http://newint.org/features/2003/11/05/epidemic/

Hale, V. G., Woo, K., & Lipton, H. L. (2005). Oxymoron no more: The potential of nonprofit drug companies to deliver on the promise of medicines for the developing world. *Health Affairs, 24*, 1057–1063.

Hanson, S., Brewster, A., & Asher, J. (2005). *Intellectual property in the AAAS scientific community: A descriptive analysis of the results of a pilot survey on the effects of patenting on science.* Washington, DC: AAAS Directorate for Science and Policy Programs.

Heller, M., & Eisenberg, R. (1998). Can patents deter innovation? The anticommons in biomedical research. *Science, 280*, 698–701.

International Energy Agency. (2010). *World Energy Outlook, 2010.* Paris, France: Author.

Jaffe, A. B. (2000). The U.S. patent system in transition: Policy innovation and the innovation process. *Research Policy, 29*, 531–557.

Johnson, J. W. (2010). Panel urges jump in energy R&D. *Government and Policy Concentrates, 88*, 32.

Knezo, G. J. (2005). *Federal research and development: Budgeting and priority-setting issues, 109th Congress.* Washington, DC: The Library of Congress, Congressional Research Service.

Kolata, G. (2010, August 12). Sharing of data leads to progress on Alzheimer's. *New York Times*, p. A1.

Kubiszewski, I., Farley, J., & Costanza, R. (2010). The production and allocation of information as a good that is enhanced with increased use. *Ecological Economics, 69*, 1344–1354.

Lanjouw, J., & Lerner, J. (1998). The enforcement of intellectual property rights: A survey of the empirical literature. *Annales d'Economie et de Statistique, 49*, 223–246.

Ledford, H. (2006). Kudos, not cash, is the real X-factor. *Nature, 443*, 733.

Lei, Z., Juneja, R., & Wright, B. D. (2009). Patents versus patenting: Implications of intellectual property protection for biological research. *Nature Biotechnology, 27*, 36–40.

Magliocca, G. N. (2006). Blackberries and barnyards: Patent trolls and the perils of innovation. *Notre Dame Law Review, 82*, 1809–1835.

Margiano, R. (2009). *Cost and duration of patent litigation. Managing intellectual property.* New York, NY: Cohen Pontani Lieberman & Pavane LLP.

Maurer, S. M., Rai, A., & Sali, A. (2004). Finding cures for tropical diseases: Is open source an answer? *PLOS Medicine, 1*, e56.

McKinsey & Co. (2009). "And the winner is…" Capturing the promise of philanthropic prizes. Retrieved from http://www.templeton.org/who-we-are/media-room/publications/reports-by-grantees/and-the-winner-is-capturing-the-promise-of-ph

McNeil, Jr., D. G. (2007, February 7). Indonesia may sell, not give, bird flu virus to scientists. *New York Times.* Retrieved from http://www.nytimes.com/2007/02/07/world/asia/07birdflu.html

Mill, J. S. (1871). *Utilitarianism, 4th edition.* London, UK: Longmans, Green, Reader, and Dyer.

National Science Foundation. (2010, March). *National patterns of R&D resources: 2008 data update detailed statistical tables*. NSF 10-314. Retrieved from http://www.nsf.gov/statistics/natlpatterns/

Paul, A. D. (2005). Can "open science" be protected from the evolving regime of IPR protections? *Journal of Institutional and Theoretical Economics*, 160, 9–34.

Pimentel, D., & Pimentel, M. (2008). *Food, energy, and society*. Boca Raton, FL: CRC Press.

Runge, C. F., & Defrancesco, E. (2006). Exclusion, inclusion, and enclosure: Historical commons and modern intellectual property. *World Development*, 34, 1713–1727.

Samuelson, P. A. (1954). The pure theory of public expenditure. *Review of Economics and Statistics*, 36(4), 387–389.

Stiglitz, J. (1999). Knowledge as a global public good. In I. Kaul, I. Grunberg, & M. A. Stern (Eds.), *Global public goods: International cooperation in the 21st century* (pp. 308–325). New York, NY: Oxford University Press.

Tansey, G. (2002). Patenting our food future: Intellectual property rights and the global food system. *Social Policy & Administration*, 36, 575–592.

Todd, M. H. (2007). Open access and open source in chemistry. *Chemistry Central Journal*, 1(3), 1–4. Retrieved from http://www.journal.chemistrycentral.com/content/pdf/1752-153x-1-3.pdf

Trouiller, P., Olliaro, P., Torreele, E., Orbinski, J., Laing, R., & Ford, N. (2002, June 22). Drug development for neglected diseases: A deficient market and a public-health policy failure. *The Lancet*, 359(9324), 2188–2194. doi:10.1016/S0140-6736(02)09096-7)

Turner, J. S. (1998). The nonmanufacturing patent owner: Toward a theory of efficient infringement. *California Law Review*, 86, 179–210.

Tyler, C. (2004, September 24). Patent pirates search for Texas treasure. *Texas Lawyer*.

United Nations Environment Program (UNEP). (1992, June 5). *Convention on Biological Diversity*, Rio de Janiero.

Vohs, K. D., Mead, N. L., & Goode, M. R. (2006). The psychological consequences of money. *Science*, 314, 1154–1156.

Vohs, K. D., Mead, N. L., & Goode, M. R. (2008). Merely activating the concept of money changes personal and interpersonal behavior. *Current Directions in Psychological Science*, 17, 208–212.

Weatherford, J. (2004). Genghis Khan and the making of the modern world. New York, NY: Crown Publishers.

Woolhandler, S., & Himmelstein, D. U. (2002). Paying for national health insurance—and not getting it. *Health Affairs*, 21, 88–98.

TWELVE

STUDYING ABUNDANCE: BUILDING A NEW ECONOMICS OF SCARCITY, SUFFICIENCY, AND ABUNDANCE

Roberto Verzola

Traditional economic thinking is blind to the value of our world's natural plenitude. Market regimes strive to turn abundance into highly managed scarcity, while humanity suffers.

It has been recognized for some time that the dynamism of the information economy comes from the diminishing cost of reproducing and transporting the next unit of an information good.[1] This incremental cost ("marginal cost" to economists) is diminishing not only for software, databases, videos, music, and other pure information goods but also products with significant information content. As more and more people acquire access to the Internet and to tools that can reproduce information on various media, the diminishing marginal cost of information goods is bound to become a universal phenomenon. With the marginal cost of reproducing and transporting information approaching zero, two major and contradictory consequences emerge.

Sharing Freely Leads to Information Abundance

The first consequence is that information now tends to be shared more freely, enhancing the altruistic tendencies usually present in most people. If my neighbours will benefit from the information I have, and I will not lose anything in sharing that information, I will more willingly share it. Perhaps, they will also do the same for me. This key feature of information—that one does not lose it when one shares it—is a strong driving force toward greater sharing. This urge to share information goods freely is so powerful that ordinary people apply it even to commercial software, regardless of what laws say.

The near-zero cost of reproducing and transporting information is the source of what is clearly an emerging abundance in the information sector. This abundance can be seen in the sheer variety and volume of information tools and content available on the Internet, much of it for free.

Intellectual Property Rights Create Artificial Scarcity

The second consequence is that as the marginal cost of an information good approaches zero, its price becomes nearly pure profit, promising information-sellers much greater potential return on investment. This is especially true if the initial price of the information good can be maintained, rather than be allowed to go down to the level of its marginal cost, as conventional economic theory says it should in a competitive market. Indeed, under current legal regimes, information prices are maintained through a system of intellectual property rights, such as copyrights and patents that take away people's freedom to make copies of information goods. In effect, this creates an artificial scarcity of information goods, enabling the information-sellers to maintain prices above marginal cost. The promise of abundance is broken by means of artificially created scarcity.

The creation of artificial scarcity through a system of patents and copyrights is usually justified as a way of ensuring the continuous creation of knowledge. Remove intellectual property rights, it is claimed, and creativity will suffer, intellectual activity will grind to a halt, and the flow of new knowledge will stop. This argument has been cited to justify the increasingly draconian measures being taken to prevent the copying of information goods. Today the single biggest obstacle to the full realization of abundance in the information sector is the legal system of intellectual property rights.

There is no better counterargument to the above claim than the dynamic generation of knowledge now occurring under the general banner of the free/open source movement, which has expanded its reach from software to publishing, databases, literature, the arts, and other information and cultural fields. Advocates of the free-sharing approach argue, in fact, that their approach is more conducive to the generation of new knowledge than the highly restrictive, secretive, and contentious attitude fostered by intellectual property rights systems. Indeed, the most actively used services on the Internet are those that are freely available and whose guiding principles include the philosophy of sharing.

Anything that can be transformed into bits and stored in digital media is an immediate candidate for abundance. Posting it on a publicly accessible Internet site for anyone to read or download makes it instantly available worldwide. People without Internet access can simply ask a friend to download it for them. In countries where the Internet infrastructure is underdeveloped, a physical distribution network of CDs and DVDs, sold close to the cost of reproduction, does a similar job, though with a greater time lag and for a much more limited range of content. What is true with digitized information is to some extent also true with books, paintings, analog audio and video, and other nondigitized information. But it is the digital approach that makes possible the unlimited and error-free reproduction of information over any number of generations of copies.

Other forms of abundance can be seen in the information sector, all feeding into the abundance of information that has become possible through digital electronic technologies.

- Silicon: The integrated circuits that lie at the very core of today's digital revolution are made of silicon. Since silicon comes from sand and is also a recyclable metal, we will not be running out of silicon for a long, long time.

- Bandwidth: Today's communication circuits are migrating from copper to optical cables, whose bandwidth capacity are orders of magnitudes greater; in fact, near infinite, according to George Gilder.[2] Optical cables are made of glass, which is also made of silicon. Again, this promises an abundance of bandwidth that may take a long time to exhaust.

- Storage: Magnetic media, optical media, and even electronic media like flash disks continually drop in price and increase their capacity, faster than we could fill them up. Storage is so cheap nowadays that the mail services of Yahoo and Google essentially give them away for free.

- Radio Spectrum: By reducing their power, transmitters free up more of the radio spectrum for other transmissions. The dramatic reduction in cost of electronics has trickled down to older technologies like radio broadcasting. It is now possible to set up a low-power FM station for about the cost of a laptop, making this medium much more accessible to civil society groups and people's organizations. This potential abundance in the broadcast spectrum, especially in underserved rural and semi-urban areas, remains mostly inaccessible mainly because of highly restrictive laws. Spread spectrum and related wideband technologies, if gradually introduced in broadcast communications, promise a new abundance of stations and channels for public broadcasting.

- IP Numbers: These are the equivalent on the Internet of private telephone numbers. The scarcity in Internet Protocol (IP) numbers should soon be a thing of the past as more and more servers migrate to the next generation protocol (IPNG), which can assign hundreds of IP numbers to every person on earth with a lot to spare.

Abundance among Living Organisms

Abundance is not exclusively confined to the information sector. It can be found in the biological sector too. Abundance in nature and, by extension, in agriculture, comes from the built-in urge—genetic program, if you will—in every organism to reproduce its own kind and thereby ensure the survival and continuity of its species.

Whenever goods consist of living organisms that inherently reproduce themselves, we find potential for abundance. As long as we manage to keep those biological processes going, we will continue to enjoy the blessings of such abundance. Earlier generations knew this, and their cultures are replete with the concepts of stewardship and caring; respect for nature; love for the forest, the land, and the soil; and strict taboos that protected ecological capital. Nature responded in kind, and rewarded earlier generations with its bounty.

Often, no effort is needed at all to make living organisms abundant, since they reproduce and multiply on their own. The key is to be aware of what the favourable conditions are, and to avoid doing anything to disrupt these conditions. In many parts of the world, if you leave any piece of land by itself, in a few years it will be teeming with plant life. In a few decades, it might have grown a forest. If you dig a pond and simply leave it alone, it will sooner or later be filled with rainwater, and algae will soon grow in it. In a year or so, without human intervention, it will have fish in it. In a few years, it will be teeming with aquatic life. Abundance in the natural world is a living force that continually asserts itself.

But if the soil or water is poisoned, then of course its potential for abundance will be undermined. Indeed, we are putting into our soils and waters toxic and other biologically harmful substances that we do not even recognize as poisons.

Biological abundance expresses itself in the following:

- The Food Web: In a finite world, nothing material can grow indefinitely. Living organisms manage to multiply endlessly, only because they have formed among themselves a food web. In this web, one species feeds another, the wastes of some species are themselves food for other species, and every species eventually reaches a dynamic balance with the rest of the living world. Nature maintains abundance indefinitely through its closed material cycles, fuelled by renewable energy from the sun. This provides valuable lessons for humans, if we want to enjoy a similar material abundance of manufactured goods for ourselves, without suffocating in our own emissions, drowning in a flood of effluents, or getting buried in mountains of wastes.

- Agriculture: Human civilization remains part of the living world, in so far as we take our food from it, we breathe its air, drink its water, and rely on its products for most of our survival needs. Thus, we need to master how to keep this living abundance flowing. Nature has shown us the way—we just need to become aware of its own methods and processes of maintaining abundance. Organic farming is showing us how poisons can be eliminated from our farms and how our soils can be regenerated. Permaculture is showing us how, through conscious ecological design, using plants and animals as farm components, we can grow forests and ponds of food and cash crops. Biodynamic farming is, in addition, showing us how to grow high-quality foods that tap the life forces of the universe.

The basic foundation of any agricultural abundance is the soil. Millions of organisms exist in a single clump of healthy soil, including decomposers and nitrogen-fixers, the true fertilizers of the soil. It is this abundance of soil life that feeds the plant—the basis of the organic dictum that one "feeds the soil, and the soil feeds the plant." What do you feed the soil with? Organic matter, of course, not chemical fertilizers or biocides that kill these soil organisms and eventually make soils virtually sterile and lifeless.

- Work Animals: Domesticated work animals not only serve as the farmer's superhuman source of pulling and carrying power, they provide in addition an abundance of milk, as well as of manure. Best of all, this source of motive power can reproduce itself every year or so, so that more farmers may have access to their abundant benefits.

- Nature's Pharmacy: Over thousands of years, humans discovered an abundance of medicinal plant and animal extracts that their healers and medicine men and women used to restore the human body and mind to balance. Though much of this knowledge has been lost, enough Indigenous peoples and herbalists around the world have retained in their Native lore substantial knowledge of the medicinal properties of various extracts from nature.

- Mother's Milk: Nature is, of course, fully prepared to nourish its young. For mammals like us, food for our young is milk, and mother's milk is best for babies. Breastfeeding not only provides babies with complete food, it also provides protection against various diseases and even serves as a mild contraceptive. Incredibly, millions of mothers miss or ignore this obvious fact. Unethical advertising and pressure from hospitals and doctors have made them abandon this priceless gift from their own bodies, a free bounty from nature, and the best for their child, in favour of expensive commercial formula that they must buy from the market, spend sleepless nights preparing, and may furthermore contain harmful substances that can lead to ill health.

More Examples of Abundance

Abundance is present not only in the information and ecological sectors. Various expressions of this phenomenon or its potential can also be seen in other sectors as well, including the energy sector and the sector of materials goods.

- Energy: It is obvious, though often taken for granted, that our most abundant source of energy is the sun. Even fossil fuels, which enabled human civilization to enjoy for a few hundred years a temporary spike in energy consumption, represent solar energy captured by biological processes millions of years ago. Through the process of photosynthesis, solar energy drives the biological processes of reproduction and growth that is the source of abundance in the living world. However, for all our vaunted intelligence, we humans have not yet been able to develop processes and technologies that can do the same in a way that is economical and sustainable enough to phase out fossil fuels. Solar energy remains a backwater of energy research and development, and we remain dangerously dependent on fossil fuels for much of our energy requirements, especially for transportation and electricity. As peak oil approaches, we will soon have no choice about weaning ourselves away from fossil fuels.

- Land: Unlike living organisms, land neither grows nor multiplies. There is only so much arable land, and as the human population grows, not only relative but absolute scarcity threatens. Yet, even in this situation, it is still possible to ensure a relative abundance of land for all. Breaking up, through land reform, huge tracts of land owned by one or a few families, and distributing these to hundreds or thousands of landless families, can give each family an economically viable piece of land for cultivation and agricultural production. Such mechanism even has a biblical precedent: the jubilee year, when all slaves are freed, debts forgiven, and land freely redistributed to give each family a piece of its own.[3] With the proper approach, relative abundance can still be created out of relative scarcity. Gandhi said it best: "Earth provides enough to satisfy every man's need, but not for every man's greed."[4]

- Water: As in land, relative scarcity can also become a problem in water, but with an important difference. Land can be subdivided and parcelled out because plants mostly stay where they are. But fish swim around, so a river or a lake has to remain communally managed, or a "common pool resource." Where fish have dwindled due to overfishing, communities have imposed measures such as banning commercial fishing in the area, or banning the use of nets, to allow the fish to regenerate and return to their prior state of abundance.

- An Abundance of Happiness: Even the poor can enjoy an abundance of happiness, if we are to believe research on happiness indices and international surveys on the happiness levels of different countries.[5] A psychic kind of abundance cannot be easily attributed to the availability of information, energy, or matter, but to a state of mind. This can be of an emotional kind, such as joy, love, contentment, or peace. It can even be of a less definable kind—which some might call spiritual. These usually result from networks of mutually supportive human relationships—family, friendships, colleagues, acquaintances, and community. We have come to a line that many scientists hesitate to cross, although these are as much a part of reality as the other types of abundance.

All these examples (except perhaps the last one) are opportunities that can bring benefits to all, if the sharing mindset becomes dominant and the abundance is managed as a commons. Conversely, the greatest benefit may be limited to a few, if the monopolistic mindset becomes dominant and the abundance is privatized for monopolistic profit-seeking.

Abundance as a Field of Study

Because abundance is clearly present in many aspects of human life, it is obviously an interesting phenomenon and its examination should logically be a major field of study. Yet economics practically denies abundance, defining itself as the study of efficient options in the context of scarcity. Economists sometimes say that when a good starts becoming abundant, it stops becoming interesting, because the economic problem has been solved. If, indeed, abundance is recognized as the solution to the problem of scarcity, should it not be studied even more? A study of abundance would include learning the conditions that lead to abundance, and the conditions that keep the abundance going. It means acquiring the knowledge and skills to generate abundance at will. It also means mastering the art and science of making one form of abundance create another, and another, to generate a cascade of abundance.

Abundance is simply one end of a continuum that has scarcity at its other end. Obviously, anything that is relatively scarce is, at the same time, relatively abundant. For completeness and by any form of logic, the entire continuum from absolute scarcity to absolute abundance should deserve our attention and study. Truly, we need a new field of abundance studies to make economic science a whole, encompassing both scarcity and abundance.

Since the first step toward such a study is to define the subject of the study, the following definition of abundance is offered: "Abundance"(or "plenitude") is the state enjoyed by a person, household, community, or society with respect to a particular good, when the quantity of the good that they can obtain approaches or exceeds their satisfaction level. This state is described quantitatively by the ratio of the obtainable quantity of the good to the quantity that represents their satisfaction level, where the "obtainable quantity" is either the quantity people can buy from the market, the quantity that one can produce for one's own consumption, or the quantity provided by a welfare state to its citizens.

If people are never satisfied with the quantity they can obtain and the satisfaction level is infinite, then the divisor in the abundance metric is infinite. Under these conditions, since infinite supply is physically impossible, abundance will always be zero. But if the satisfaction level is finite, then abundance can be less than one when the quantity obtained is below the satisfaction level, equal to one when the quantity obtained equals the satisfaction level, and greater than one when the quantity obtained exceeds the satisfaction level. The term "relative abundance" can be used to describe the first two cases, and "absolute abundance" to describe the third case. The second case might also be described as a state of "sufficiency."

Thus, the whole range of availability of a good may be described as follows: absolute abundance when the obtainable quantity exceeds the satisfaction level; sufficiency (also relative abundance) when the obtainable quantity equals the satisfaction level; relative abundance/relative scarcity when the obtainable quantity is below the satisfaction level but above the survival level; and absolute scarcity when the obtainable quantity is equal to or below the survival level.

The term "satisfaction" itself may have a range of meanings, from "satiation," where any excess is actually less preferred to the satisfaction level, to "satisficing," where the person is indifferent to excess goods available for consumption. Note that as abundance becomes absolute, the price of the good under consideration approaches zero. This tendency and its consequences for business are the subject of two books by *Wired* editor-in-chief Christopher Anderson.[6]

Since most definitions of economics assume scarcity of resources, some economists may balk at the introduction of the concept of abundance because it is contrary to a fundamental economic assumption. However, such skeptics will hopefully be convinced by the following argument.

Among scarce resources, some may be very scarce while others may only be somewhat scarce. Thus, the concept of relative scarcity should be uncontroversial. Now, consider a glass whose water level reaches half its height. The glass may be considered half-empty, which is a perspective of relative scarcity, or it may be considered half-full, a perspective of relative abundance. Thus, economists who acknowledge relative scarcity should be driven by logic to acknowledge relative abundance too. After all, half-empty and half-full describe the same reality. With this minor leap in logic, the concept of abundance can be introduced among those who have always taken the fundamental assumption of scarcity as gospel truth. In fact, the concept has already entered mainstream economic literature through the term "natural resource abundance." While this term has triggered a curious debate as to whether such abundance is a curse or a blessing, this chapter suggests that one goal of economies should be abundance for all.

Abundance in the History of Economic Thought

James Peach and William Dugger, who provide a detailed history of the concept of abundance in economic thought, say, "many of the great economists wrote convincingly about the possibility of an economy of abundance."[7] The attitudes toward abundance of some of these economists are quoted or described as follows:

- Adam Smith ("It is the great multiplication of the productions of all the different arts, in consequence of the division of labour, which occasions, in a well-governed society, that universal opulence which extends itself to the lowest ranks of people"); Karl Marx, who

believed that modern technology was already capable of attaining
an economy of abundance but that capitalism held it back;

- Thorstein Veblen, who thought that only a small section of
the community, which he called the "leisure class," enjoyed the
economy of abundance;

- Joseph Schumpeter ("If capitalism repeated its past performance
for another half-century ... this would do away with anything that
according to present standards could be called poverty, even in the
lowest strata of the population, pathological cases alone excepted");

- John Commons ("The Industrial Revolution divided economic
history into three periods. ... Scarcity, abundance, and
stabilization periods");

- John Maynard Keynes, who expected that the increases in per
capita living standards in his time were likely to continue, leading
to economic abundance;

- Stuart Chase, who wrote a book *The Economy of Abundance* in 1934;

- Clarence Ayres ("No one any longer doubts the physical and
technological possibility of a world-wide economy of abundance");

- John Kenneth Galbraith, who thought that abundance was
not only feasible for the future but was already a feature of the
present; and

- Amartya Sen ("We live in a world of unprecedented opulence, of
a kind that would have been hard even to imagine a century or
two ago").[8]

After defining the subject of abundance studies and a short list of past economists who accepted abundance as an economic concept, our next step might
be to see how the different manifestations of abundance may be classified.

Classifying Abundance

Abundance may be classified in various ways, each way revealing additional
facets about the phenomenon and giving us hints as to how it may be tapped
for the human good. Abundance may be classified in the following ways.

Space
Is it, like a waterfall, available to a few communities only? Local sources need
local management, where face-to-face interaction between acquaintances,

neighbours, and friends may ease the tension of resource conflicts. In fact, many resources are actually local, though nation-states have appropriated these for themselves and turned them into national patrimony. The regalian doctrine that favours national over local control of resources is, in many countries, a vestige of their colonial past. The continuing debates between local and national decision-making in the case of forests, dams, and mine sites reflect this ongoing tension between local and national management of sources of abundance. This conflict becomes ever more complicated with the entry of corporations, which range the globe for resources to tap until these are depleted. Then they move on. Some sources of abundance, like seas and great rivers, bring benefits to more than one country, and therefore require even more delicate and sensitive negotiations. Resource conflicts may erupt into wars, especially over resources that are gradually running out. The truly global sources of abundance, like our atmosphere and the oceans, require complex international management, as can be seen today in the climate change negotiations. Each of these types needs skill and knowledge, not just in the scientific aspects of abundance but in a whole range of areas that include political, economic, social, cultural, and historical perspectives. Negotiations between potential beneficiaries and other stakeholders involving spatially limited abundance can be highly unequal due to existing asymmetric power relations. This is even truer in the case of abundance that is spread over the time dimension, as explained below.

Time
Is the abundance precarious? Precarious abundance is one whose collapse is imminent and might be gone soon, and we had better do something about it quickly if we want to continue enjoying its benefits. Is it temporary? This would refer to phenomena that last for less than a human lifetime, perhaps a gold rush in some mountainside, or a discovery of a huge pile of guano in an isolated island or cavern. Will it last for a few human lifetimes? Then it is a short-term abundance, like oil is turning out to be. If it will last many lifetimes more, then it is a medium-term abundance, like, possibly, coal. Forests, rivers, lakes, seas, and other long-term sources of abundance should last beyond human existence. Because of our own profligacy, ignorance, or indifference, many of these medium- and long-term resources have instead been turned into short-term resources that will be gone in a few generations. These are huge challenges that should be of interest to all. How do we stop a precarious resource from imminent collapse? How do we turn a temporary abundance into a long-lasting one that can serve not only a few but many generations,

if not every generation that is yet to come? The seventh-generation principle of Native American Indians, it is said, reckoned decisions in terms of their effects up to the seventh generation.[9] Should not our generation, given the greater power of its technologies, look even farther into the future?

Future generations cannot negotiate for themselves. Neither can plants and animals. Thus, some humans must take up the cudgels for these voiceless stakeholders. Negotiating for access is hard enough when a resource is abundant, how much more when it becomes scarce, and furthermore, one has no role in decision-making? This situation demands not only the utmost of intergenerational and cross-species empathy from us but also the deepest appreciation of the interconnectedness of generations and species.

Social Sectors

Certain types of abundance are accessible to all, others are accessible only to those who have the wealth to exploit them. When the sun is up, poor and rich alike can enjoy the warmth and the vitamin D. Due to higher entry costs, the very poor might be precluded from setting up a solar water heater, a solar food cooker, or a photovoltaic panel. But only corporate giants can access the coal, oil, and gas deep underground or beneath the sea, and then process these into the various fuels and other oil-based products they currently sell. It should thus be obvious which abundant energy source should receive the highest priority in terms of government research, subsidy, and preference.

Across Species

Appropriating the world's abundance of matter and energy exclusively for the human is a utilitarian perspective that is increasingly under question. A less anthropocentric view concedes the right of other species to exist, and therefore to survive. It further concedes other species the right to their own living space, a concession that everyone must eventually make, if not for the sake of these species, then also for the sake of future generations. This explicit concession is already enshrined in the design principles of at least one farming system. Permaculture parcels every farm into several zones. For example, Zone 5 is wilderness, for creating favourable conditions for the emergence of a cascade of abundance reserved for other species and not to be casually intruded upon even by its so-called human owners, and then only as visitors.[10] Reserved wilderness areas within the permaculture farm allow us to witness, study, and appreciate at close range how nature's abundance, left to its own, plays itself out.

Elemental Basis

Prehistory has seen stone-based, as well as iron-based, eras featuring a specific set of abundance that characterize them. Information abundance is silicon-based, dependent on technological advances in semiconductors, of which silicon is one, together with the benefits of digital technologies, which make the reproduction of any number of identical copies over unlimited generations. Ecological abundance is carbon-based. Carbon's natural affinity to hydrogen, oxygen, and a few other elements created organic substances that formed the basis of life and of reproductive processes. These led to the great abundance in nature that is ultimately our very own basis for existence. The abundance of solar energy is hydrogen-based. Hopefully, in the future, another hydrogen-based energy economy, using hydrogen extracted from water to run fuel cells, can replace the unsustainable fossil fuel-based energy economy we have today.[11] It would be interesting to find out if there are other elements with a potential to support new types of abundance.

The Building Blocks of the Universe

These fundamental building blocks are matter, energy, and information. Using these as a basis for a typology of abundance, I offer the following additional classification in this chapter.

Material Abundance

Matter exists both in animate and in inanimate—living and nonliving—form. Biological goods become abundant because they have evolved, over eons, the built-in means to reproduce themselves and yet to maintain a dynamic balance that does not overwhelm the finite world in which they exist. While the means of reproduction of information goods is external, usually through human agents or automatons on the information network, the means of reproduction of biological organisms is internal. They contain their own programs for reproducing themselves.

BIOLOGICAL ABUNDANCE. Maintaining ecological abundance is less a problem of ensuring the right conditions for the reproduction of life and more a problem of ensuring that we humans do not destroy those conditions which are favourable to the reproduction of life. Over millions of years, various life forms have evolved to optimize their capacity to reproduce themselves under existing ecological conditions. All we need to do is to respect these conditions and make sure our human activities do not modify them to the extent of threatening the ecological abundance that promises us a perpetual stream of ecological benefits. Furthermore, we must learn from the way ecological systems reproduce themselves indefinitely without having to grow without limit. The secret is in establishing closed material loops fuelled by the sun. These closed loops are cyclical food chains that encompass every element of the system. Together, they form a food web that eventually reaches a dynamic balance that is highly resilient to environmental stresses and provides human communities with a continuous stream of goods, services, psychic rewards, and other benefits.

Think of depositing money in the bank, where it earns a fixed interest. As long as you do not touch the principal and withdraw only the interest earnings, you will get a perpetual stream of benefit out of that fixed amount. This used to be the situation in most of the living world, where our natural capital gave us a perpetual flow of natural income. As long as human communities protected the principal and withdrew from nature only a small portion of its products, we would have been able to enjoy nature's abundance indefinitely. Today, with most of our renewable resources, we are drawing not only the interest but portions of the principal, often large portions of it. In the future, there will be less interest earnings to enjoy, and if we continue with our unsustainable way, the principal itself will soon be gone. This is the situation today with many of our renewable resources.

MINERAL ABUNDANCE. Though nonliving objects like metals, sand, rock, and so on do not reproduce, there are other means of keeping them abundant. We must remember that matter is never created or destroyed, only transformed. Consider metals. Even if the world's metallic reserves were all eventually mined and used up (this would be an environmental disaster!), the metals would not be gone. The millions of tons of gold, silver, iron, copper, aluminum, tin, and other metals that have been mined from the bowels of the earth for human use on the ground are still around us. All we need to do is locate them, gather them, and reprocess them into usable forms once again. The key to abundance in inanimate matter is durability, reusability, and recycling: closed material loops fuelled by renewable energy, using natural ecosystems as models.

INDUSTRIAL ABUNDANCE. A derivative of ecological and mineral abundance is industrial abundance. Taking raw materials provided by these two sources, the industrial sector transforms these raw materials into finished products through human and machine labour, creating an abundance of manufactured goods. Mid-twentieth century interest in abundance usually referred to this type of abundance.[12] Unfortunately, where it exists, industrial abundance today relies unsustainably on linear, one-way processes that transform raw materials from nature at the input end to finished products and waste by-products at the output end, fuelled mainly by fossil and radioactive fuels instead of closed material loops fuelled by renewable energy. Thus, industrial abundance has been highly disruptive of living ecosystems and is the major cause of their destruction and, in some cases, extinction. The onset of peak oil likewise threatens industrial societies that have been largely dependent on oil and related fuels.

Industrial production can be made more sustainable by taking advantage of advances in information technologies. If the machines used in creating an abundance of material goods are made programmable by software, then industrial production can take advantage of the potential of information abundance by essentially eliminating the cost of product design and thereby drastically bringing down the cost of manufactured products to the cost of the raw materials and energy that go into the product.

Imagine, for instance, a programmable weaving machine with built-in facilities to cut and sew, such that threads go in at one end of the machine and shirts, pants, coats, dresses, and other wearables come out at the other end. The process is software-driven. You can go to the Internet, where people might share their own designs for a particular style of wear, download the software freely, customize the dimensions to their specific requirements, and run the program on the machine. One can easily imagine a similar programmable fabricator for, say, wood. Give it as many pieces of plywood or lengths of 2x4s, as necessary, and with the right software downloaded from the Internet, you can make your own chair, frame, shelf, table, and other furniture or toys. This approach is already possible with metal, using software-controlled universal milling machines.

Instead of cutting, chipping, or scraping away material from a workpiece, one can also work from the other end and add material to a workpiece. As early as the 1990s, a three-dimensional ("3D") printer that deposited epoxy layer by layer to a workpiece, to build up any three-dimensional shape, was already commercially available.[13] It could make toys, gears, intricate parts, moulds, and a thousand other things. The only limit was one's imagination, captured in software. Such 3D printers have since become common commercial items. If the working raw material were made nontoxic and recyclable, too, then this could be another answer to the challenge of making material abundance accessible to more people. Enabling the machine to handle a mix of plastic, wood, metal, and electronics could turn it into a software-controlled personal fabricator. This is what MIT's Media Lab has been working on since the turn of the century.[14] It does not even have to be a *personal* fabricator. A whole community can share one and manage it as a common pool resource.

ABUNDANCE IN HUMAN SERVICES. Another type of abundance is created out of human labour—the provision of what are often called services. Typical examples would be education, health, and miscellaneous personal services. These may require information as input and may result in psychic benefits, but they are basically human services that are produced and consumed at the same time. Abundance in these services means, for instance, the assurance that all of one's health and medical needs will be taken care of, or that one's children will get enough education and can take any course they choose and can excel in. Where these services are provided through public funds, through schools, universities, gyms, clinics, and hospitals, for instance, they can be made accessible to all. However, when these services are privatized, the quality and quantity of service available get pegged to one's ability to pay. The key toward abundance in human services seems to be the human division of labour—which requires a minimum level of population—together with a certain level of assurance that each type of labour is sufficiently and fairly compensated relative to other types. This type was placed under material abundance because it requires an actual person to provide the service at the point of consumption.

As the cost of information goods approaches zero, the economic phenomenon of substitution (lower-cost goods/technologies replacing higher-cost ones) leads to these services being increasingly automated. This may possibly create more abundance but at the cost of lost jobs for those who had been personally providing these services in the past, undermining not only livelihoods but also social relations arising from the provision of these services. It has been suggested that one path to abundance is universal employment, to ensure a minimum income for all members of society.[15]

Energy Abundance
Energy may be derived from renewable or nonrenewable sources, with differing challenges and consequences.

RENEWABLES. Although it is one of the least tapped by modern technologies, our greatest source of energy abundance is the sun. Solar energy is a source that is incredibly immense and practically infinite in terms of human scales. It continuously provides a steady source of diffuse energy, from a distance that is far enough to spare us most of the damaging side effects of the infernal processes that fuel the stupendous generation of that energy. Through the appropriate use of collectors and concentrators, the sun's diffuse energy may be transformed into medium- to high-quality heat that can then be converted into other forms for a wide range of uses.[16] Solar energy is still not absolute in abundance. It is not available at night, for instance.[17] So, in addition to collectors and concentrators, storage devices are also needed to make it available when the sun is below the horizon.

NONRENEWABLES. Nonrenewable sources of energy are a special challenge. Once gone, they are gone forever. That is a huge ethical burden to a society with a conscience. We have built our civilizations on the shaky and short-term foundations of fossil fuels, or the shakier foundations of radioactive fuels. As a result of this flawed decision, we have reached a dead end, ending up with a global greenhouse problem resulting in climate change, sea-level rise, and other threats to our very survival. There is urgent need to shift gears, change direction, and to focus on various renewable energy sources that can provide us with comparable abundance in the long term rather than the short term. Only the energy from the sun, perhaps, given its stupendously massive stock of hydrogen, can be considered as good as infinite, even if it will likewise use up its fuel billions of years from now.

Nonmaterial Abundance
This aspect of abundance is manifested almost always in both tangible and nontangible forms.

INFORMATION ABUNDANCE. This is truly a special type of abundance, because information is not lost whenever it is shared. In fact, sharing information multiplies it, and enables everyone to create even more of it. Because of what economists call the "substitution effect" (people tend to shift from higher-priced goods to lower-priced ones that can more or less do the same job or fulfill the same need), the information content of other goods will also keep rising as long as using information is cheaper than other approaches. Information abundance can be expected to lead to a cascade of other types of abundance.

The main problem today with information abundance is the mismatch between two trends: diminishing cost and the promise of universal access on one hand, and, on the other hand, the legal regime of intellectual property rights that threatens information abundance with restrictive laws that unrealistically prohibit sharing, copying, and other forms of reproducing information. The second challenge is how to encourage intellectual activity without intellectual property. The success of free/open source software and the extension of this concept to other fields has already shown that monopoly is not the only way, or even the best way, to encourage intellectual activity. More varied ways of rewarding intellectual work need to be evolved.

PSYCHIC ABUNDANCE. The term "psychic" is used here not in the context of extrasensory perception but in the same psychocultural sense as "psychic rewards" (i.e., nonmonetary, nonmaterial). It refers to certain human feelings and thoughts, variously described as "emotional" or "spiritual," which are likewise intangible but not captured by the term "information." These include love, happiness, companionship, peace, joy, tranquillity, beauty, wisdom, and related concepts that are often associated with a certain kind of abundance, as well as an altruistic perspective or a simpler lifestyle. Psychic abundance covers phenomena that cannot be quantified, digitized, copied, and reproduced like information. These ideas and feelings usually emerge from webs of positive social relationships or an individual's relationship with nature or the cosmos. Many references to abundance on the Internet are of this kind. These references clearly express certain human needs that cannot be met with information, energy, or material phenomena but require a special human response that must also be studied, learned, and mastered.

Abundance Studies: More Areas for Practical and Research Work

Case Studies
Another potentially fruitful area involves studies of specific cases of possible, actual, or lost abundance, as well as cases of artificially created scarcity. Nature, agriculture, and the information sector will provide students and researchers a rich field in which to explore for such cases. Earlier sections of this chapter have already referred to some of these. Under each type, more cases can be identified. From each case study, specific, as well as general, lessons can be drawn that will enrich our understanding of the phenomenon.

Economic Models
Some economic schools of thought pride themselves on building models that idealize real economic processes, from which insights might be drawn

not only for descriptive but also for normative purposes. It will be interesting to find out what kind of models might be appropriate for the various types of abundance listed in this chapter.

A multiplicative model—where consumers of a particular good have themselves the wherewithal to become producers, and where the market for this good starts as a monopoly but soon becomes a competitive market as consumers turn into producers, until the good's price becomes so low that it becomes "too cheap to matter"—might describe accurately the dynamics of most information goods in the absence of statutory measures that protect monopolies. A self-reproductive model—where a natural process, with minimum human intervention, is able to extract on its own both matter and energy from its immediate environment to provide consumers a perpetual stream of benefits, at the same time creating the means to regenerate the productive process itself—might describe accurately the dynamics of most biological goods. As is or with some modification, existing models for renewable and nonrenewable energy and mineral resources can be integrated into a more general model for describing processes of abundance.

Commons
Because abundance creates commons, abundance studies will mesh perfectly with the renewed interest in the commons in mainstream social science circles (as evidence of the latter, take, for example, the awarding of the 2009 Nobel Prize in Economic Science to Elinor Ostrom for her work on common pool resources). Common pool resources in the past involved mostly forests, fishing grounds, pasture lands, irrigation canals, lakes, parks, public plazas, and similar location-specific commons and public spaces. Today the increasing public awareness of serious threats to global commons, such as oceans, the atmosphere, and biodiversity, as well as the new possibilities for cultural production and social interaction created by the Internet, have made these commons an equally exciting area for practical and academic studies. Studies in the two distinct but closely related areas of abundance and commons are bound to feed on each other, possibly opening up new areas for further research.

More Research Areas
Several other related areas offer opportunities for researchers looking for the less-travelled paths. Under a state of plenty, the desire for efficiency and minimizing waste recedes in importance and several other equally important considerations start taking greater priority:

- Universal Access: This might also be called fairness, equality, or social justice. In a way, an abundant resource that is not accessible to some sectors of society is a failure for them, which links this concept to the concept of reliability.

- Reliability: The need to preserve the sources of abundance, to protect them from threats and risks of failure, and to make them last for generations, preferably indefinitely.

- Quality: The need to enhance the quality of the goods, services, and other benefits that are being provided in a perpetual stream by the sources of abundance.

- Cascading Abundance: Once we become intimately familiar with the phenomenon, we can learn to create conditions that can make new abundance emerge, and then create cascades of abundance.

- Dynamic Balance: This is the answer to doubts if abundance can continue indefinitely in a finite world. The ecosystems of the natural world show us how: biological abundance does not lead to runaway growth but to dynamically balanced food webs of closed material cycles fuelled by renewable energy, creating ecosystems that are able to regenerate themselves, are resilient to environmental stresses, and are a rich source of perpetual streams of goods, services, psychic rewards, and other benefits to human communities.

- Abundance Ethic: The management of abundance usually starts from a common rule set that binds all beneficiaries; in time, the rule set should lead to a mindset—or an ethic—that respects, values, and nurtures abundance and its sources.

Institutional Mechanisms for Managing Abundance

Historically, the management of abundance has been approached in various ways, which may roughly be categorized into supply-side and demand-side approaches. Supply-side approaches include:

- Free/Open Access: These arrangements essentially involve opening up a resource to anyone, with a minimum of rules governing access. This approach may apply to certain universally accessible resources like solar energy and wind energy. Likewise, access to public domain software, versions of free software like the BSD licence, and various freely/openly accessible Internet services fall under this category. Some health, social, or public services may be provided under free/open access without encouraging waste. No one, for instance, will request tooth extraction or an appendectomy simply because it is free. Neither will commuters on a mass transport system travel an extra station or two just because it costs little to do so. But where a resource is exhaustible, local, limited, or in a precarious state, the free/open approach may, indeed, lead to a collapse. Another area where free/open access can work is in self-provisioning: a family with a substantial backyard to maintain several fruit trees and a vegetable garden will enjoy occasional abundance from the harvest. Given large enough land and knowledge, the family can enjoy true agricultural abundance.

- Common Pool Resource or Commons: This approach relies on rule-based arrangements enforced collectively or by a community. Common pool resources (CPR) have gained much attention in the past few decades with the debate about the "tragedy of the commons." More recent studies have debunked the idea that commons management will inexorably end in tragedy.[18] The success of the GNU Public License, a CPR version of free software, Wikipedia, and other information and Internet commons have given new impetus to the commons approach.

- Government Control: The government itself takes over the resources, relying on a bureaucratic command structure to implement policies, rules, and regulations. Government utilities and services, like the common pool approach above, can provide a more equitable allocation even under conditions of scarcity—which is important for essential goods—in contrast to market approaches that allocate goods based on capacity to pay.

- Market Competition: Market-based approaches rely on free interactions between self-interested sellers and buyers to determine access, levels of exploitation, and other parameters. The government defines, protects, and enforces private property rights but otherwise interferes minimally in the market.

- Private Monopolies: The government bids out the management of the resource to private monopolies that ensure the protection and maintenance of the resource while they make reasonable profit in managing it.

The above supply-side approaches may also be complemented by demand-side approaches:

- Population Balance: One way to bring a society closer to abundance is to correct the gross imbalance between the human population and the rest of the living world. While determining a sufficiently balanced population level based on the current state of nature, technology, and other factors is hard, and finding acceptable ways to bring the population down to such a level is probably even harder, we must face up to the challenge if we are to fully realize the gains from supply-side efforts to manage abundance. That a huge literature exists about the population imbalance, and a big debate is going on about how a better balance can be attained, indicates how important this matter is to many others.

- Changing Mindsets: Cultural approaches have also been tried successfully in many cases. These approaches enhance the community spirit, develop an ethic of sharing and co-operation, encourage generosity and altruism, and reduce consumption and demand by extolling simpler or even ascetic lifestyles, and as a result they prolong the life of nonrenewable resources and reduce the pressure on renewable resources. While most of the earlier approaches are mutually exclusive, this demand-side approach can complement any of the other approaches listed above, though it may work better with some approaches than with others.

A number of promising areas for research within the new field of abundance studies have now been identified. Wolfgang Hoeschele has also proposed an agenda for abundance studies that includes research on property regimes, such as the pooling of resources in common; self-provisioning as well as exchange systems, such as barter systems, local exchange trading systems, gift exchange, mutual aid, time dollars, and other nonmonetary exchange systems; monopolies, oligopolies, and other "scarcity-generating institutions"; nonviolence, for providing the necessary context for "free, unco-erced economic exchange"; health-promoting environments, institutions, methods, and financing; knowledge and the conditions that further foster its pursuit; educational contexts, approaches, and content; and vehicles for promoting abundance and "changing the world without taking power."[19]

Juliet B. Schor likewise listed four principles of plenitude (her preferred term for what this chapter calls abundance), which can be research topics in themselves: a new allocation of time; self-provision as a way to diversify from the market; an environmentally aware approach to consumption that she calls "true materialism"; and reinvesting in one another and in one's communities.[20]

Note that both Hoeschele and Schor refer to self-provisioning, which earlier writers have called "production for one's own consumption," or the do-it-yourself (DIY) movement. This also includes the whole area of household production and consumption, a major interest of feminist economics. The concept of provisioning, if it includes state provisioning, market provisioning, mutual provisioning (commons and peer-to-peer exchanges), and self-provisioning, is such a wide area for study that economics itself has been defined as a study of "how society provisions itself."

It was pointed out at the start of this chapter that abundance leads to two consequences and generates two mindsets: 1) a mindset of sharing and co-operation; and 2) a mindset of self-interest and monopoly. Thus, all areas above should be studied in the context of these two opposing perspectives. Since the principal carrier of self-interest and monopolistic thinking is the corporate mind, this suggests another fertile ground for research: corporate power. It has been pointed out that corporations now dominate the world economy, with fifty-one of the one hundred largest economies in the world belonging to corporations and only forty-nine to countries. Elsewhere, I have also pointed out that corporations now occupy the top of the food chain and—if they were counted as a man-made species—could now be considered the dominant species on this planet. Research in corporate power will probably bring fresh insights about artificial scarcity and scarcity-generating institutions.

Conclusion

It should be clear by now that the phenomenon of abundance deserves careful study, so that we may learn how to create, maintain, prolong, and even build cascades of abundance for the benefit of human communities and societies. In the past, we have evolved various institutional mechanisms for managing abundance. We should learn from our rich trove of experiences and from the emerging field of abundance studies to master this phenomenon for the human good.

Notes

1   U.S. Congress, Office of Technology Assessment, *Intellectual Property Rights in an Age of Electronics and Information*, OTA-CIT-302 (Washington, DC: U.S. Government Printing Office, 1986), 24.

2   George Gilder, *Telecosm: How Infinite Bandwidth Will Revolutionize Our World* (New York: The Free Press, 2000).

3   See Leviticus 25.

4   As cited in Pyarelal Nayyar, *Mahatma Gandhi: Poornahuti*, vol. IV (Ahmedabad, India, 1973), 166.

5   Nora Schultz, "Why the World Is a Happier Place," *New Scientist*, August 27, 2008, http://www.newscientist.com/channel/being-human/mg19926714.100-why-the-world-is-a-happier-place.html.

6   Christopher Anderson, *The Long Tail: How Endless Choice Is Creating Unlimited Demand* (London: Random House Business Books, 2006); Christopher Anderson, *Free: The Future of a Radical Price* (London: Random House Business Books, 2009).

7   James Peach and William Dugger, Economic Abundance: An Introduction (Armonk, NY: M. E. Sharpe, Inc., 2009), 3.

8   Ibid., 6–20.

9   Harvey Martin Jacobs, *Who Owns America: Social Conflict over Property Rights* (Madison, WI: University of Wisconsin Press, 1998), 221.

10 Bill Mollison, *Permaculture: A Designer's Manual* (Hyderabad, India: Deccan Development Society, 1990), 50.

11 For a thorough discussion, see Jeremy Rifkin, *The Hydrogen Economy* (New York: Tarcher/Penguin, 2002).

12 See, for instance, Robert Theobald, *The Challenge of Abundance* (New York: Clarkson N. Potter, 1961) and Robert Theobald, *Economizing Abundance* (Athens, OH: Swallow Press, 1970).

13 Neil Gershenfeld, *When Things Start to Think* (New York: Henry Holt and Co., 1999), 71.

14 Gershenfeld, *When Things Start to Think*; Neil Gershenfeld, *Fab: The Coming Revolution on Your Desktop—From Personal Computers to Personal Fabrication* (New York: Basic Books, 2005).

15 Dugger and Peach, *Economic Abundance*, 173–194.

16 Barry Commoner, *The Poverty of Power: Energy and the Economic Crisis* (New York: Knopf, 1976), 135.

17 Strictly speaking, reflected solar energy is also available on some nights as lunar light. This is the basis for a number of agricultural practices based on the phases of the moon.

18 Elinor Ostrom, Thomas Dietz, Nives Dolšak, Paul Stern, Susan Stonich, and Elke Weber, eds., *Drama of the Commons* (Washington, DC: National Academy Press, 2002).

19 Wolfgang Hoeschele, "Research Agenda for a Green Economics of Abundance," *International Journal of Green Economics* 2, no. 1 (2008): 29–44.

20 Juliet B. Schor, *Plenitude: The New Economics of True Wealth* (New York: Penguin, 2010).

THIRTEEN

SEEDS, SOIL, AND GOOD GOVERNANCE: A MESSAGE TO GOVERNMENT

Doug Bone

It appears as if my days as a farmer may be numbered in this Wild West stampede to carve up the commons.

The theme running through this chapter is based on an idea put forward by Allan Savory, the originator of Holistic Management. He says from poverty to genocide, most of humankind's problems stem from the soil degradation caused by failing to incorporate a proper regard for land health into our decision-making process.[1]

And if you think about it, although the sun is ultimately the source of all human wealth, soil and water are the necessary medium by which energy from the sun becomes the abundance of our natural commons. As Savory points out, there is no source other than the sun acting through soil and water that produces human wealth.[2] This perspective sheds a whole new light on the importance of soil, and, indeed, of farmers and ranchers. If a society took all measures necessary to restore and protect the integrity of its soil and water, the abundance of the commons would then largely take care of humans' economic and social problems, almost by default.

I want to focus on ideas for how governments can help us protect soil and water, but first I want to address the impact of an assault on our commons. That assault is by corporations, and I will use my own farm as an example.

Like most small-scale farmers in any country, I have what I think are pretty modest hopes and goals:

- I want to make a living from the land I farm.
- My family and I want to be a part of a vibrant, caring community, free from fear. After all, the best security is happy and well-cared-for neighbours.
- I want the ability to grow healthy, uncontaminated food.
- I want my family and everyone else to have clean air, clean water, and have the choice to eat food that is not contaminated.
- Lastly, like most farmers, I want to pass on the land in my care, *undamaged*, to the next generation.

In the mid-1990s, I thought simply by farming organically, I could achieve these goals by avoiding the high-input/low-price treadmill of industrial agriculture; but, of course, the likes of Monsanto had other ideas to block this end run around their control.

Enter the new reality of biopatenting, genetic engineering, and the threat of terminator technology—all enabled by governments acting as boosters for corporate interests, propelled by various international trade agreements. For instance, the North American Free Trade and World Trade Organization agreements have meant that trade-related intellectual property rights and patent regulations regarding genetic engineering have been harmonized and forced on member nations. This allows the corporate agenda to trump the rights of communities to their genetic heritage, and prevents governments from using the "precautionary principle"—described by the Canadian Environmental Law Association as "a duty to prevent harm, when it is within our power to do so, *even when all the evidence is not in*"[3]—to regulate industry and technology use.

From a corporate standpoint, sustainable and subsistence farming are forms of resistance and threats to their bid to dominate the food system. In response, the strategy of the transnationals has become clear. First, co-opt the political and regulatory systems, then deliberately contaminate our fields and our food as rapidly as possible, with the hope that the damage from their transgenic varieties will soon be too widespread to be halted or reversed by a resigned public. Worldwide, culturally key crops like maize, rice, beans, and wheat are being targeted. Field test plots for genetically modified (GM) wheat are dotted across Western Canada. If wheat seed stocks become contaminated, Prairie organic farms will likely not survive, being unable to supply the GMO-free food organic customers pay us to grow.

Jonathon Rowe, of the commons policy think tank, the Tomales Bay Institute, says the enclosure and privatization of the commons has become the dominant fact of our lives.[4] Current Canadian public policy reflects this trend, to the detriment of the public good, as universities and government regulatory agencies are shifted to a philosophy of "cost recovery." At universities, public agricultural research is being abandoned in favour of partnership arrangements with corporations. The result is compromised academic freedom and skewed research, as private companies profit from the huge investment of public taxpayers' money. A further example of the degeneration of public policy is the schizoid mandate given to the Canadian Food Inspection Agency (CFIA). The CFIA is required to act as both the regulator *and* the promoter of industries such as biotechnology. This is clearly a conflict of interest. Canadians should be alarmed.

So it appears as if my days as a farmer may be numbered in this Wild West stampede to carve up the commons. A review of the past decade presents a sobering picture. For example, Monsanto's seeds and biotech traits accounted for 88 per cent of the total area planted with genetically modified seeds worldwide in 2004, and by 2005, Monsanto controlled 41 per cent of the global market share in commercial corn maize, and 25 per cent of the world market in soybean seeds.[5] On the animal side, that same year, Monsanto filed an application with the World Intellectual Property Organization (WIPO), claiming patent rights in 160 countries, to give them widespread control over pig breeding. According to the information and analysis organization, the ETC Group, in 2008, just ten firms controlled over half the world's seed sales.[6] By 2013, the top ten firms' market share had increased to 75 per cent, with two firms—Monsanto and Dupont—together holding 44 per cent of sales.[7] Some U.S. markets have reached almost total monopoly saturation, with 80 per cent of U.S. corn and 93 per cent of soy grown from Monsanto's patented seeds.[8] And if patenting the building blocks of life was not enough to make your blood run cold, contemplate the feeding frenzy surrounding nano-technology, the next great commercial frontier.

However, globally it appears there is a citizens' movement to reassert their power and defend the sovereignty of both the natural and intellectual commons. John Ralston Saul says that apart from the "small, closed world of economists and officials and interest group associations," a shrinking number of people believe that the predetermined economics of globalization will chart the future course for civilization.[9] Contrary to the technocrats, there are alternatives. There are things we can do as individuals, of course, but this chapter concentrates on the role of our governments. Here are a few ideas for how we, as citizens, might direct our representatives to protect the natural commons.

1. First, the seeds we plant and eat are a gift, a common heritage passed down from past generations. We can insist our provincial governments lobby for federal legislation against the patenting and privatization of genetic plant and animal material, and lobby for the overturning of the international trade agreements that helped biopatenting happen. Internationally, there are some jurisdictions that have declared themselves GMO-free zones. This has given them an economic advantage in the marketplace.

2. Second, we can push provincial and federal governments to rededicate themselves to supporting publicly funded agricultural education, information, and research at universities. Governments should permanently remove themselves from research partnerships that line the pockets of private corporations with public dollars.

3. Third, governments could take leadership in funding public research on sustainable and low-input crop and animal production. I want to stress this should be geared to our rainfall and climate. Technological quick fixes like mega-dam and irrigation projects promoted in the Saskatchewan Agrivision Corporation's 50-Year Water Development scheme are all about the privatization of a public resource and ignore the social and environmental aspects of rural development. By focusing only on economics, these schemes are doomed to be expensive failures.

4. Fourth, provincial governments can develop policies that encourage socially and environmentally responsible food production. Good-quality locally produced and consumed food fosters urban-rural links, creates jobs, builds communities, and reduces environmental costs such as hauling food long distances.

Government subsidization of intensive livestock operations, *and* developing so-called economic clusters strung along the South Saskatchewan River will not save rural communities.

5. Fifth, a provincial government with a functioning and effective regulatory system would apply the "precautionary principle" to all development projects and new technologies. This "go-slow" approach takes into account that things *can* go wrong and the unexpected *can* happen. A fair regulatory system would also include a "polluter will pay for damages" policy.

6. Sixth, press your provincial government to support and rejuvenate essential rural services and infrastructure such as roads, rail lines, telecommunications, schools, and hospitals in an even-handed manner. The success of any rural enterprise depends on a functioning infrastructure. In the case of my own home province, companies doing business in Saskatchewan should pay their fair share of taxes to support this. It is time to recognize that businesses need functioning communities at least as much as those communities need businesses.

7. Seventh, one of the foundations of a *socially*, *economically*, and *environmentally* sustainable province could be a "Food Charter," which would target food security for all its citizens. The World Food Summit in 1996 declared, "Food security exists when all people, at all times, have physical and economic access to sufficient, safe, and nutritious food to meet their dietary needs and food preferences for an active and healthy life."[10] Through policy, governments could play an active role in making such a charter a reality and a driving force. The health, social, environmental, and economic spin-offs would be enormous and serve as the underpinning of a vibrant society.

8. Finally, I urge readers to not give up on the political process. Pressure your favourite political party to make some type of proportional representation reform part of its platform. There is much to learn from the ground-up, holistic approach of the Wixarica people of Mexico. They say the defence and reclamation of their maize from GMO contamination cannot be understood

in isolation from the web of life and culture in which it is enmeshed. They see the world as a magic circle in which nothing can operate alone. They are working for the replenishment of their communities with maize as the heart of their resistance. The defence of their common and their maize began by rebuilding their soil. This led them to farming without chemicals. Then rebalancing the water cycle called them to hold back erosion by taking care of the forest. To do that, they say, "We have to defend our territory...and our rights to land as a people. *That means our* [political] *representatives must really obey the community's mandate*" (emphasis added).[11] So by first tending to the needs of seed and of soil, there is hope of prosperity, and good human governance, flowing to the Wixarica people. Here in Canada we, too, can reassert our rights as citizens.

I will end with a quotation from farmer and author, Wendell Berry: "The only answer to any of our problems is a way of life that is not corrupt, not violent, not wasteful nor toxic. That calls for a lot of small, mostly personal and local steps that probably have to be taken...one at a time."[12]

Notes

1   Allan Savory, "The Ecology of Food Production," *World Business Academy Perspective* 12, no. 4 (1998): 55.
2   Ibid.
3   Canadian Environmental Law Association, "The Precautionary Principle," http://www.cela.ca/collections/pollution/precautionary-principle.
4   Jonathan Rowe, "Reclaiming the Commons," *Canadian Perspectives* (Winter 2003): 8–9.
5   ETC Group, *Global Seed Industry Concentration 2005*, Communiqué No. 90 (September–October 2005); National Farmers' Union, *The Farm Crisis and Corporate Profits: A Report from the National Farmers' Union*, Farm Crisis Series No. 4 (2005).
6   ETC Group, *Who Owns Nature? Corporate Power and the Final Frontier of the Modification of Life*, Communiqué No. 100 (November 2008).
7   ETC Group, *Putting the Cartel before the Horse...and Farm, Seeds, Soil, Peasants, etc. Who Will Control Agricultural Inputs, 2013?* Communiqué No. 111 (September 2013).
8   Organic Consumers Association, "U.S. and Monsanto Dominate Global Market for GM Seeds," August 7, 2013, http://www.organicconsumers.org/articles/article_28059.cfm.

9   John Ralston Saul, *The Collapse of Globalism and the Reinvention of the World* (London: Atlantic Books, 2005), 86.

10 World Food Summit, *Rome Declaration of World Food Security* (Rome, Italy: Food and Agriculture Organization of the United Nations, 1996), para. 1.

11 Cited by Silvia Ribeiro, "The Day the Sun Dies: Contamination and Resistance in Mexico," *Seedling*, July 2007, http://www.grain.org/article/entries/423-the-day-the-sun-dies-contamination-and-resistance-in-mexico.

12 Wendell Berry, quoted in "The Next Millennium? How About the Next Year!" *World Watch* 12, no. 6 (November–December, 1999): 9.

FOURTEEN

OPEN ACCESS TO SCHOLARLY KNOWLEDGE: THE NEW COMMONS

Heather Morrison

An old tradition and a new technology have converged to make possible an unprecedented public good. The old tradition is the willingness of scientists and scholars to publish the fruits of their research in scholarly journals without payment, for the sake of inquiry and knowledge. The new technology is the internet. The public good they make possible is the world-wide electronic distribution of the peer-reviewed journal literature and completely free and unrestricted access to it by all scientists, scholars, teachers, students, and other curious minds. Removing access barriers to this literature will accelerate research, enrich education, share the learning of the rich with the poor and the poor with the rich, make this literature as useful as it can be, and lay the foundation for uniting humanity in a common intellectual conversation and quest for knowledge.

—Budapest Open Access Initiative (BOAI), 2002

This is a vision of a knowledge commons, a common pool of all of the knowledge of humankind from which all can draw freely and to which all qualified scholars are welcome to contribute. This chapter highlights some of the history, successes, issues, current status, and future priorities for achieving a sustainable, global, open access (OA) knowledge commons.

Access Expansion from Print to Online Open Access

The expansion of access to knowledge made possible by the web is almost incomprehensible. The thesis provides an excellent example. Until recently, there would be a very limited number of print copies of a thesis, as little as one or two, and perhaps microfiche. Access was, of necessity, extremely limited. Even finding out about the existence of a thesis on a topic was limited to those with access to specialized tools such as the Dissertation Abstracts database; subscriptions to such tools are common only in research-intensive organizations. Even when the existence of a thesis was known, libraries were often reluctant to interlibrary loan theses, as the library typically only had one copy. The current trend is for theses to be made publicly available to anyone, anywhere over the Internet through institutional repositories. Access to theses has shifted dramatically in the past few years from extremely limited access to almost ubiquitous access.

In the mid-1990s, the United States National Institutes of Health (NIH) made PubMed available. PubMed is a freely available version of the United States National Library of Medicine's *Medline*, the world's premiere index to medical literature, previously available only through subscription.

The purpose of releasing *Medline* to the public was so that every doctor in the United States (and elsewhere) would have access. The NIH was astonished at the usage—a hundredfold increase. There were more PubMed users than doctors in the United States. Clearly, opening up access meant more than a few more readers. This expansion of access to a key resource preceded the move to evidence-based medicine, and, in the author's opinion, may be a causal factor.

The Open Access Movement

While open access is, by definition, online, an online journal per se is not necessarily open access. There are many online journals that are only available through subscription. For many scholars, this type of access may *look* very similar to open access. When the scholar's library has a subscription, users onsite are seamlessly connected to the journal, at no cost to the user. From home, all that is needed is to enter a username and password. It may not be obvious to scholars in the developed world that when others try to access the same content—whether colleagues in other universities and colleges, their own former students as alumni, scholars in the developing world, professionals, patients, civil servants, journalists, and others—they are asked either to subscribe, at costs of hundreds or thousands of dollars per journal subscription for academic journals, or to pay to view each article at costs around $30 per article.

The work of a scholar that is published in an open access journal is much more accessible than work that is published in an online subscription-based journal. While access to the scholarly literature is generally excellent at large research universities, not even the largest and best libraries can afford to subscribe to every journal. To illustrate the difference, let us look at the difference in access even to scholars at research universities between the open access *Journal of Medical Internet Research* and the subscription-based *Canadian Journal of Anesthesia*, which, like many subscription-based journals, provides free access to back issues after an embargo period. When an article is published in the fully open access *Journal of Medical Internet Research*, it is immediately available to anyone, anywhere. Articles are included in PubMedCentral (PMC), with links from the popular PubMed search service. The *Journal of Medical Internet Research* is listed in the *Directory of Open Access Journals* (DOAJ); it costs nothing for libraries to add the journal to their title lists, so the *Journal of Medical Internet Research* will be found through most library journal lists.

At Harvard University Library and California State University Library, both the *Journal of Medical Internet Research* and the *Canadian Journal of Anesthesia* are listed in the e-journals collections. However, neither Harvard nor Cal State subscribes to the *Canadian Journal of Anesthesia*, so articles are only freely available after the embargo period. If one author publishes an article in the *Journal of Medical Internet Research*, it is immediately and freely available to scholars at Harvard and Cal State. If another author publishes an article in the *Canadian Journal of Anesthesia*, for the first couple of years after publication, scholars at Harvard and Cal State are told that the article is restricted and are invited to buy online access.

With this difference in access at some of the world's largest academic library collections, it is not hard to imagine the difference open access makes at smaller libraries and in the developing world. While there are good programs, such as the World Health Organization's HINARI Access to Research in Health Programme and OARE (Online Access to Research in the Environment), to increase access in the developing world to subscription-based journals, these are not equivalent to open access. For example, countries like India and China that should qualify for these programs on the basis of low gross domestic product are excluded because there are a few institutions that can afford subscriptions.

The progress of the open access movement around the globe is phenomenal. The movement for open access coalesced around three major international meetings that included a focus on defining open access. The resulting definition of open access is often called the BBB definition for the three meetings (Budapest, Bethesda, and Berlin). The Budapest Open Access Initiative (2002) offered up the following definition of open access:

> By "open access" to this literature, we mean its free availability on the public internet, permitting any users to read, download, copy, distribute, print, search, or link to the full texts of these articles, crawl them for indexing, pass them as data to software, or use them for any other lawful purpose, without financial, legal, or technical barriers other than those inseparable from gaining access to the internet itself. The only constraint on reproduction and distribution, and the only role for copyright in this domain, should be to give authors control over the integrity of their work and the right to be properly acknowledged and cited.

The BBB definition has been an inspiration to the open access movement for many years. Recently, the author has come to view the definition as slightly flawed and a perceived rigid adherence to the technical element of the definition as problematic. I now use a brief, simpler definition of open access based on the one long posted by Peter Suber (n.d.) on his much-perused Open Access Overview: open access is scholarly literature that is digital, online, free of charge, and free of most copyright and licensing restrictions.

My reason for abandoning the BBB definition reflects to some extent a persistent confusion of this definition of open access with the Creative Commons—Attribution Only (CC-BY) licence. In spite of the superficial similarities of CC-BY and the BBB definition, there are some very important differences, and ongoing open access to scholarly works needs to happen in a real world where not everyone shares the noble goals expressed at the original BOAI meeting. Notably, none of the CC licences are restricted to works that are free of charge; the blanket commercial rights granted by the CC-BY licence could be giving license for downstream enclosure. If open access to the original works is not maintained, CC-BY could lead from open to toll access.

Tempting as the simplicity of equating open access with the CC-BY licence may be, in depth examination of what is really needed to achieve the BOAI vision is one of the important tasks for open access in the next few years. While re-use of materials such as graphs and charts is likely highly desirable in many instances, blanket permission to change scholarly works (create derivatives as allowed by most CC licences) could be problematic in some areas. For example, in the medical literature small changes in wording, if used as the basis for patient treatment, could have major negative implications. Useful open sharing of research data likely depends more on format and standardization of metadata than on specific licensing issues.

Open Access Archives

While the terms "repository" or "institutional repository" are more common, the author prefers the term "open access archives" to highlight that the purpose of the archive is open access, and also to emphasize the archival or preservation function of these services. The Directory of Open Access Repositories (OpenDOAR) is a vetted list of open access archives, listing over 2,600 archives as of November 2014.

The world's largest open access archive is PMC, with over 3.2 million items. The purpose of PMC is both access and preservation; PMC carries forward into the online environment the preservation function of the United States National Library of Medicine, which has long had a role in preserving the medical literature in paper format. Authors sometimes deposit articles; many of these authors are *required* to deposit in PMC by their research funders, a topic that will be covered later in this chapter. Many journals also deposit articles in PMC. Close to two thousand journals voluntarily contribute contents to PMC; over 1,350 of these journals make access through PMC free immediately on publication. Some journals will submit articles covered under open or public access policies on behalf of authors.

PMC is one example of a disciplinary or subject repository. The majority of repositories are not discipline-based but rather institutional in nature. One example is the Max Planck Society's E-Doc Server, developed for Max Planck authors to self-archive research output, with over two hundred thousand open access items as of November 2014 according to OpenDOAR. Most university libraries host a repository for their institutions.

arXiv.org is one of the oldest, largest, and most heavily used of the open access archives. Developed in the 1990s by Paul Ginsparg, the arXiv self-archiving tradition flows naturally from a tradition of sharing preprints among physicists that predates the electronic environment. arXiv is hosted by Cornell University Library and has eighteen mirror sites around the world. In physics, arXiv is heavily used—hits of more than half a million per day at the main site alone are not uncommon. While formal publication continues to be valued for formal certification, it tends to be arXiv that is read. Building on this tradition, the SCOAP³ Sponsoring Consortium for Open Access Publishing in Particle Physics has achieved the remarkable feat of switching all of high-energy physics publishing from a subscription to an open access basis, after forming a global consortium to coordinate the funding for OA publishing.

Open Access Journals

A fully open access journal is one that makes articles freely available from the moment of publication, in contrast with subscription-based journals that make articles freely available but only after a delay or embargo period. Open access journals, like subscription journals, vary in quality, age, discipline and region of origin, and business model. Some open access journals are new journals, while others have converted from a subscription model. There are open access journals with high impact factors. For example, several of the Public Library of Science journals are at or near the top ranking in their fields—very impressive, indeed, for relatively new journals. There are disciplinary differences in the trend toward open access, with relatively more open access journals in fields like genomics, but there are open access journals in every discipline.

As for a business model, it is important to emphasize that the vast majority of open access journals do not charge publication fees. As of May 2014, only 26 per cent of the journals listed in DOAJ had publication fees (Morrison, Salhab, Calvé-Genest, & Horava, in press). Indeed, publication charges are less common with open access journals than was the case with subscription journals (Kaufman-Wills Group, LLC, 2005; Suber & Sutton, 2007). Many open access journals rely on subsidies from their parent organizations. It is not uncommon, for example, for a society journal to rely on revenue from society members to subsidize a journal; this was often the case even with print journals.

The efficiencies of an online-only, open access journal make it much easier for a scholarly society to produce and disseminate an open access journal at minimal cost. Many academic libraries provide free or low-cost hosting and support services for journals that their faculty are involved with (Hahn, 2008).

Author's Rights and Self-Archiving

Traditionally, authors have transferred copyright to publishers, usually with a copyright transfer agreement. Copyright is not all-or-none, and in the electronic environment, it is increasingly common for authors to retain some of the copyright to their works. Many publishers are moving away from copyright transfer to a licence to publish. The licence to publish approach *tends* to leave more rights with authors, but this is not always the case. Currently, there is a wide variety of practices, ranging from full copyright transfer to authors transferring to publishers only the right to publish (or right of first publication) and retaining all other rights, to Creative Commons licensing.

It is important that authors retain rights to their work to allow for maximum dissemination through self-archiving, and also to allow authors to make full use of their own works. If an author has transferred full copyright to a publisher, it will not be legal for the author to post a copy on the author's website or distribute copies of the work to the author's own students without permission. Many publishers will not grant such permission without payment, even to the author of the work. Authors should consider the rights publishers expect even before submitting a paper, read the transfer agreement, and use an author's addendum to ensure retention of rights.

The SHERPA/ROMEO Publisher Copyright Policies and Self-Archiving provides brief summaries of the policies of the majority of publishers and journals, as well as links to the policies. This is a time of transition in this area for publishers, so authors should really read the publication agreement or licence to publish carefully before signing, or use an author's addendum to indicate the rights they wish to retain. There are a number of author's addenda available, including the Scholarly Publishing and Academic Resources Coalition (SPARC) and the SPARC Canadian Authors' Addendum, among others.

One of the reasons for retaining rights is to ensure maximum access to one's work by self-archiving a copy for open access. There is a substantial body of evidence demonstrating the open access impact advantage (Hitchcock, 2010). Another good reason is the strong preference by research funders for open access, increasingly expressed through open access policies.

Open Access Policies

The Registry of Open Access Repositories Mandatory Archiving Policies (ROARMAP) listed 503 mandates in total as of November 2014, up from 415 in November 2013. There are many more open access mandate policies in the works. There are two basic types of policies: institutional/funder or top-down policies and scholar-led permissions policies.

While the exact details of each policy varies, the basic idea of institutional or funder policies is that researchers funded or employed by the mandating body are required to make their work publicly or openly accessible, preferably immediately on publication, although most allow for some delay period if required by a publisher. Open access policies ideally require the researcher to deposit their own final manuscript into an open access archive. The deposit is usually required immediately, even if public access must be delayed.

The United States National Institutes of Health is the largest medical research funder in the world, and the largest funder to have implemented a public access policy. NIH-funded researchers are required to make their work publicly accessible in PMC, no more than twelve months after publication. The NIH Public Access Policy was among the first policies in the world. NIH learned a valuable lesson; the first form of the policy, which only requested, but did not require, public access, resulted in a dismal compliance rate of less than 4 per cent in the first year. In April of 2008, NIH implemented a much stronger policy, clearly requiring compliance.

All of the United Kingdom's Research Councils (RCUK) have some form of an open access policy. In 2013, the RCUK implemented a controversial open access policy strongly encouraging publication in open access journals with block funding provided to UK higher education institutions to pay article processing charges. In my submissions to the RCUK policy consultations, I have emphasized the distortion that this subsidy will cause in the market, one of the controversial aspects of this policy (Morrison, 2013).

The Harvard Faculty of Arts and Sciences' open access policy was a breakthrough, as it was the first policy initiated by faculty members. With the Harvard policy, faculty members grant to Harvard a nonexclusive licence to make their work open access through the Harvard open access repository (under development), "but not for a profit" (Mitchell, 2008). MIT's (2009) policy is the one I point to as a model, based on Harvard's but specifying open access. This is an improvement because "not for a profit" leaves the door open to charges for cost recovery.

To understand the commitment of research funding agencies to open access, it helps to look at the opposition, which has been substantial. Scholarly communication resembles a gift economy in some respects (e.g., neither authors nor peer reviewers are paid). At the same time, the highly lucrative science, technology, and medicine (STM) scholarly journal publishing market is worth $8 billion a year (Ware & Mabe, 2009). A few of the companies and the more profitable of the society publishers of this highly lucrative business have a history of actively lobbying against open access.

Lobbying efforts are aimed both at governments and at scholars, and sometimes take the form of deliberate deception. One notable example is the Association of American Publishers' hiring of Eric Dezenhall, known as the "Pit Bull of Public Relations," as reported by Jim Giles in *Nature* (2007). Giles reported that executives from Elsevier, Wiley, and the American Chemical Society met with Dezenhall, who subsequently sent some strategy suggestions to focus on simple messages such as "public access equals censorship" and "attempt to equate traditional publishing models with peer review." The Association of American Publishers confirmed the hiring of Dezenhall, and subsequent communications and lobbying efforts make it very clear that the publishing industry has followed Dezenhall's advice. It is obviously ludicrous to claim that public access equals censorship; this is probably not a tactic meant to withstand reflection, rather one designed to cause hesitation by someone with little time to consider the message. It is nonsense to claim that open access journals are not peer reviewed when there are thousands of peer-reviewed, fully open access journals included in the DOAJ, and even at the time, the journals of many of the anti-open-access lobbying companies provided options for authors to make their work open access. Peter Suber offered a thorough rebuttal to the argument that open access threatens peer review in the September 2007 SPARC *Open Access Newsletter*.

That so many open access policies have been, and are being, implemented in spite of this fierce opposition is one of the indications of the strength of the open access movement. Another is the phenomenal growth of open access resources. In addition to the over ten thousand journals, a DOAJ search includes over 1.7 million articles. The newer Directory of Open Access Books lists over 2,200 books from over seventy publishers and is growing at a rate of more than 40 per cent annually. The Bielefeld Academic Search Engine searches thousands of open access archives, containing more than sixty-four million documents, adding over fourteen million documents in 2014 alone (Morrison, 2014).

Conclusion

The Internet makes possible an unprecedented public good: open access to the world's scholarly knowledge, a commons where our collective knowledge can be accessed by anyone, and to which any qualified scholar can contribute. In the period just over a decade since the first defining moment of open access in the Budapest Open Access Initiative, the growth of the global movement toward open access has been phenomenal. There are more than ten thousand fully open access journals, seventy publishers of open access scholarly monographs, and millions of documents available through thousands of repositories. The issues and challenges for the next few years for open access will be revisiting and refining the technical definition of open access and refreshing the vision of "sharing the learning of the rich with the poor and the poor with the rich." Finding the means to sustain open access economically will be key to a stable open access scholarly publishing system; this is the main focus of my current research, *Sustaining the Knowledge Commons* (2014).

References

Budapest Open Access Initiative (BOAI). (2002, February 14). Retrieved from http://www.soros.org/openaccess/read.shtml

California State University Library website. Retrieved January 31, 2009, from http://www.calstatela.edu/library/

Giles, J. (2007). PR's "pit bull" takes on open access. *Nature, 445,* 25.

Hahn, K. (2008). *Research library publishing services: New options for university publishing*. Washington, DC: Association of Research Libraries. Retrieved September 25, 2010, from http://www.arl.org/sc/index.shtml

Harvard University Library website. Retrieved January 31, 2009, from http://e-research.lib.harvard.edu/

Hitchcock, S. (2010). *The effect of open access and downloads ("hits") on citation impact: A bibliography of studies*. Retrieved September 25, 2010, from http://opcit.eprints.org/oacitation-biblio.html

Kaufman-Wills Group, LLC. (2005). *The facts about open access*. The Association of Learned and Professional Society Publishers. Retrieved September 25, 2010, from http://www.alpsp.org/ngen_public/article.asp?id=200&did=47&aid=270&st=&oaid=-1

Massachussetts Institute of Technology (MIT). (2009). *MIT faculty open access policy*. Retrieved November 25, 2014, from http://libraries.mit.edu/scholarly/mit-open-access/open-access-at-mit/mit-open-access-policy/

Max Planck Society E-Doc Server. Retrieved September 25, 2010, from http://edoc.mpg.de/

Mitchell, R. (2008, February 14). Harvard to collect, disseminate scholarly articles for faculty. *Harvard University Gazette Online*. Retrieved from http://news.harvard.edu/gazette/story/2008/02/harvard-to-collect-disseminate-scholarly-articles-for-faculty/

Morrison, H. (2013). Predicting increased costs and reduction in open access: Comments on the Research Councils UK revised OA policy and guidance. *The Imaginary Journal of Poetic Economics* (blog). Retrieved November 25, 2014, from http://poeticeconomics.blogspot.ca/2013/03/predicting-increasing-costs-and.html

Morrison, H. (2014, October 1). Dramatic growth of open access: Some useful figures for open access week 2014. *The Imaginary Journal of Poetic Economics* (blog). Retrieved November 25, 2014, from http://poeticeconomics.blogspot.ca/2014/10/dramatic-growth-of-open-access.html

Morrison, H., Salhab, J., Calvé-Genest, A., & Horava, T. (in press). *Open access article processing charges: DOAJ survey May 2014.* Retrieved November 25, 2014, from http://sustainingknowledgecommons.files.wordpress.com/2014/10/oa-apcs-article-2014-october-171.pdf

OpenDOAR. Retrieved November 25, 2014, from http://www.opendoar.org/

PubMedCentral. Retrieved from http://www.pubmedcentral.nih.gov/

Registry of Open Access Repositories Mandatory Archiving Policies (ROARMAP). Retrieved September 25, 2010, from http://www.eprints.org/openaccess/policysignup/

Research Councils UK. (2013). RCUK policy on open access and supporting guidance. Retrieved November 25, 2014, from http://www.rcuk.ac.uk/RCUK-prod/assets/documents/documents/RCUKOpenAccessPolicy.pdf

Scholarly Publishing and Academic Resources Coalition (SPARC). *Author's rights.* Retrieved September 25, 2010, from http://www.arl.org/sparc/author/addendum.shtml

SCOAP3—Sponsoring Consortium for Open Access Publishing in Particle Physics. Retrieved November 25, 2014, from http://scoap3.org/

SHERPA/ROMEO Publisher Copyright Policies and Self-Archiving. Retrieved September 25, 2010, from http://www.sherpa.ac.uk/romeo/

SPARC Canadian Authors' Addendum. Retrieved September 25, 2010, from http://www.carl-abrc.ca/projects/author/author-e.html

Suber, P. (n.d.). Open access overview. Retrieved from http://legacy.earlham.edu/~peters/fos/overview.htm

Suber, P. (2007, September). Will open access undermine peer review? *SPARC Open Access Newsletter.* Retrieved September 25, 2010, from http://www.earlham.edu/~peters/fos/newsletter/09-02-07.htm#peerreview

Suber, P., & Sutton, C. (2007, November). Society publishers with open access journals. *SPARC Open Access Newsletter.* Retrieved September 25, 2010, from http://www.earlham.edu/~peters/fos/newsletter/11-02-07.htm#list

Sustaining the Knowledge Commons (blog). (2014). Retrieved November 25, 2014, from http://sustainingknowledgecommons.org/

Ware, M., & Mabe, M. (2009). The stm report: An overview of scientific and scholarly journal publishing. Oxford, UK: STM: International Association of Scientific, Technical and Medical Publishers. Retrieved 2010 from http://www.stm-assoc.org/document-library/

ACKNOWLEDGEMENTS

The editors wish to thank the contributors to this collection for their generous offering of two most precious resources: time and critical thought. The same thanks are due our reviewers, who lent invaluable feedback on early drafts. This collection has passed through many caring and competent hands at the University of Regina Press, including Brian Mlazgar, Bruce Walsh, Donna Grant, and Karen Clark. This book would not have been possible without the Free Knowledge meeting held in November 2005, and funded by the University of Regina's Transdisciplinary Project Fund, that featured keynote speaker Brewster Kneen and panelists: the late Ian Black, Doug Bone, Helen Clarke, Patricia Elliott, Brad Fox, Michael Francis, Peter Garden, Rod Haugerud, Sally Mahood, Roger Petry, Claire Polster, and Winona Wheeler. We further acknowledge the encouragement and moral support of the University of Regina, in particular our home departments, the School of Journalism and the Department of Computer Science. Finally, we are eternally grateful to our colleagues, friends, and families for offering ideas, rallying our spirits, and helping cheer on this project to completion.

CONTRIBUTORS

Jane Anderson is an assistant professor of anthropology and museum studies. She specializes in the fields of intellectual property law, Indigenous rights, and comparative histories of colonialism and intercultural exchange. Her work focuses on the production, reproduction, and translation of property regimes in controlling knowledge and visual culture alongside current legal and political claims for the return, repatriation, and restitution of cultural property held in cultural institutions around the world. Anderson's publications include *Law, Knowledge, Culture: The Production of Indigenous Knowledge in Intellectual Property Law* (2009) and the United Nations policy document, *Safeguarding Cultural Heritage and Protecting Traditional Cultural Expressions: The Management of Intellectual Property Issues and Options—A Compendium for Museums, Archives and Libraries* (2011). Her current collaborative project, Local Contexts (www.localcontexts.org), involves the development of Traditional Knowledge licences and labels. This is a legal and educational strategy that addresses culturally specific conditions for accessing and using Indigenous cultural heritage materials.

Leonzo Barreno is a Mayan from Guatemala. He holds an MA (justice studies) from the University of Regina and is a Ph.D. student in the University of Saskatchewan Native Studies Program. He coordinated the International Indigenous Program (1994–1997) and directed the Saskatchewan Indian Federated College's (now First Nations University of Canada's) Indigenous Center for International Development (2000–2005). He wrote *Higher Education for Indigenous People in Latin America* (2003), used as a working document by UNESCO-Latin America. He is an adjunct professor in the School of Journalism, University of Regina, where he has taught various courses dealing with Indigenous and new immigrant issues since 2003.

Doug Bone is an organic farmer from the Elrose area of west-central Saskatchewan, and grows organic cereals and pulses. He is a member of the National Farmers Union and also a member of the Saskatchewan Organic Directorate (SOD's Organic Agriculture Protection Fund) committee that coordinated the class action lawsuit in Saskatchewan that organic farmers launched against Monsanto and Bayer Crop Science for damages caused by contamination from genetically engineered canola. The committee remains actively involved in various endeavours to halt the introduction of genetically modified alfalfa.

Mitch Diamantopoulos is a Centre Scholar with the Centre for the Study of Co-operatives at the University of Saskatchewan and an associate professor at the University of Regina's School of Journalism, where he also serves as department head. He cofounded Hullabaloo Publishing Workers' Co-operative, which publishes independent city papers *Prairie Dog Magazine* in Regina (since 1993) and *Planet S Magazine* in Saskatoon (since 2002).

Patricia W. Elliott is an assistant professor at the School of Journalism at the University of Regina. In addition to being a freelance magazine journalist and author, her background includes alternative media practice and community-based research. Her PhD dissertation, undertaken through the University of Saskatchewan's Centre for the Study of Co-operatives, examines paths to sustainability among independent nonprofit and co-operative media enterprises. She coproduced an independent documentary film on underground journalism, *Breaking Open Burma* (2012), and is the author of *The White Umbrella: A Woman's Struggle for Freedom in Burma* (2003), a biography of a political exile who became a rebel army leader.

Joshua Farley is an ecological economist, professor in community development and applied economics, and Fellow at the Gund Institute for Ecological

Economics at the University of Vermont. He holds degrees in biology, international affairs, and economics. His broad research interests focus on the design of an economy capable of balancing what is biophysically possible with what is socially, psychologically, and ethically desirable. He is co-author with Herman Daly of *Ecological Economics, Principles and Applications*, originally published in 2003 and now in its second edition (2010).

Daryl H. Hepting is an associate professor in the Department of Computer Science, associate member of the Department of Film, and associate director of the Regina Integrative Cognitive Experimentation (RICE) lab, all at the University of Regina. He is the coordinator of the Farming and Local Food Production, Consumption and Waste Minimization Theme Area Working Group within the Saskatchewan Regional Centre of Expertise on Education for Sustainable Development. He is interested in how information technology can engage and empower citizens.

Brewster Kneen is the author of six books on agriculture, genetic engineering, and corporate control, drawing on his fifteen-year experience as a commercial sheep farmer in Nova Scotia. He and his wife Cathleen have published a monthly newsletter, *The Ram's Horn*, since 1980. Kneen's most recent books include *Journey of an Unrepentant Socialist* (2014), focusing on social justice movements of the 1950s and 1960s, and *The Tyranny of Rights* (2009), a critical discussion of the concept and language of rights, including the idea of a "right to food."

Ida Kubiszewski is a senior lecturer at the Crawford School of Public Policy at Australian National University. She was also a United Nations negotiator on climate change, specifically around adaptation and loss and damage, for the Dominican Republic at the Conference of Parties (COP) in Warsaw in November 2013. She is the founding managing editor and current co-editor-in-chief of a magazine/journal hybrid called *Solutions*. She is also the cofounder and former managing editor of the *Encyclopedia of Earth*, an electronic reference about Earth, its natural environments, and their interaction with society. She is the author or co-author of over a dozen scientific papers. She is a Fellow at the National Council for Science and the Environment, on the board of the Veblen Institute (Institut Veblen), and sits on the steering committees or advisory boards of various organizations, including the Ecosystem Service Partnership and the Environmental Information Coalition.

Sally Mahood is a family physician and associate professor of family medicine at the University of Saskatchewan Department of Family Medicine. She teaches and practises at the Family Medicine Unit of the College of Medicine, University of Saskatchewan, in Regina and is on staff at the Women's Health Centre and Planned Parenthood in Regina. She has special interests in women's health, primary care, the preservation of public health care, and has teaching and research interests in the pharmaceutical industry and physician-industry interactions.

Heather Morrison is an assistant professor at the School of Information Studies, University of Ottawa, and is a well-known open access advocate. Her current research program, Sustaining the Knowledge Commons, funded by Canada's Social Sciences and Humanities Research Council (SSHRC), focuses on the economics of transition from subscriptions and purchase of scholarly materials to production- (supply-) side economics to support open access. This program demonstrates an open research approach through the *Sustaining the Knowledge Commons* blog (sustainingknowledgecommons.org). She obtained her PhD from Simon Fraser University's School of Communication, authoring the dissertation, "Freedom for Scholarship in the Internet Age." She also writes the scholarly blog, *The Imaginary Journal of Poetic Economics* (http://poeticeconomics.blogspot.com).

Claire Polster is a professor of sociology and social studies at the University of Regina. Her research focuses on the ongoing transformation of Canadian higher education and its implications for the public interest. She has published widely on various higher education issues, including government policy related to universities, the commodification of academic research, and the erosion of university autonomy and democracy. She is also a co-editor of *Academic Callings: The University We Have Had, Now Have, and Could Have* (2010) and was a cofounder of the University of Regina's Community Research Unit.

Arthur Schafer is a Canadian ethicist specializing in bioethics, philosophy of law, social philosophy, and political philosophy. He is the director of the Centre for Professional and Applied Ethics at the University of Manitoba. He is also a full professor in the Department of Philosophy and an ethics consultant for the Winnipeg Regional Health Authority, Department of Child Health. For ten years he was head of the Section of Bio-Medical Ethics in the Faculty of Medicine at the University of Manitoba.

Marian van der Zon founded a pirate radio station (TAR: Temporary Autonomous Radio), hosts *Be the Media* (CHLY), and teaches in the Media Studies and Women's Studies departments at Vancouver Island University. She has contributed sound documentaries and audio art to sound festivals, art galleries, and pirate, community, and public radio (CBC); is co-editor of the anthology, *Islands of Resistance: Pirate Radio in Canada* (2010); played in the band Puzzleroot; and performs in the multimedia project Meridian.

Roberto Verzola, an activist since the early 1970s, spent three years in prison as a political prisoner of the Philippine martial law regime. Educated and trained as an engineer, he has worked closely with civil society organizations on issues such as intellectual property rights, information technology, genetic engineering, the environment, nuclear power, election automation, and sustainable farming and renewable energy. He ran an e-mail service for several nongovernmental organizations for almost a decade (1992–2000), receiving an industry award as "the father of Philippine e-mail." He is a founder of the Philippine Greens (1996) and author of *Towards a Political Economy of Information* (2004). He coordinates a sustainable rice-farming network and a think tank promoting an energy transition to 100 per cent renewable electricity, and is working on a book on the political economy of abundance. He also teaches mathematics to humanities students at the University of the Philippines.

Joel Westheimer is University Research Chair in Democracy and Education and a professor in the social foundations of education at the University of Ottawa, and a principal investigator for Democratic Dialogue, a research collaborative dedicated to the critical exploration of democratic ideals in education and society. He received his PhD from Stanford University and his BSE from Princeton University. His award-winning books include *Among Schoolteachers: Community, Autonomy, and Ideology in Teachers' Work* (1998) and *Pledging Allegiance: The Politics of Patriotism in America's Schools* (foreword by the late Howard Zinn) (2007). His most recent book is *What Kind of Citizen?* and will be published in 2015 by Teachers College Press. He is the recent recipient of the Canadian Education Association's Whitworth Award "for research that matters" and serves as the education columnist for CBC Radio's *Ottawa Morning*.

Gregory Younging is a member of the Opaskwayak Cree Nation in northern Manitoba. He has an MA from the Institute of Canadian Studies at

Carleton University, a master's of publishing degree from the Canadian Centre for Studies in Writing and Publishing at Simon Fraser University, and a PhD from the Department of Educational Studies at the University of British Columbia. He has worked for the Royal Commission on Aboriginal Peoples, the Assembly of First Nations, the Committee of Inquiry into Indian Education, the Native Women's Association of Canada, and from 1990 to 2003, was the managing editor of Theytus Books. He is a former member of the Canada Council Aboriginal Peoples Committee on the Arts (1997–2001) and the British Columbia Arts Council (1999–2001). He is the former assistant director of research for the Truth and Reconciliation Commission of Canada and currently is the Indigenous studies program coordinator at University of British Columbia Okanagan.

INDEX